D0908337

# T H E
# LOST CHORD

# T H E
# LOST CHORD
## Essays on Victorian Music

EDITED BY

# Nicholas Temperley

INDIANA UNIVERSITY PRESS
Bloomington and Indianapolis

FB

&
. LIT.
INDEX

Manufactured in the United States of America

Library of Congress Cataloging-in-Publication Data
The Lost chord.
Includes index.
1. Music—Great Britain—19th century—History
and criticism.   I. Temperley, Nicholas.
ML285.4.L68   1989      781.741       88-45456
ISBN 0-253-33518-3

1   2   3   4   5   93   92   91   90   89

# CONTENTS

# PREFACE

This book originated in the Autumn 1986 issue of *Victorian Studies*—a special issue devoted to music in the Victorian age. The first essay is a slightly revised version of an introductory article, "The Lost Chord," which I wrote for that issue, while the next five are taken from it without change. Robert Bledsoe's essay appeared in an earlier issue of *Victorian Studies* (Summer 1985). The final chapter is a version of a paper delivered at a conference on Nineteenth-Century Musical Theatre in English held at the Pierpont Morgan Library, New York, in June 1985; it is published here by agreement with Greenwood Press and F. Woodbridge Wilson.

I am greatly indebted to Patrick Brantlinger, editor of *Victorian Studies*, for taking the positive step of commissioning the special music issue, which was the first of its kind anywhere. I am also deeply grateful to the University of Illinois Research Board and the Indiana University Research and Development Office for jointly financing the production of the cassette recording that accompanied both the journal and this volume. Thanks are also due to William Burgan, Catherine Hoyser, Thomas Prasch, Annette Sisson, and Keith Welsh, of the VS editorial staff, and to Luanne Holladay for preparing the index.

Nicholas Temperley

# THE
# LOST CHORD

*Nicholas Temperley*

# INTRODUCTION: THE STATE OF RESEARCH ON VICTORIAN MUSIC

ANYONE WHO HAS STUDIED VICTORIAN HISTORY OR LITERATURE IS LIKELY TO BE well aware of the presence of music, for it played a prominent part in Victorian life. Yet music has played little part in Victorian studies. This is a fact that needs some explaining. It also needs remedying, and this collection of essays is intended to open up the territory and to encourage further exploration.

The importance of music in Victorian life is easy to demonstrate. We already know how much it meant to writers like Charles Dickens, Alfred Tennyson, Edward Lear, George Eliot, Thomas Hardy, and George Bernard Shaw. One aspect of music in fiction is treated in this volume by Mary Burgan, while Linda Hughes analyzes a major musical setting of a Tennyson poem. Public figures like Prince Albert, William Gladstone, and Arthur Balfour also attached due importance to music, as did many leaders in other fields like Isambard Kingdom Brunel, William Dyce, and Herbert Spencer. To these names we may add that of John Ruskin, whose musical ideas are explored in William J. Gatens's essay.

More systematic evidence shows that music was no laggard in the general bigger-and-better trend of the age. The number of music editions copyrighted per year climbed steeply from 151 in 1835 to 8,063 in 1901 [1]; the number of pianos manufactured yearly rose from 23,000 in 1850 to 75,000 in 1910 [2]; the proportion of London parish churches maintaining choral services increased from under five percent in 1858 to over 38 percent in 1882 [3]; and the number of professional musicians and music teachers grew from about

---

[1] See D. W. Krummel, "Music Publishing," in Nicholas Temperley, ed., *The Romantic Age,* Volume 5 of *The Blackwell History of Music in Britain,* 6 vols. projected (London: Athlone Press, 1981; repr. Oxford: Blackwell, 1988), pp. 46–59, especially Table 1 (p. 49).

[2] Cyril Ehrlich, *The Piano: A History* (London: Dent, 1976), p. 210.

[3] Nicholas Temperley, *The Music of the English Parish Church,* 2 vols. (Cambridge: Cambridge University Press, 1979), I, 279.

6,600 in 1841 to about 39,300 in 1901.[4] Still more significant are the completely new developments originating in that dynamic period: the mass sight-singing movement, musical education in state-supported schools, cheap octavo editions of choral works, colleges of music,[5] university courses in music (Rainbow, "Music in Education," pp. 29–34), diploma-granting professional organizations, and the Musical Association (now Royal) for the scholarly study of music.[6]

Music, then, was hardly slighted by the Victorians. But Victorian music has been slighted by scholars and writers of later years. In its forty years of existence, the *Journal of the American Musicological Society* has never printed an article on any aspect of Victorian music; neither has *Acta Musicologica,* the journal of the International Musicological Society; neither has the eleven-year-old journal *19th Century Music.*[7] Even the *Proceedings of the Royal Musical Association* yield only eight historical papers on Victorian subjects in the eighty-seven years since 1901, not counting obituary tributes. *Victorian Studies* itself, until the Autumn 1986 issue which is the basis of this book, had published only two articles on music in its twenty-nine years.[8] The first time, to my knowledge, that a panel of speakers on Victorian music was ever assembled at an interdisciplinary conference was at the meeting of the Midwest Victorian Studies Association at Ann Arbor, Michigan, in May 1984. The Institute of Victorian Studies at Leicester University organized the first known conference devoted to Victorian music in September 1979. Scholarly editions of Victorian music, too, are a very recent development.[9]

If music meant so much to the British in the nineteenth century, why has the twentieth shown so little interest in the music they produced? In an attempt to answer this question I must first discuss the scholarly study of mu-

---

[4] Cyril Ehrlich, *The Musical Profession in Britain Since the Eighteenth Century: A Social History* (Oxford: Clarendon Press, 1985), p. 235, Table 1.

[5] Both the sightsinging movement and the introduction of music in schools are treated by Bernarr Rainbow in his essay and also in *The Land Without Music: Musical Education in England 1800–1860 and Its Continental Antecedents* (London: Novello, 1967). See also his "Music in Education," in Temperley, ed., *The Romantic Age,* pp. 29–45, especially pp. 34–39. One college, the Royal Academy of Music, is pre-Victorian (1822). For information on inexpensive octavo editions, see Anon., *A Short History of Cheap Music* (London: Novello & Co., 1887).

[6] Founded in 1874, the Musical Association had two predecessors, the Musical Institute of London (1851–53) and the Musical Society of London (1858–67). See A. Hyatt King, "The Musical Institute of London and Its Successors," *Musical Times* 117 (1976), 221–223. For diploma-granting professional organizations, see Ehrlich, *The Musical Profession,* pp. 116–120.

[7] The subject is touched on, however, in David B. Levy, "Thomas Massa Alsager, Esq. [1779–1846]: A Beethoven Advocate in London," *19th Century Music* 9 (1985–86), 119–127. An article "Schumann and Sterndale Bennett" is due to appear in 1989.

[8] These were Temperley, "The English Romantic Opera," 9 (1965–66), 293–301, and Robert Bledsoe, "Henry Fothergill Chorley and the Reception of Verdi's Early Operas in England," 28 (1984–85), 631–655, which is included in this volume.

[9] The series *Musica Britannica: A National Collection of Music* began publication in 1951, but broached the Victorian period only with its 37th volume, *William Sterndale Bennett: Piano and Chamber Music,* edited by Geoffrey Bush (London: Stainer & Bell, 1972). A volume of Romantic Songs (1800–60) followed in 1979, and several volumes of late Victorian songs, edited by Bush, are now in progress. Other scholarly

sic in general—the discipline of musicology. There are two distinct goals in the study of the music (or any other art product) of a period: one for its value in itself, as art; the other for what it may tell us about the culture it represents. The conflict between them runs through the history of musicology and is very much with us today, with its overtones of a larger tension between the humanities and the social sciences.

Musicology is one of the youngest disciplines in the humanities. It is not to be confused with music theory, an ancient field of speculation. Musicology, in its historical phase, arose out of antiquarianism. When people began to feel curious about the music of past ages, they created a demand for experts who could interpret obsolete musical notation and explain early theoretical treatises and instruments. The earliest efforts centered on the music of classical Greece, but the sixteenth-century humanists found insuperable difficulties in resurrecting that defunct art. With the dawn of Romanticism in the eighteenth century, antiquarians began to turn to the music of the Middle Ages and Renaissance. Here the English took the lead in developing the necessary knowledge and began to revive early music in both publication and performance well before 1800.[10] The first two general histories of music were also the work of English authors.[11] These pioneers were musicians and men of letters; they never dreamed of calling themselves musicologists. It was the Germans who elevated musical scholarship into a distinct discipline (*Musikwissenschaft*) and developed its theoretical and philosophical framework, and many of its systems and methods. The seminal article for the new discipline was published by Guido Adler a century ago, to open a new journal.[12] British scholars long resisted such codification of their work. Edward Dent, professor of music at Cambridge from 1926 to 1941, is said to have pronounced that "German musicologists write only for other German musicologists".[13]

The distinction between English and German styles of musical scholarship has been lucidly drawn by Vincent Duckles, who concludes: "The truth of the matter is that Englishmen, in their thought about music, have always

series that substantially cover the music of the Victorian period are Gerald H. Knight and William L. Reed, eds., *A Treasury of English Church Music*, Vol. 4: 1760–1900 (London: Blandford Press, 1965); Nicholas Temperley, ed., *The London Pianoforte School, 1766–1860*, 20 vols. (New York: Garland, 1984–86), of which vols. 16–18 are wholly, and vols. 19 and 20 partly, Victorian; and William S. Gilbert and Arthur S. Sullivan, *The Operas*, ed. Steven Ledbetter and Percy M. Young, 13 vols. (New York: Broude Brothers, forthcoming). See also note 39.

10 See Vincent Duckles, "Musicology," in Temperley, ed., *The Romantic Age*, pp. 483–502, especially pp. 492–494.

11 These were John Hawkins, *A General History of the Science and Practice of Music*, 5 vols. (London: T. Payne and Son, 1776); and Charles Burney, *A General Hisotry of Music*, 4 vols. (London: n.p., 1776–89).

12 Guido Adler, "Umfang, Methode und Ziel der Musikwissenschaft," *Vierteljahrschrift für Musikwissenschaft* 1 (1885), 3–20. For discussion see Barry S. Brook and others, eds., *Perspectives in Musicology* (New York: Norton, 1972).

13 A tradition at Cambridge University. I personally recall R. Thurston Dart (1921–71), Dent's successor in the Cambridge chair of music from 1962 to 1964 and perhaps the leading British musicologist of his generation, categorically denying that he was anything other than a "musician."

taken greater interest in the *artistic* than in the *scientific* aspect of their discipline. They have never ceased to regard music as a realm of concrete experience, not a field for philosophical speculation" (Duckles, "Musicology,"
p. 484). Suspicion of systems has tended to persist in modern British musicology, although there are exceptions. Thus, we find today that London is the
world capital of the movement for historically authentic performance of early
music. The kind of scholarship needed for the recovery of music of the
Baroque and earlier periods is perfectly suited to the talents and inclinations
of the modern British musicologist, who is often a gifted performer as well:
such a person as Christopher Hogwood, or the late David Munrow. But when
we come to the more methodical study of musical history as a part of social
history or the history of ideas, to the systematic study of musical documents,
or to the analysis of musical styles, we frequently find that more real progress
is being made elsewhere, especially in Germany and the United States.
American musicology has inherited both British and German traditions, to
its great benefit, but if anything it has leaned towards the German, thanks to
the influence of German-trained refugees in the 1930s and 1940s who were
the second founders of American musicology.

When nineteenth-century music began to be opened up for scholarly
study, the obvious subject matter was the music of genius—of Beethoven,
Schubert, Berlioz, Wagner, Verdi. Nineteenth-century music, more than any
other, presents itself as a succession of masterpieces of great composers, who
reduce their contemporaries to insignificance. It happens that none of these
giants were British.[14] Nevertheless, it would have been a natural thing for
British scholars to take an interest in the music of their recent forebears, as
they have conspicuously in that of the more distant past. If few have done so,
it may be partly due to this very tendency to focus on the artifact, described
so clearly by Duckles. After all, there is little stimulus to work towards the
revival of Victorian music in performance. For one thing, we already know
how to perform nineteenth-century music—or we think we do; there are few
problems of notation, obsolete instruments, or performing practice that require the intervention of scholars. For another thing, there is already an
abundance of first-rate nineteenth-century masterpieces in the standard repertory. So there is little to interest the British scholar who is oriented towards
revival of historical music. And if British scholars have not taken a strong
lead in the revival of Victorian music in performance, there is the less reason
for Continental or American scholars to follow.

It is not surprising, then, that much of the best recent scholarship on
Victorian music has been of the kind that does not deal with the performance

---

[14] Edward Elgar (1857–1934) comes nearest to the pantheon. He is only just a Victorian: his two most
widely acknowledged masterpieces are the "Enigma" Variations (1899) and *The Dream of Gerontius*
(1900).

and critical evaluation of music itself, but with music as a reflection of society; and a good part of this work had been done by American rather than British scholars, and by people who are not musicologists by profession. Three good examples are Donald W. Krummel's work on music printing and publishing, Martha Vicinus's on industrial folksong, and William Weber's on concert life and middle-class values.[15] Among British scholars Bernarr Rainbow has done pioneering work on music education and the sightsinging movement, and Cyril Ehrlich on piano manufacture and more recently on the organization of the musical profession.[16] Good biographical research has been done on Victorian composers such as Edward Elgar, John Stainer, Arthur Seymour Sullivan, and Samuel Sebastian Wesley.[17]

But sooner or later it becomes necessary to deal with the music itself: to evaluate Victorian music as art. Naturally this side of the matter is concerned with art music.[18] Popular and functional music, almost by definition, do not invite critical evaluation; instead they are judged by their popularity or their functional utility, as the case may be. The evaluation of Victorian art music has been traditionally negative. Prejudice against serious Victorian music has persisted long after the general reaction against things Victorian peaked and subsided.

Much of this attitude stems from the Victorians themselves. They were prejudiced against native products in music much more than in the other arts. The sobriquet "Das Land ohne Musik," coined as the title of a German book about Britain (not about British music) published in 1914,[19] was founded squarely on the Victorians' estimation of themselves. Although some critics like James William Davison championed English art music and asserted its equal status with that of any other nation, they were clearly on

[15] Krummel, "Music Publishing"; Martha Vicinus, *The Industrial Muse* (London: Barnes & Noble, 1974); William G. Weber, *Music and the Middle Class: The Social Structure of Concert Life in London, Paris, and Vienna Between 1830 and 1848* (New York: Holmes and Meier, 1975). One recent study by a professional musicologist suggests that the tide may be turning: William J. Gatens, *Victorian Cathedral Music in Theory and Practice* (Cambridge: Cambridge University Press, 1986). Stephen Banfield, in *Sensibility and English Song: Critical Studies of the Early Twentieth Century* (Cambridge: Cambridge University Press, 1985), provides a serious appraisal of late Victorian art song, but only as an introduction to later music.

[16] Rainbow, *The Land Without Music*; Ehrlich, *The Piano* and *The Musical Profession*.

[17] Jerrold Northrop Moore, *Edward Elgar: A Creative Life* (Oxford: Oxford University Press, 1984); Peter Charlton, *John Stainer and the Musical Life of Victorian Britain* (Newton Abbot: David & Charles, 1984); Arthur Jacobs, *Arthur Sullivan, A Victorian Musician* (Oxford: Oxford University Press, 1984); Peter Horton, *Samuel Sebastian Wesley* (Oxford: Oxford University Press, forthcoming).

[18] The boundaries between folk, popular, and art music are the subject of constant discourse among musicologists. For the purpose of the Victorian period I have found it convenient to define folk music as that which people make for themselves without training or rehearsal; popular music, made for a population by professional musicians as music to listen to, but without intellectual challenge to ordinary members of that population; functional music, similarly produced, but designed as an accompaniment to other activity such as dancing, marching, or worship; art music, composed by professional musicians for a restricted population that will accept intellectual challenge on the basis of its familiarity with a body of established classics.

[19] Oscar A. H. Schmitz, *Das Land ohne Musik: englishche Gesellschaftsprobleme* (Munich: G. Müller, 1914).

the defensive. George Alexander Macfarren, composer, writer, and musical scholar, published an article in the *Cornhill Magazine* in 1868 expressly to refute the "almost proverbial saying—'The English are not a musical people.'"[20] Indeed the belief that English music was inferior, or even nonexistent, goes back more than a century before Victoria's reign, to the overwhelming prestige that Italian music enjoyed in the Augustan age, when the supreme exponent of Italian opera in London was a German, George Frideric Handel. During the nineteenth century Italy maintained its hegemony in opera; in instrumental music and the art song it gave way not to English but to German dominance, while France continued to be the main source for dance music and, later, operetta.

Many countries besides Britain experienced foreign domination of their music, and several in the nineteenth century produced a strong reaction that is known as musical nationalism. One of the first to do so was Germany: composers like Carl Maria von Weber, Robert Schumann, and Richard Wagner devoted much of their energies to establishing German music as the equal or superior of Italian. In this they were supremely successful. Poles, Russians, Czechs, Hungarians, Norwegians, and Spaniards also looked for what was distinctive in the music of their own cultures and emphasized it in their compositions, building styles based on recognizable and colorful rhythms, scales, and instruments of their nations' folk song and dance. Musical nationalism was often linked with political independence movements, and, like them, was not truly a phenomenon of the "folk," but of intellectuals of the professional classes and the civil service. Frédéric Chopin, exiled in Paris from his native Poland, which was under oppressive Russian occupation, vented his patriotism in mazurkas, polonaises, and Polish songs. Later, in Russia itself, Modest Mussorgsky and Alexander Borodin, tired of the exclusively West-European musical tastes of the Russian aristocracy, asserted native values in the 1850s and 1860s in works like *Boris Godunov* and *Prince Igor.*

There was a corresponding movement in Britain. The cultivation of Scottish and Irish songs by Robert Burns, Thomas Moore, and their colleagues is certainly an example of it. Even in England, where the political motive was lacking, there was some manifestation of musical nationalism, as we will see in the final chapter.[21] But it did not develop strongly until the turn of the century, as Plantinga has pointed out.[22] It was then a reaction to Ger-

---

[20] George A. Macfarren, "The English are not a Musical People," *Cornhill Magazine* 18 (1868), 344–363. Ralph Waldo Emerson, in *English Traits* (Boston: Phillips, Sampson, and Co., 1856), 251, n. 1, wrote: "England has no music. It has never produced a first-rate composer, and accepts only such music as has already been decided to be good in Italy and Germany." For some earlier British expressions of similar opinions, see *Musical Times* 116 (1975), 439, 625, 877.

[21] See also Henry C. Banister, *George Alexander Macfarren: His Life, Works, and Influence* (London: George Bell, 1891), chap. 7.

[22] Leon Plantinga, *Romantic Music* (New York: Norton, 1984), p. 400. This is, by the way, the first general book on nineteenth-century music that accords adequate consideration to British music.

man domination and was linked to the increasing political hostility between the two countries; it is perhaps best exemplified in the music of Ralph Vaughan Williams.[23]

But beyond the weakness of the nationalist impulse lay the rooted belief that the English were by nature unmusical. It was even stated categorically that there was no such thing as English folksong. William Chappell, in the 1855 preface to his pioneering collection of English folksong, wrote: "I have been at some trouble to trace to its origin the assertion that the English have no national music."[24] This astounding illusion could only be sustained by a kind of selective deafness, for there was English folk music to be heard everywhere: in city streets as well as country lanes; in theatres, taverns, churches, dance halls, warehouses, and factories, and for that matter in drawing rooms, where young ladies vied with each other in playing fantasias and variations on English airs. The trouble seems to have been that English folk music was not recognized as such. It was too close to the mainstream of art and popular music, and lacked those exotic, colorful traits that distinguished the songs of Ireland and Scotland or, for that matter, of Poland, Hungary, and Spain. By the same token, European art music, however much it was dominated by Italian and German composers, did not sound to the English like an alien imposition. It was their idiom too, and they had played a part in its development.

For all these reasons the concert-going public was highly receptive to Continental music, performed if possible by Continental singers and players; and increasingly, they preferred the "classics"—music of dead composers accepted permanently into the repertory, in a temple where they were enshrined above criticism (Weber, pp. 61–69). In the first tier of this monumental structure Handel stood alone. He was thought of as "our great national composer," but far beyond the reach of imitation. In the later Victorian period, Bach began to challenge this position, as his great choral works became widely known. In a second tier were Haydn, Mozart, and Beethoven, soon joined by Spohr, Weber, and Mendelssohn—Germans all, representing the modern era. This hierarchy is not only revealed by statistics from Victorian programs and writings. It was carved in stone in the architecture of the old St. James's Hall, opened in 1858, and can also be found in a neoclassical decorative design on the covers of Novello's vocal scores (see figure 1).[25]

---

[23] For a full discussion see Frank Howes, *The English Musical Renaissance* (New York: Stein and Day, 1966), chaps. 12 and 13.

[24] William Chappell, *The Ballad Literature and Popular Music of the Olden Time*, 2 vols. (London: Chappell, 1855, 1859), I, xiv.

[25] The cover border shown in figure 1 was used by Novello & Co. for their octavo choral scores from about 1870. The covers are buff with dark brown lettering. Shortly after 1900 the names Weber and Spohr were dropped and replaced by Brahms and Purcell (the first English name). A parallel series of opera scores used the same design, but with orange lettering and a different selection of names: Mozart in the top panel, Beethoven at the bottom, and at the sides Auber, Cherubini, Gluck, Wagner, Rossini, and Weber.

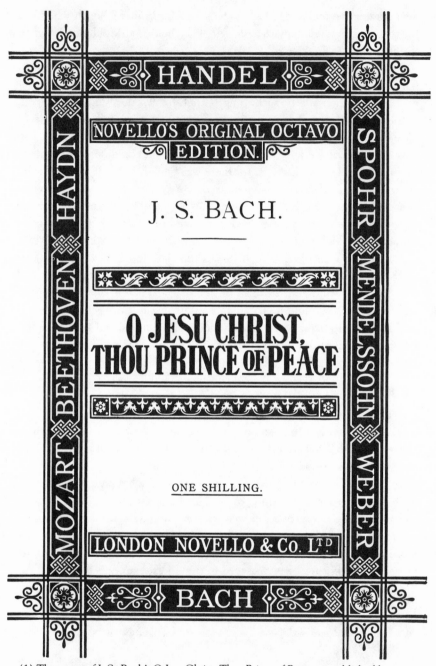

(1) The cover of J. S. Bach's *O Jesu Christ, Thou Prince of Peace,* as published by Novello & Co.

Again, our cover illustration, representing an amateur musical gathering in 1849, has books of music strewn about the floor in front of the players, showing a similar assortment of names: Bach, Beethoven, Cherubini, Handel, Haydn, Mendelssohn, Mozart, Palestrina, Pergolesi, Sphor [sic], Spontini, and Weber. There is not an English name among them.

Was it the case that there were no talented English composers? As far as inborn musical ability goes, we can discount this possibility. England had just as many precocious musical children and prodigies as any other country, and they were brought before the public at a time when this was fashionable. William Crotch (1775–1847) far exceeded even Mozart in precocity: there is excellent evidence that he publicly performed "God Save the King" with a bass of his own devising at the age of two and a half.[26] He was also a talented painter. He became professor of music at Oxford and then an ultraconservative early Victorian composer. One of Crotch's successors at Oxford, Frederick Ouseley (1825–89), had had two compositions—one a full-length Italian operatic *scena*—reviewed in print before he was nine.[27] George Aspull (1813–32) was also famous for his precocity as pianist and composer.[28] The works of all these, and of others like them, are almost entirely forgotten today.

The problem surely lay in the lack of encouragement for English composers. In the eighteenth century, and still in the early nineteenth, the attitudes of the landed aristocracy were decisive in this as in most other matters. Unlike the petty princes of Germany and Italy, whose rivalry did so much to provide support for music and musicians at their courts, English noblemen did little to promote the art at home. Instead, they demonstrated their superiority by their knowledge of foreign languages and music. The Italian opera was their great musical stronghold—at the King's Theatre in the Haymarket (later Her Majesty's Theatre), and from 1848 also at the Royal Italian Opera House, Covent Garden, from which the word "Italian" was not dropped until 1892. In his essay, Robert Bledsoe discusses the Victorians' reception of the operas of the greatest Italian composer of their time, Giuseppe Verdi. French, German, Russian, and even English operas had to be translated into Italian before they could be performed there: Wagner's *Der fliegende Holländer*, for instance, appeared as *L'Ollandese dannato*.[29] Only one opera by a British (in this case, Anglo-Irish) composer was ever commissioned for either Italian opera house during the Victorian period: Michael William Balfe's *Falstaff*, to

[26] Dr. Charles Burney's "Account of an Infant Musician" was published in *Philosophical Transactions of the Royal Society* 69 (1779), 183ff. There is also an account in Daines Barrington, *Miscellanies* (London, 1781), pp. 311ff.

[27] *Harmonicon* 11 (1833), 102; *Monthly Supplement to the Musical Library* 1 (1834), 66.

[28] See Muriel Silburn, "The Most Extraordinary Creature in Europe," *Music and Letters* 3 (1922), 201–205.

[29] It is a bizarre fact that one of the first British piano arrangements of Wagner's music, a medley by Arthur O'Leary, appeared in 1871 in a series, published in London, entitled *Les charmes de l'opéra italien*.

an Italian libretto by the in-house poet, S. Manfredo Maggione, had its premiere at Her Majesty's in 1838.

Together with this affectation of Italian taste came the aristocratic idea that music was no pursuit for a gentleman, except as a dilettante. Mary Burgan finds this attitude in the writings of John Locke; it is also trenchantly expressed in Lord Chesterfield's letters to his son.[30] Music, by this standard, was something to be provided for one's entertainment by lesser breeds, among which Italians and ladies were certainly included. Young ladies in bourgeois and aristocratic families were encouraged to study the piano, the harp, and singing, as a superficial accomplishment valued in the marriage market.

Not all these attitudes were adopted by the increasingly formidable middle classes, from whose ranks one might have hoped that great English composers would emerge. There were, of course, many different strains within the middle classes, and one must beware of easy generalization. A substantial fraction of professional business men belonged to religious denominations that had a long history of proscription of the theatre; this included evangelical Anglicans as well as most dissenters. They would not countenance opera and would accept oratorio only when it moved out of the theatres and into the churches, or into such respectable venues as Exeter Hall and the town halls of Birmingham and Leeds. Reared perhaps on unadorned hymn singing, they gradually came to accept instruments and elaborate musical forms if associated with Biblical or other uplifting texts.

More widespread in middle-class circles was a prejudice against Italian music, associated as it was with the theatre, the Catholic church, and the more frivolous pursuits of the nobility. Those who did cultivate music tended to turn instead to the Protestant, sober, and serious music of northern Europe. It was indeed in middle-class organizations such as the Philharmonic Society (founded in 1813) that the dominance of German instrumental music was established.[31] The beginning of serious and profound appreciation of music as an art was also evidently a middle-class phenomenon, supported perhaps by a handful of aristocrats. A telling indicator is audience behavior. At the fashionable concerts attended by the nobility, according to a French observer in 1829, "Hardly has the accompanist given the signal by preluding on the piano, when colloquies are established throughout the room; the chattering soon becomes similar to that of a public place or market, and lasts till the end of the piece."[32] In the middle-class chamber music concerts established

---

[30] Philip D. Stanhope, 4th Earl of Chesterfield, *Letters . . . to his Son* (London: J. Dodsley, 1774), letter 175 (April 1749).

[31] This is clearly stated in the *Quarterly Musical Magazine and Review* 4 (1821), 252. For further discussion see Weber, p. 64. An observer in 1837 noted that when Mozart's *Don Giovanni* was put on at the King's Theatre instead of the usual fare of Rossini and his imitators, a very different audience came, drawn mainly "from the East of Pall Mall"—that is, from the mercantile part of London (*Musical World* 5 [1837], 124).

[32] François J. Fétis, letter to his son on the state of music in London, printed in translation in *Harmonicon* 7 (1829), 276. It is part of a discussion of the social exclusiveness of the Italian opera and the concerts ancillary to it.

in London in the 1830s, a very different atmosphere prevailed—one familiar
enough today, but considered worthy of description in 1838: "The prolonged
silence indicates the deepest interest; the subdued whisper acknowledges the
sympathy felt at particular points of the performance; and the cordial applause, at the close of each piece, appears a relief to the high-wrought enthusiasm of the hearers." [33]

Some newly rich people, on the other hand, were known for philis-
tinism, for a tendency to esteem things only for their palpable practical or
social utility. That meant giving music a low rating in general, and, insofar as
they valued it at all, looking only for what had social prestige or displayed
mechanical dexterity, while ignoring inner meaning. Such attitudes were
satirized in this mock-antique excerpt from "Mr. Pips his Diary" in *Punch* for
21 April 1849, which was printed below the caricature by Richard Doyle re-
produced on our cover:

> To Mr. JIGGINS's, where my Wife and I were invited to Tea and a little Musique . . . I do
> prefer a stronger kind of Musique as well as Liquor. Yet it was pleasing enough to the Ear
> to hear the fashionable Ballads, and the Airs from all the new Italian Operas sung by the
> young Ladies; which, though they expressed nothing but common-place Love and Senti-
> ment, yet were a pretty Sing-Song . . . Besides the Singing, there was Playing of the
> Piano Forte, with the Accompaniment of a Fiddle and Bass Violl, the Piano being played
> by a stout fat Lady with a Dumpling Face . . . They did call this Piece a Concerto, and I
> was told it was very brilliant; but when I asked what Fancy, Passion, or Description there
> was in it, no one could tell . . . After the Concerto, some Polkas and Waltzes, which did
> better please me, for they were a lively Jingle certainly, and not quite unmeaning.
> Strange to find how rare a Thing good Musique is in Company; and by good Musique I
> mean such as do stir up the Soul . . . My Wife do Play some brave Pieces in this Kind, by
> Mynheer Van Beethoven, and I would rather hear her perform one of them, than all I did
> hear to-night put together . . . But every one to his Taste; and they who delight in the
> trivial Style of Musique to theirs, as I to mine, not doubting that the English that have
> but just begun to be sensible to Musique at all, will be awake to the nobler Sort of it
> by and by. [34]

Middle-class people in general were probably no more anxious than
their social betters to have their children become professional musicians. For
men, any serious interest in music was thought effeminate as well as unprac-
tical, and the subject was not included in most public-school curricula, as
Bernarr Rainbow points out in his essay. Women might pursue music as an
accomplishment, but it was taken for granted that they were incapable of serious attainment, particularly as composers. [35]

Thus, although there were plenty of English men and women who
were gifted in music, most of them failed to get a fair hearing if they attempted serious work. Their lives were often a heartbreaking series of disap-

---

[33] *Musical World* 8 (1838), 50.

[34] "Mr. Pips his Diary," *Punch* 16 (21 April 1849), 164.

[35] See Derek Hyde, *New Found Voices: Women in Nineteenth-Century English Music* (London: Belvedere, 1984). Hyde does, however, list forty-nine known women composers from this period in an appendix. See also Ehrlich, *The Musical Profession*, 156–161.

pointments. A prime example is William Sterndale Bennett (1816–75), whose career began in a blaze of excitement and enthusiasm. The most promising student coming out of the Royal Academy of Music in the 1830s, Bennett went to Germany and was hailed by Mendelssohn and Schumann as the bright new star from the West. In those early years he was producing some three major orchestral works every year, as well as songs, chamber music, and piano pieces, and was getting them performed and published in both England and Germany. But when he settled down to his career in London the hard reality soon came home to him: the British public at large did not support his serious aims. He wrote to his Leipzig publisher, Friedrich Kistner, in 1840: "You know what a dreadful place England is for music; and in London, I have nobody who I can talk to about such things, all the people are mad with Thalberg and Strauss, and I have not heard a single Symphony or Overture in one concert since last June. I sincerely hope that Prince Albert our Queens husband will do something to improve our taste."[36] Bennett's output soon dwindled, and the quality of his compositions declined, because he was forced to devote all his energies to teaching and, later, administration. The other alternative, to resort to popular music, was against the high artistic principles he shared with the German Romantics. Although he gained growing official recognition and status, culminating in a knighthood recommended by Gladstone in 1871, he never recovered his early brilliance as a composer.[37]

But there were some exceptions to the lack of encouragement and opportunity that Victorian composers generally faced. One was the Church of England, which supported a large number of musicians, and which was still an almost exclusive preserve of native composers, with traditions largely independent of Continental music. Several Victorians who devoted their energies to the composition of cathedral music achieved both frequent performance of their works and some critical acclaim: for instance, besides Ouseley and Stainer, John Goss (1800–80), Thomas Attwood Walmisley (1814–56), and Charles Villiers Stanford (1852–1924). For the same reasons, their works have continued to be heard occasionally in our own time, and others could easily be revived by cathedral choirs. One cathedral musician, Samuel Sebastian Wesley (1810–76), was a composer of genius, particularly inspired in his response to the words of the Bible. He is the subject of Peter Horton's essay. On a less exalted level, many female as well as male organists had part-

---

[36] From an album of hand-copied letters, entitled "W.S.B.'s Letters to Kistner," in the Sterndale Bennett family collection at Longparish, Andover, Hants. I am grateful to Mr. Barry Sterndale-Bennett for allowing me access to this collection.

[37] For more detailed analysis of Bennett's career, see James R. Sterndale Bennett, *The Life of William Sterndale Bennett: By His Son* (Cambridge: Cambridge University Press, 1907); Geoffrey Bush, "Sterndale Bennett: The Solo Piano Works," *Proceedings of the Royal Musical Association* 91 (1964–65), 85–97; Nicholas Temperley, "Bennett, Willaim Sterndale," in *The New Grove Dictionary of Music and Musicians* (London: Macmillan, 1980).

time employment in parish churches and nonconformist chapels, and the huge market for hymn tunes was a forum for hundreds of British composers.[38]

There was, secondly, a school of Engligh-language opera, which continued to flourish, though at a far lower level of prestige and finance than the Italian opera. It enjoyed something of a rebirth in the 1830s when a new school of English romantic opera was founded (Temperley, "English Romantic Opera"), and Balfe's *Bohemian Girl* (1843) and William Vincent Wallace's *Maritana* (1845) enjoyed a success that lasted a hundred years, well into the era of the radio and phonograph. Some of the songs and ballads from these operas were perennially popular; one of these, "I dreamt that I dwelt in marble halls" from *The Bohemian Girl,* is included on the cassette accompanying this book. In later years, of course, Sullivan found a place in the sun for his comic operas. Like Balfe and Wallace, he was of Anglo-Irish stock. Studies of William Schwenk Gilbert tend to slight Sullivan's contribution to their joint triumph, but his music was original, technically brilliant, and often passionate. It supplied the lyric warmth that Gilbert himself conspicuously lacked. Sullivan's idiom is not sharply distinguished from the general European style of the day; there is nothing nationalistic about it. It was Gilbert who gave the Savoy operas their thoroughly English complexion and who, partly by avoiding all suggestions of impropriety, won over a new opera public who had originally avoided opera altogether.

The Savoy operas show no signs of losing their popularity, even with the decline of British government subsidy and the demise of the D'Oyly Carte company. As with cathedral music, the survival of some examples makes the revival of others a comparatively risk-free proposition, and there have been recent performances of little-known late works like *Utopia Limited,* and of Sullivan's pre-Gilbert operetta *Cox and Box.* But Sullivan composed seriously in many other fields—oratorio, church music, incidental music, symphonies, songs, and piano music—and he wrote one grand opera, *Ivanhoe* (1891). The time seems to have come when some of this music will at last get a fair hearing.

At the turn of the century another composer, Edward Elgar, broke the barriers and entered the realms of the great: the decisive factor here was that his music was taken up in Germany shortly after 1900.[39] Now a great Elgar revival is in progress in Britain. It can be interpreted as part of the nostalgia

---

[38] For discussion of cathedral music see "Cathedral Music" in Temperley, ed., *The Romantic Age,* pp. 171–213, and Gatens, *Victorian Cathedral Music.* For women organists see Hyde, pp. 32–35. For hymn tune composition see Temperley, *Music of the English Parish Church,* I, 296–310, and Erik Routley, *The Music of Christian Hymns* (Chicago: G.I.A. Publications, 1981), pp. 89–110.

[39] See Michael Kennedy, *Portrait of Elgar* (London: Oxford University Press, 1968), pp. 97–102. A critical edition of Elgar's works is in process of publication: Jerrold Northrop Moore and others, eds., *Elgar Complete Edition,* 43 vols. projected (London: Novello, 1981–    ). It is the first of its kind for any British composer later than Henry Purcell (1659–95).

for the imperial high noon that is now engulfing the country, seen also in the many films and television productions dealing with the Edwardian period, the Great War, the twenties and thirties, and the Raj. But Elgar has been given no more than his due.

In all these cases—cathedral music, the Savoy operas, Elgar—upward reevaluation can build on a living tradition of performance. It is quite another matter with music that has dropped out of the repertory. When we try to revive and revalue neglected writers, thinkers, artists, and architects, the process can be easily initiated within the academic community; we can all read the books for ourselves, while paintings, drawings, and buildings are readily available to be looked at with fresh eyes. It is much more difficult to revive music, and the degree of difficulty escalates as we go from piano music and songs, through chamber music and partsongs, to orchestral music, oratorio, and grand opera. The number of people who can read a score in a library and imagine how it would sound is quite small. For wider assessment, one needs performances and recordings. They cost money, time, and trouble, which few are willing to invest on untried bodies of music.

This inherent difficulty has tended to perpetuate the judgments of previous generations. It is the final reason for the backwardness of musical scholarship in opening up the Victorian age. Serious Victorian music is a Lost Chord: the sound of it is out of our reach, in a way that the sight and message of other Victorian arts is not. The chord was heard only faintly by the Victorians themselves, being drowned out by sounds coming across the Channel; after their time, in the words of Adelaide Procter's song, it "trembled away into silence."

It is in the hope of overcoming this handicap that we are attaching a specially recorded cassette to this volume, containing music which, for the most part, is difficult or impossible to hear on commercial recordings.

First, I have recorded a few songs to illustrate some of the points made in this introductory essay.[40] Edward James Loder (1813–65) was another victim of prejudice against serious music by English composers. Having no source of income except his composing, he tried to make a living by writing popular ballads under contract with a London publisher, but he made a sharp distinction between these and his art songs. "Invocation to the Deep" is one of the latter, with a text by the then-fashionable Felicia Hemans, who asks the sea to restore its victims. Not a great poem, it is yet well suited to music, and Loder makes the most of his opportunity to illustrate the swelling waves in a way that also conveys passionate feeling.

Next, Charles Stanford was a figure of the late Victorian musical es-

---

[40] Phyllis Hurt, who sings the five songs on this recording, also sang them in a presentation, "Victorian Songs for Every Taste," given at the Midwest Victorian Studies Association, Bloomington, IN, 28 March 1980, and at the Northeast Victorian Studies Association, Hartford, CT, 25 April 1981.

tablishment who composed prolifically in many branches of music. In 1892 he published a set of songs from Robert Louis Stevenson's *Child's Garden of Verses.* "Foreign Children" illustrates that ineffable cultural superiority of the English to which allusion has been made; but it is here combined with some delicate touches of musical exoticism.

Several late Victorian women joined the ranks of serious British composers, among them Maude Valérie White, Ethel Smyth, and Liza Lehmann. Lehmann (1862–1918), like Loder, spread her talent over a spectrum of musical styles from the drawing-room ballad to the art song. The setting of Shelley's "Widow Bird" is one that succeeds in powerfully conveying landscape and atmosphere on a small scale; if Loder's song is comparable to Mendelssohn's or Schumann's, Lehmann's need not be ashamed to stand beside Hugo Wolf's.

To exemplify middle-class popular music I have chosen Balfe's "I dreamt that I dwelt in marble halls," from *The Bohemian Girl.* In the opera it makes a strong dramatic point, in that the heroine, brought up among gypsies, is really remembering her patrician childhood when she thinks she is dreaming. But ballads were placed in operas primarily for subsequent sale as sheet music, in association with the name of the primadonna who had launched them on the stage: hence their nickname "music-shop ballads." Alfred Bunn's text, taken out of its stage context, neatly expresses the dreams of a middle-class Victorian girl: riches, social standing, admiration, romance, and a constant lover. Balfe writes a smooth melody and a murmuring, static accompaniment to induce a state of dreamy fantasy.

The last example is of working-class popular music, and was sung by perhaps the greatest of all music-hall singers, Marie Lloyd, "the expressive figure of the lower classes".[41] As many have pointed out, both the verses and the music of such songs were quite ordinary; the poets and composers were nonentities. Everything depended on the spirit and personality of the singer and her rapport with the audience,[42] which we can only do our best to echo. In "Buy Me Some Almond Rock" Lloyd is indulging in a pleasant fantasy of social aspiration. She imagines herself flirting with the political leaders of the day, and so cuts them down to size.

To illustrate the essay by Mary Burgan, the recording continues with two contrasted piano pieces such as Victorian young ladies played. "The Battle of Prague," an old war-horse by the Bohemian Franz Koczwara, was first published at London in about 1788, presumably to commemorate Frederick the Great's victory of 1757. It is difficult to say why this piece of claptrap remained so popular long after the general fashion for illustrative battle pieces

---

[41] T. S. Eliot, "Marie Lloyd," in *Selected Essays, 1917–1932* (New York: Harcourt Brace, 1932), pp. 369–372, especially p. 371.

[42] See Richard Middleton, "Popular Music of the Lower Classes," in Temperley, ed., *The Romantic Age,* pp. 63–91, especially p. 86.

had abated, and it was a frequent subject of jokes and parodies in the Victorian period. Mendelssohn's "Fantasia on a Favorite Irish Melody" was also first published in London—in 1830, when the composer was deeply stirred by his direct experience of the wilder Celtic parts of Britain.[43] "'Tis the last rose of summer," on which it is based, was perhaps the most popular of all Thomas Moore's *Irish Melodies*. This wonderfully romantic piece is a superior example of the countless fantasias and variations on "national airs" that so many lady pianists delighted in; and many, the young queen among them, retained for Mendelssohn a special place in their affections.

The six songs composed by Ruskin, though nobody would claim for them high musical merit, are interesting curiosities which, so far as we know, have never before been recorded. To some extent they are experimental, as William Gatens explains. By contrast, we have in Samuel Sebastian Wesley a composer who has always been recognized as a genius, if an erratic one, and who is arguably the greatest master of Anglican cathedral music since the time of Purcell. Peter Horton has found new significance in the connection between the style of these three works and Wesley's employment at Leeds parish church.

Finally, the Tennyson song cycle by the late Victorian composer Arthur Somervell marks what some have called the English Musical Renaissance of that time,[44] and certainly demonstrates a new sensitivity on the part of British composers to the meaning of poetry on many levels. That is the subject matter of Linda Hughes's essay.

These assorted fragments of Victorian music—high and low, professional and amateur, original and conventional—can give some echo of the immensely varied and vital musical life the Victorians knew. But a fully informed and considered judgment on the sum of their musical achievement can only be made after their greatest works have been made available once more to the scholarly community and the public at large.

---

[43] See Roger Fiske, *Scotland in Music: A European Enthusiasm* (Cambridge: Cambridge University Press, 1983), pp. 116–149; R. Larry Todd, "Mendelssohn's Ossianic Manner," in *Mendelssohn and Schumann: Essays on Their Music and Its Context*, ed. Jon W. Finson & R. Larry Todd (Durham, N.C.: Duke University Press, 1984).

[44] See Ernest Walker, *A History of Music in England* (Oxford: Clarendon Press, 1907; 3d ed., revised and enlarged by Jack A. Westrup, 1952), chap. 11; Frank Howes, *The English Musical Renaissance* (New York: Stein & Day, 1966).

Bernarr Rainbow

# THE RISE OF POPULAR MUSIC EDUCATION IN NINETEENTH-CENTURY ENGLAND

IN THE YEAR OF VICTORIA'S SUCCESSION TO THE THRONE, THOMAS WYSE, A vigorous advocate of educational reform in the House of Commons, drew attention to the longstanding neglect of music teaching in the nation's schools:

> Music, even the most elementary, not only does not form an essential of education in this country, but the idea of introducing it is not even dreamt of. It is urged, that it would be fruitless to attempt it, because the people are essentially unmusical; but may not they be anti-musical because it has not been attempted? The people roar and scream, because they have heard nothing but roaring and screaming — no music — from their childhood. Is harmony not to be taught? . . . No effort is made in any of our schools; and then we complain that there is no music amongst our scholars. It would be as reasonable to exclude grammar and then complain that we had no grammarians. [1]

The national struggle to reverse that position took place during the queen's reign in conjunction with gradual acceptance by the state of responsibility for popular education as a whole.

Such limited educational progress as in fact occurred in Britain between 1800 and 1837 was largely due to private endeavour. Much of it concerned elementary education, was purely local in effect, and found its inspiration in some particular individual's awareness of continental developments. The rival monitorial systems introduced by Joseph Lancaster and Andrew Bell, each administered by opposing religious bodies, first received a meagre government subsidy to support them in the provision of elementary education in 1833. But the state still failed to accept responsibility for the education of its subjects along lines similar to those of most northern European countries.

The first major effort to readmit music teaching to the elementary curriculum in England since its virtual banishment at the Reformation had occurred in 1790 when Bishop Porteus of London advised the clergy of his di-

---

[1] Thomas Wyse, *Education Reform* (London: n.p., 1836), p. 186; quoted in J. Mainzer, *Music and Education* (1848; rpt. ed. Kilkenny: Boethius, 1985), p. 106. Wyse uses the term "harmony" here to indicate "music," not the skill of chord writing.

ocese that the provision of singing lessons in the nation's many Sunday Schools would go a long way toward correcting the deplorable standard of singing in parochial churches. [2] On the other hand, the first stirrings of an awareness that music deserved a place in its own right in every child's general education can safely be traced to Robert Owen and the model for infant education first presented in his experimental school at New Lanark on the Clyde before its disbanding in 1824. Though evidently unaware of the writings of Rousseau and Johann Heinrich Pestalozzi on education, Owen had formed ideas of his own virtually identical with many of theirs. In his school, memorization and "book-learning" were replaced by deliberate exercise of the senses. Practical experiment and observation, play, physical drill, dancing, and singing all became essential features of his little pupils' daily programme; and among the wall charts enlivening their classrooms were found not only pictures of exotic animals and plants, but copies of the tunes they sang written out in musical notation. [3]

Owen's educational experiment was shortlived, and though his ideas were taken up elsewhere in Britain by such disciples as David Stow and Samuel Wilderspin, enlightened teaching received its next important stimulus more directly from Pestalozzi through the activities of enthusiasts who had travelled to Switzerland to work under his direction before setting up private schools of their own in Britain. Charles Mayo at Epsom and J. P. Greaves at Ham, are best known among those who brought Pestalozzian methods — including recreational song — into currency. And in his *Letters on Early Education Addressed to J. P. Greaves* Pestalozzi expressed his regret that in spite of its beneficial influence music did not form a more prominent feature in general education in England. [4]

But before music could earn a place in subsidized schools run by the supporters of Bell and Lancaster middle class scepticism had to be persuaded. Hard-headed school governors who failed to respond to Pestalozzi's declaration that music was "beneficial" were more readily convinced when it could be shown that music teaching was "useful." And the first school music textbook to appear in England in modern times was careful to underline this functional aspect on its title page. John Turner's *Manual of Instruction in Vocal Music* (1833) was subtitled *chiefly with a view to Psalmody*. Its immediate successor, Sarah Glover's *Scheme for Rendering Psalmody Congregational* (1835), was even more specifically titled. And only when W. E. Hickson's *The Sing-*

---

[2] Beilby Porteus, *Works*, 6 vols. (London: Cadell and Davies, 1811), VI, 243.

[3] H. Silver, ed., *Robert Owen on Education* (London: Cambridge University Press, 1969), pp. 162-163.

[4] Johann Heinrich Pestalozzi, *Letters on Early Education Addressed to J. P. Greaves* (London: Sherwood, Gilbert and Piper, 1827), Letter 23, 18 February 1827, pp. 93-99.

*ing Master* (1836) followed, was the connection between singing in school and singing in church less heavily emphasized, to be replaced by the argument that something more was required "to improve the mind, and hearts, and promote the happiness of the rising generation than has hitherto been attempted."[5] All three books were soon enjoying local use in a few areas.

Each of the pioneers concerned in these prime ventures, from Bishop Porteus onward, sought (often unwittingly) to restore music teaching to the place it had held in popular education before the Reformation swept away the song schools, chantry, and monastic schools providing it. As Thomas Wyse's statement suggests, early efforts in this direction remained little known nationally. But in the warmer educational climate that followed the passing of the first Reform Bill, it is no coincidence to find three school music textbooks making their unprecedented appearance within as many years. For when the first state grant for education was belatedly approved by Parliament in 1833, a turning point had been reached. Subsequently, governmental apathy in such matters steadily gave place to reluctant awareness that educational provision in Britain was shamefully inadequate. The situation was slowly corrected during Victoria's reign.

I

One striking feature of the century's educational advance was its initial polarity. At the outset, reforming energy was centred upon schools catering to extreme elements in the population: the children of the labouring poor and of the aristocratic rich were its principal beneficiaries, leaving the sons and daughters of a rapidly growing middle class largely unprovided for. Religious differences complicated the situation. According to whether their parents subscribed to Prayer Book or Dissent, the children of the poor went to "National" or "British" elementary schools; the sons of the wealthy folk either to ancient public schools or those nonconformist academies established during the previous century. The curriculum content, religious instruction, and methods of teaching in these schools varied greatly, and no music was taught in any of them.

An increase in the government grant subsidizing voluntary elementary schools heralded the appointment in 1839 of school inspectors whose reports were soon exposing conditions of scandalous neglect and incompetence in existing schools and their teachers. Six years previously a special committee

---

[5] W. E. Hickson, *The Singing Master* (1836; rpt. ed. Kilkenny: Boethius, 1984), p. 3. John Turner, *Manual of Instruction in Vocal Music* (1833; rpt. ed. Kilkenny: Boethius, 1983); Sarah Glover, *Scheme for Rendering Psalmody Congregational* (1835; rpt. ed. Kilkenny: Boethius, 1982).

of the Privy Council had been appointed to consider educational provision; and in 1835 £10,000 was voted for the building of a state training college for teachers. But it was not until the true scale of educational shortcomings was revealed during 1839 that urgent remedies were sought and the new Committee of Council on Education braced itself to undertake substantial reform of elementary education. An indirect consequence was the reinstatement of the music lesson in schools for the children of the poor. Meanwhile, following the example of Thomas Arnold at Rugby, reform began from within the almost equally ill-conducted schools of the wealthier classes. But it required the courageous unorthodoxy of another famous headmaster, Edward Thring of Uppingham, before music was admitted to the curriculum of a public school a generation later.

Although much of the substance of the Education Bill of 1839 may be traced to earlier proposals made by Wyse, the principal architect of the policy implemented by the Committee of Council on Education was its secretary, James Kay. A medical man rather than a teacher and later to become Sir James Kay-Shuttleworth, he owed his influential appointment to his known devotion to progressive educational ideals and the success with which he had applied them in his capacity as assistant poor law commissioner to improve the lot of pauper children immured in the workhouses of rural England.

The members of the committee itself — Henry Petty-Fitzmaurice, John William Ponsonby, John Russell, and Thomas Spring Rice — relied heavily upon their secretary for the formulation of educational strategy. To prepare himself for the responsible task of advising them, Kay undertook in 1839 a three-months' tour of Holland, France, Prussia, and Switzerland, to examine for himself the methods and conditions prevailing in the schools of the four countries which had already introduced state systems of education. On his return, armed with a substantial collection of the primers and manuals employed in those schools, Kay's belief in the automatic superiority of continental teaching methods was reinforced, and his faith in Pestalozzi as the inspired fount of educational wisdom confirmed.

During Kay's absence abroad, however, Parliament again deferred the establishment of a national training college for teachers. No compromise could be reached between Church and Dissent upon their differences over religious instruction in the proposed institution, and the issue was shelved. Faced with this obstacle, Kay promptly and boldly decided to found a private institution himself, to demonstrate how such an establishment could be conducted without sacrificing religious principles. With the financial backing of his friends he set up a small-scale training college to accommodate a dozen youths in what was then the Thames-side village of Battersea. There he put into practice the lessons learnt during his recent educational tour and laid the framework of a model curriculum for the elementary schools of the future. No longer restricted to religious instruction and the three "Rs," Kay's enlarged syllabus included both music and drawing, taught according to methods which he attributed to Pestalozzi. At that time Kay's conception of the nature of Pestalozzian teaching was summarized by him as "leading children from the known to the unknown by gradual steps."[6] Valid so far as it went, that definition failed to recognize the method's sensory and synthetic characteristics. As a result Kay often tended to attribute to Pestalozzi teaching methods which owed little or nothing to his tenets.

An example of this misconception can be seen by comparing the methods adopted at Battersea for teaching reading, writing, drawing, and music. The reading primer was an English adaptation of the German method devised by a pupil of Pestalozzi named Lautier. The writing primer was by another of his pupils named Mühlhauser. Both were authentic applications of the Swiss educationist's principles.[7] But drawing was taught using Alexandre Dupuis' geometrical objects, and this had no connection with Pestalozzian theories, though Kay justified their use as allowing the student "to proceed by gradual steps through a series of combinations until he was able to draw faithfully any object, however complex."[8] And music was also taught by a French system, devised for use in the monitorial schools of Paris by Guillaume Wilhem and owing nothing at all to Pestalozzi's principles, in spite of Kay's confident declaration that "the method of Wilhem is simply an application of the Pestalozzian method of ascending from the simple to the general through a clearly analyzed series" (Minutes, 1842-43, p. 226).

To staff his training institution, Kay relied for the most part upon volunteers among his friends; but the choice of a musician able to teach by means of an unfamiliar continental method presented a very real problem. Eventually, however, Kay met John Hullah, a young composer who had for some time been attracted to the idea of setting up in London a series of public singing classes similar to those which were then enjoying remarkable popularity in Paris.[9] Begun in 1836, two rival courses for adults were attracting hundreds of aspiring singers from the Parisian labouring classes. One course was directed by Joseph Mainzer, a German ex-priest who had formerly taught music in the seminary in Trier. The other was run by Wilhem, employing the

---

[6] James Kay-Shuttleworth, *The Training of Pauper Children* (London: Clowes, 1839), p. 5.

[7] James Kay-Shuttleworth, *Minutes of the Committee of Council on Education* (London: Clowes, 1841), pp. 33-51.

[8] James Kay-Shuttleworth, *Four Periods of Public Education* (London: Longmans, 1862), p. 345.

[9] Frances Hullah, *Life of John Hullah* (London: Longmans, 1886), p. 25.

monitorial system which he had already introduced for teaching music in the *commune* schools of Paris. [10]

Hullah had first become aware of the singing classes in Paris from an article in the *Athenaeum*, London's leading journal treating the arts, late in 1837. Written by H. F. Chorley, the paper's music critic, it spoke of Mainzer's classes with sufficient enthusiasm to make Hullah decide to visit Paris to witness so unusual an educational venture for himself. Chorley had written: "I was present at one of the meetings of M. Mainzer's singing class of workmen and artizans, at a room in the Place de l'Estrapade. This gentlemen's success should encourage all those who wish to diffuse a musical taste among the humbler orders." [11] Making Chorley's acquaintance, Hullah sought further details; and in 1839 the two men journeyed to Paris to enable Hullah to see Mainzer at work. They were disappointed because Mainzer's classes had just been discontinued; but they were able to visit those of Wilhem instead (F. Hullah, p. 25).

It was thus through accident rather than design that Hullah became acquainted with the Wilhem system which was to occupy his labours for the next forty years. Soon after his return home he was introduced to Kay, presented with the challenge of adapting Wilhem's system to English use, and invited to instruct the apprentice teachers at the new institution in Battersea. Hullah's own description of these events is revealing:

> Shortly before this the Normal School for schoolmasters had been opened at Battersea — the only school for schoolmasters then existing in England. It consisted at first of some ten or twelve youths, two or three of whom only had any knowledge of music, and as many any voice or apparent knowledge of the subject. Any beginning less encouraging could hardly be conceived. I remember, after walking some time before the gates of the establishment, at length summoning up courage to make my appearance . . . and I found myself, for the first time in my life, called upon to give a lesson in music. In this, I believe, I was considered to have been fairly successful.
>
> (F. Hullah, pp. 25-26).

Completely inexperienced as a teacher, at the age of twenty-seven Hullah was able to rely on a combination of charm, enthusiasm, and a natural talent for exposition for his early success. His pupils, handpicked boys just rescued from the workhouses where their future had seemed without hope, reacted eagerly to his kindly instruction. Visitors to Battersea, many of them eminent, expressed their surprise at the efficiency with which these youngsters were soon performing the exercises from Wilhem's course. The boys were soon called upon to demonstrate their powers to the public at large. On witnessing these unsophisticated lads displaying musical skill beyond that of

[10] F. J. Fétis, *Biographie universelle des musiciens* 8 vols. (Paris: Fournier, 1835-1860), "Mainzer," VI, 231; (Brussels: Meline, Cans et Cie, 1844), "G. B. Wilhem," VIII, 563-566.

[11] Henry Fothergill Chorley, "Foreign Correspondence," *Athenaeum* no. 527 (2 December 1837), 881.

most adults, delighted audiences in London and the provinces responded with incredulous applause. The Battersea Boys, clad in their green uniforms, were soon known nationally as "Hullah's Greenbirds."[12]

Encouraged by this early success, Kay urged the Committee of Council to approve the foundation of a singing school for schoolmasters where the teachers of London might be taught the secrets of Hullah's triumph. Sanction was given, and on 1 February 1841 the first class was enrolled at London's largest public arena, Exeter Hall. Two further classes were formed in the following March, when the first course for schoolmistresses also began. Each class met twice weekly for sixty nights under Hullah's personal tuition; the course cost fifteen shillings, thus making the venture self-supporting.[13]

The *Minute* of the Committee of Council on Education that announced the formation of the Exeter Hall Singing School was a substantial document designed not only to publicize Hullah's classes, but to justify the inclusion of the music lesson in schools generally. In it Kay summarized the arguments employed to sway influential opinion in government circles and public debate. He reiterated them in a single sentence when he declared that vocal music was an "important means of forming an industrious, brave, loyal, and religious working class" (quoted in J. Hullah, *Method*, p. iv). He also emphasized the merit of song as a promoter of patriotism, civilizing agent, innocent pastime, counter-attraction to the beerhouse, and the means of making attendance at public worship more attractive to the uneducated. "A relish for such pursuits," Kay's *Minute* went on, "would in itself be an advance in civilisation, as it would doubtless prove in time the means of weaning the population from debasing pleasures, and would associate their amusements with their duties" (quoted in J. Hullah, *Method*, p. v). It was with this moralistic preamble — in itself a seasoned foretaste of the high Victorian manner — that Hullah's adaptation of a French method of teaching music was first presented to the public at large.

Just how warmly it was received may be discovered from the way in which the initial success of the classes for teachers at Exeter Hall promptly led to the formation, at vigorous public demand, of additional classes "wherein the working classes, and the apprentices and foremen of shops and handicraft trades" might acquire this innocent and useful recreation (*Minutes*, 1841-42, p. 75). By the end of 1841, according to a contemporary estimate, at least 50,000 children of the working classes in London had also begun to receive instruction at school in singing from notes (*Minutes*, 1841-42, p. 75). Just as their teachers had so recently been, those children were led

[12] T. Adkins, *History of St. John's College, Battersea* (London: National Society's Repository, 1906), p. 80ff.

[13] John Hullah, *Wilhem's Method of Teaching Singing adapted to English Use* (2d. ed. 1842; rpt. ed. Kilkenny: Boethius, 1983), p. xiv.

through the pages of Hullah's *Method*, slowly learning to find their way up and down the scale and to sing such edifying ditties as:

> How pleasant it is, at the close of the day,
>   No follies to have to repent;
> But reflect on the past and be able to say,
>   My time has been properly spent!
> When I've finished my business with patience and care,
>   And been good, and obliging, and kind.
> I lie on my pillow, and sleep away there,
>   With a happy and peaceable mind.
>
> (J. Hullah, *Method*, p. 65).

## II

Some witnesses of this apparent triumph for Kay's idiosyncratic musical policy were less than enthusiastic. Few professional musicians were persuaded that Hullah's singing school would achieve worthwhile results. Ultra-conservatives among the upper classes clung to their conviction that any attempt to educate the humbler members of society must lead to an increase in discontent and subversion. Even staunch advocates of the development of popular education, and of music education in particular, voiced their disapprobation of the Committee of Council's haste in putting Kay's recommendations into practice without first consulting informed opinion as to the suitability of the French method he had chosen. Soon after the publication of Hullah's adaptation of Wilhem's manual, a stern but well-informed criticism of it appeared in the *Westminster Review*:

> In our visits to continental schools we have accumulated among other school books, a great number upon singing, but we have not one in our collection so overlaid with the technical pedantries of the science, so abounding in difficulties insuperable to children, so little of the character of a work adapted for the self-instruction of an adult, as this English adaptation of Wilhem's method. Indeed without a master to explain it, the book is perfectly useless. [14]

The writer was W. E. Hickson, the vigorous promoter of the cause of national education whose *Singing Master* has already been mentioned. Since its publication, however, Hickson's wider philanthropic and educational activities had included service on a government commission to examine the circumstances of unemployed handloom operators (1837) and an educational tour of North Germany and the Low Countries (1839). [15] These pursuits had

---

[14] W. E. Hickson, "Music, and the Committee of Council on Education," *Westminster Review* 37 no. 1 (January 1842), 29.

[15] *Dictionary of National Biography*, 2 vols. (compact ed., London: Oxford University Press, 1975), I, 969.

increased his stature as a public figure, lending added authority to the pronouncements on educational matters which he published in the *Westminister Review*, a journal he had purchased in 1840 as a vehicle for his utterances.

Hickson's detailed criticism of Hullah's singing manual took exception to several of its essential features and was restated in subsequent articles in the *Spectator* in 1841 and the *Illustrated London News* two years later. [16] For Hullah's natural talent as a teacher Hickson spoke with unqualified approval; his objections were wholly against the government for overlooking indigenous methods within their reach while prepared to occupy themselves in "rambling researches" in Switzerland, Holland, the German States, Prussia, Austria, and France. And contrary to the Committee of Council's declaration that no method had previously existed to simplify the teaching of vocal music in elementary schools, Hickson pointed out the existence of many such works, "fully as clear and quite as useful as the one now adopted," not a few of them native products. There were, moreover, other treatises of a more authentically Pestalozzian cast in use both in Germany and America.

Perhaps the most radical of Hickson's objections was directed against Hullah's adoption of French nomenclature for the degrees of the scale. Instead of employing the customary alphabetical note-names, in his manual Hullah justified the continental usage in these terms: "In England the eight sounds of this scale are called C, D, E, F, G, A, B, C; and it may be useful, at some future time, to become familiar with these names. The syllables . . . (commonly used in France and Italy) have, however, many advantages over the letters, and will therefore be used throughout this method. . . . Thus, by using the syllables Do, Re, Mi, Fa, Sol, La, and Si over and over again, we find names for as many sounds as we need" (J. Hullah, *Method*, p. 6). Hickson justifiably questioned this policy, pointing out that a pupil taught in this way would "begin and finish his course of lessons without being acquainted with the names of the notes as they are universally used in England" ("Singing Classes," p. 77). He would be unable to sing or understand anything but the contents of his own singing manual.

Later experience was to expose an even more damaging disadvantage of the use of this continental system. The whole of the first course of lessons in Hullah's manual was limited to the key of C, where the sol-fa names established a sense of note-relationships. And the marked success of his early teaching occurred while pupils were at this initial stage. But when keys other than C were introduced in the second course of lessons, the sol-fa names no longer identified familiar note patterns, and pupils grew increasingly confused as a result. Thereafter, only the naturally talented were able to progress.

[16] W. E. Hickson, "Wilhem's Method of Teaching Singing," *Spectator* 14 (10 July 1841), 667-668; "The Singing Classes of Exeter Hall," *Illustrated London News* 1 (11 June 1842), 76-77.

In undertaking his search on the continent for the means to redeem England from her educational sloth, Kay more than once exposed his own limited understanding of technical considerations. Nowhere was the discrepancy more obviously revealed than in his choice of Wilhem's system of teaching music. Because he had selected in Hullah a man with no previous teaching experience to introduce the new method, its most obvious shortcomings were left unexplained to him before he sought for it the government's approval. The chosen method was to prove deficient; and Hickson's castigation of it was more than justified by the consistent failure of the Hullah-Wilhem system to develop real competence in either the average child or his teachers. After its first dramatic success, the survival of Hullah's manual was assured only by the official backing of the Committee of Council on Education who insisted on its being taught to teachers in training. Twenty years after its first introduction, most practicing teachers had abandoned using it in their classrooms. Yet the importation of Wilhem's method to the schools of early Victorian England should not be hastily dismissed as heralding a false dawn. However misguided the policy formulated by Kay and followed by his lieutenant, Hullah, their joint efforts were to prove far from fruitless. Ten years after the first lessons at Battersea and Exeter Hall had begun to arouse unprecedented public interest in learning to sing at sight, Dickens's *Household Words* recorded the appearance of a new attitude toward music in the school curriculum: "Music is becoming a regular branch of popular education. . . . Already its effects are striking and encouraging. Music — well, badly, or indifferently taught — forms a part of the business of the great majority of schools, national, public, and private, throughout the country."[17]

By 1850 — when those words were written — a considerable number of alternative methods of teaching music were employed. The annual reports issued by government inspectors of schools during the 1840s reveal that in spite of the official recognition accorded to Hullah's manual, outside the metropolis itself individual teachers were still using one of the earlier primers published by the three native pioneers in the field: Turner, Glover, or Hickson (see *Minutes*, 1841-42, p. 179). The accepted aim of the music lesson in all these primers was to teach children to sing melodies at sight while acquiring a growing repertory of moral texts. But examination of their books shows that Turner and Hickson both assumed that by explaining the meaning of the symbols of notation to children they were automatically enabling them to read music. Only Sarah Glover made use of movable sol-fa, anglicizing the syllables as Doh, Ra, Me, Fah, Sole, Lah, and Te, and using those initial letters as an ancillary form of notation from which her pupils gradually learned to sing with confidence.

---

[17] [George Hogarth?], "Music in Humble Life," *Household Words* 1 (1850), 164.

Elsewhere, individual teachers who chanced to be members of church choirs made what use they could of the methods by which they themselves had been trained. The most common of these was the traditional "fasola" system which named the notes of the scale fa, sol, la, fa, sol, la, mi, and consequently presented the beginner with ambiguities likely to baffle all but the brightest child. [18] Another more straightforward method then being taught nationwide to nonconformists by one of their ministers, the Reverend J. J. Waite, used numerals as a form of notation, representing the degrees of the major scale by the figures 1-7, as Rousseau had recommended. [19] A third system, the "interval method," introduced no ancillary notation but attempted to reduce the element of chance in reading from standard notes by drilling the pupil in striking different intervals from a given keynote. This was the method favoured by most professional singing teachers and the one also adopted by John Turner in his *Manual*.

The range of possible approaches to teaching sight-singing in schools was yet further increased in May 1841, when Joseph Mainzer — whose singing classes in Paris appear to have been regarded as potentially treasonable assemblies and were thus closed by the police — crossed to London and started classes in rivalry to those which Hullah had then been holding for four months at Exeter Hall. Mainzer's classes were held in assembly halls in various London districts under the catch phrase "Singing for the Million." [20] They each attracted hundreds of devotees and contributed decisively to producing the "singing mania" which was to become one of the most remarkable social phenomena of early Victorian England.

Mainzer used the same catch phrase as the title of his teaching manual, *Singing for the Million* (1841), a much less pedantic treatise than Hullah's and one clearly based upon many years' practical teaching experience. Mainzer summarized his policy as follows:

> To impart a general knowledge of the principles of music, a different method of teaching is indispensable to distinguish it from a purely musical education; and it is a great error to apply to elementary schools, or public classes, methods which are not founded on this rigorous distinction. . . . In the latter, it is only necessary to communicate a general knowledge of the art, to incite a taste for it, to prepare the physical organs, — the ear and the throat, — to awaken the intelligence and the heart, and to afford to infancy and youth a participation in the attractions and noble sentiment inspired by its mysterious power. To attain this object, it suffices to study the few rules applied to the reading of music, explained in this little work. . . . These are the simple and only means I have employed in gratuitious classes opened in Paris in favour of workmen.
>
> (Mainzer, *Singing*, pp. i-ii).

The straightforwardness of Mainzer's early lessons and the simple vocal exercises they employed made encouraging progress possible for the begin-

---

[18] B. Rainbow, *English Psalmody Prefaces* (Kilkenny: Boethius, 1982), pp. 4-6.

[19] J. J. Waite, *The Hallelujah* (London: Snow, 1852), preface.

[20] J. Mainzer, *Singing for the Million* (1841; rpt. ed. Kilkenny: Boethius, 1984), introduction, pp. 4-5.

ner. But as the course continued and the singer began to meet sharps, flats, and key signatures, the French background to Mainzer's method and its consequent use of fixed sol-fa no longer provided a reliable method of pitching intervals correctly. It was at this stage that enthusiasm began to wane and attendance at Mainzer's classes began to fall off. As with Hullah's method (and for precisely the same reason) Mainzer's *Singing for the Million* encouraged many thousands of ordinary folk to become aware of the pleasure that choral music could afford, without enabling them to take more than the first steps into mastering its demands. Hullah and Mainzer both depended more upon their own enthusiasm, natural aptitude for teaching, and personal charm for their success than upon the merits of their systems of instruction. Yet it was natural for schoolteachers attending their classes to attempt to pass on to their own pupils what little skill they had managed to acquire themselves.

By 1846 the number of alternative methods of teaching sight-singing had grown so profuse that James Turle, the organist of Westminster Abbey, and Edward Taylor, Gresham Professor of Music, joined forces to produce *The Singing Book* (1846) which emphasized that there were no short cuts to proficiency, that once the essentials of musical rudiments had been acquired by a pupil, practice must do the rest, and that the existence of so many different systems led to nothing but confusion. [21] There were few subjects, their preface declared, which the wit and ingenuity of man had encumbered with more needless words and presented to a young mind in a less attractive form than the art of singing from notes. Instead of removing gratuitous obstacles to progress, individual teachers seemed determined to multiply them — not least by the addition to the regular musical alphabet of a host of arbitrary and unmeaning syllables. Usually called, and often supposed to be, "the Sol-fa system," no description of it could be more incorrect. For scarcely any two writers in modern times had used the system in the same way. The Italians and the French had their own ways of handling it; the English were not only at variance with both but with each other.

Examination of various elementary works on singing showed that far from being founded upon any well-established and universally accepted principle, the details and application of sol-fa varied in different countries and were "altered according to the fancy of individual instructors" (p. iv). Recent attempts (such as Hullah's) to substitute sol-fa names for the alphabetical names of the notes simply exasperated Turle and Taylor: "The alphabetic notation *must* be known by every musician, because it is of universal employment. No other is used in any choir or orchestra in the kingdom. The student may add to it some other, but he *must* learn this" (p. v). For all these reasons

---

[21] James Turle and Edward Taylor, *The Singing Book* (London: Bogue, 1846), pp. i-vii.

*The Singing Book* dispensed with sol-fa altogether, adopting instead, for its preliminary exercises numerals together with alphabetical note names printed beneath the staff. In this way, it was claimed, "a correct idea of distance" was developed in the mind of the beginner (p. v). Thus the multiplicity of methods was further increased.

### III

In the hands of a talented and musical teacher each of the methods that have so far taken our attention offered a possible approach to teaching sight-singing. But it seems evident today that something more specific was required to enable the teacher to overcome personal musical limitations and then satisfactorily guide pupils. What was needed was not so much a textbook prepared by an expert musician as one prepared by an expert teacher. Only then would the accomplished musician's innate tendency to underestimate the learner's problems be avoided and recent advances in the techniques of teaching other subjects be applied to music also.

Even so earnest a music teacher as John Turner, the pioneer who produced the first school music text in English in 1833, had underestimated the task he was undertaking, as this summary of his aims makes clear: "It is proposed that the children should be taught the names of the notes, and other marks of music, their nature and their use; that they should be practised in singing the scale, and in the proper use of the voice; that they should learn to pronounce words so as to preserve the organs of the throat in free exercise, and be by these means instructed in the rudiments of melody and harmony" (Turner, p. 26). Faith in rote-learning of facts had long dominated all teaching in schools. Understandably, it dominated most early attempts to teach music there. Indeed, Sarah Glover alone among those whose work has been considered revealed an awareness of the need to organize her teaching along other than factual lines: "In teaching children music, I think it best to instruct them on the same principle as they are taught speech; viz., by deducing theory from practice, rather than practice from theory." [22] She also deliberately chose to employ movable sol-fa (which emphasizes the regular pattern of tones and semitones in the major scale whatever the key) instead of fixed sol-fa, the continental counterpart adopted by both Mainzer and Hullah. As the name implies, the latter system attached the sol-fa names permanently to the key of C, thus robbing them of their value in other keys. It fell to John Curwen, a young man in his early twenties already known in Congregational-

---

[22] Sarah Glover, *A Manual of the Norwich Sol-fa System* (London: Hamilton, Adams, 1845), p. 66.

ist circles for his remarkable skill in teaching young children and his insight into educational theory, to contrive a method of teaching music which made it available to musically inexperienced teachers and their pupils. The fact that when he undertook the task he was equally inexperienced himself was to prove an advantage rather than a handicap in the long run.

Even as an undergraduate at London's new University College in 1833, Curwen's intense interest in teaching children impressed his fellow students. Every Sunday he taught in a school held in the Barbican for children obliged to work on weekdays, developing there his "Look and Say" method of teaching them to read words as a whole instead of spelling them out letter by letter. This ability to analyze the processes of instruction and then plan teaching procedures to accommodate them was partly instinctive and partly the result of conscious study of the writings of the progressive teachers of his day. Perhaps above all he was indebted to Pestalozzi for his radical views on teaching; but that influence came to him at first indirectly through the books of Elizabeth Mayo, David Stow, Horace Grant, and Jacob Abbott. [23]

In 1838 Curwen was appointed assistant minister at the Independent Chapel at Basingstoke, Hampshire, where once again it was his remarkable powers with children that impressed local people. The amazing success of a deliberately simple storybook for children which he now published soon made his name widely known among parents and teachers. As a result he found himself invited to address meetings and conferences of teachers in many parts of the country. On one such occasion in 1841, when the rival classes of Hullah and Mainzer were first attracting general public interest, a conference chairman, impressed by Curwen's evident grasp of educational values, commissioned him to review existing methods of teaching singing and to "recommend some simple method to the churches which should enable all to sing with ease and propriety." [24] Aware of his own musical limitations, Curwen accepted the task with misgiving. But he regarded it as a solemn undertaking and, though he could not anticipate the consequences, it was to become his life work.

A year later Curwen published the first results of his investigation in a series of "Lessons on Singing" in a Congregationalist journal, the *Independent Magazine*. [25] Utterly unlike the standard music primer which traditionally began by defining the difference between "noise" and "music" and then introduced the symbols of notation, Curwen's approach was essentially practical, dispensed with rote-learning, and was couched in the simplest language.

[23] B. Rainbow, *John Curwen: A Short Critical Biography* (London: Novello, 1980), pp. 10-13.

[24] John Curwen, *The Teacher's Manual* (1882; rpt. ed. Kilkenny: Boethius, 1986), p. 153.

[25] John Curwen, "Lessons on Singing," *Independent Magazine* 1 (January 1842), 23-24.

He presented his lessons in the form of "letters to a friend who had undertaken to train a class of children":

> I must suppose you, with your blackboard and chalk at your side. . . . I shall enclose your words in inverted commas, and where I suppose a pause while anything is done, I will mark it by an asterisk.
>
> "Now, children, we are going to learn the art of singing in tune. What are we going to learn? First, then, you must remember that any musical sound is called a *note*. What is a musical sound called? This is a note." (I hear you singing to the sound *ah* any note you please.) "I will sing another note. • Now I will sing another note. • Could not some of you sing a note? Hold up hands — those who can sing a note. Do you — • and you. • I want you now to distinguish the *same* note from a *different* one. Sing the *same* note as this. • Sing the *same* note as this. • Hold up hands — those who will sing me a note, and I will sing the same. Do you — • and you.

(J. Curwen, "Lessons," pp. 23-24).

Curwen had found so many shortcomings in existing methods — particularly in Hullah's — that he decided to develop one of his own. For its basis he chose Sarah Glover's "Norwich Sol-fa" with its simple notation of sol-fa initial letters and movable do. But he amended many of its details before incorporating further material from other methods which his own experience — first as learner, then as teacher — showed to be valuable. Curwen acknowledged indebtedness for "borrowed" teaching devices and other intrinsic matter to his fellow countrymen, J. J. Waite, and W. E. Hickson; to the Irish teacher, R. J. Bryce; to the Frenchmen, Jue de Berneval and Aimé Paris; the American, Lowell Mason; the Swiss, H. G. Naegeli; and the Bavarian, M. T. Pfeiffer. Thus began the process of synthesis by which, over a period of thirty years or more, Curwen's Tonic Sol-fa system was engendered. [26]

Following its first tentative introduction to the limited readership of the *Independent Magazine* early in 1842, the Tonic Sol-fa method slowly became more widely known through meetings and classes for Sunday school teachers and temperance workers. Evening classes for adults were also started and, as a result, Curwen was invited to contribute a series of articles on music to John Cassell's new magazine, the *Popular Educator*, in 1851. The magazine's enormous circulation among readers anxious for "self-improvement" brought Curwen's first article, published in April 1852, into thousands of homes, marking a welcome upward trend in his affairs. Further classes were soon begun in London's Crosby Hall attended by many teachers and educationists; and though Curwen's solitary crusade had neither the government support accorded to Hullah nor the resources of Exeter Hall at its disposal, during the following three years he had attracted some twenty thousand pupils. [27] By 1860 Tonic Sol-fa had eclipsed both the Hullah and Mainzer methods to stand alone in public estimation as the humble person's method of

[26] B. Rainbow, *The Land Without Music* (London: Novello, 1967), pp. 139-155.

[27] J. S. Curwen, *Memorials of John Curwen* (London: J. Curwen & Sons, 1882), p. 153.

learning to sing from notes. Following the passing of the Forster Education Act of 1870 and the introduction of compulsory elementary schooling, Tonic Sol-fa became the accepted method of teaching singing in the nation's new Board Schools.

The testing ground where the viability of music as a subject in the modern school curriculum was first demonstrated and the merits and disadvantages of alternative methods of teaching it were gradually assessed was thus found in the elementary schools established and developed during the first half of Victoria's reign. And although the apparent success of Hullah's early teaching encouraged the headmaster of Eton College to invite him to teach there experimentally in 1842, the venture was shortlived and not repeated in other independent schools. No doubt partly because the boys at Eton lacked the docility of their humbler counterparts, once the novelty of learning to sing faded, the pedestrian progress of Hullah's lessons quickly lost their interest. Nor was the opportunity taken to link the singing lessons with the music of the college chapel. The services there were sung by the choir of St. George's Chapel, Windsor, the youthful congregation — like their high-born parents — convinced that it was "not genteel to sing in church."[28]

IV

The first successful attempts to introduce music teaching in secondary education came with the development of a new type of boarding school for the sons of middle-class parents during the 1840s. The new energy in educational matters which had first given rise to the establishment of schools for the children of the poor was now turned to the provision of others where less expensive secondary education was made available, particularly to the sons of the clergy. Founded as boarding schools, both Marlborough (1843) and Rossall (1844) were sufficiently influenced by the model of Arnold's Rugby to attach great importance to the influence of well-chosen prefects and the sobering impulse of daily worship. But at Radley (1847) the daily chapel service was made a central feature of the school's life. The chapel building was furnished with elaborate care and contained "one of the finest organs in the country."[29] One of the first four members appointed to its staff was E. G. Monk, the chapel organist and school music master, under whose direction a musical tradition was steadily built up in which the whole school shared in choral worship whether from choirstall or pew.

---

[28] John Hullah, *The Psalter* (London: Parker, 1843), preface.

[29] E. Bryans and T. D. Raike, *History of St. Peter's College, Radley* (London: Blackwell, 1925), chap. 1.

This new ideal, further stimulated by the liturgical reforms associated with the Oxford Movement, was taken up in other new boarding schools at Lancing (1848), Hurstpierpoint (1849), Bradfield (1850), and elsewhere, to establish a generally accepted view of music in the curriculum of a Victorian boarding school as the natural adjunct to well-ordered communal worship. [30] Because music was taught in such schools by specialists rather than novices, the lengthy struggle to select and test teaching methods which had complicated the introduction of music lessons in elementary schools was avoided. Much of the chapel repertoire, however, was learned by rote, natural ability rather than systematic coaching having to provide the sight readers necessary to maintain the choir. Far less attention was given to formal teaching of music in class than was the case in elementary schools.

In the older public schools there was no similar call to entrust the choral element in worship to the boys and masters. At Eton, as we have seen, visiting choristers from Windsor Castle sang the chapel services; at Winchester the cathedral choir sang in the college chapel; at Westminister the boys of the school attended services in the Abbey; at Harrow they went to the adjacent parish church; at Rugby the simple congregational service familiar to Thomas Arnold was jealously preserved. There was thus no immediate demand to introduce music lessons in these schools as a means of enhancing choral worship. Moreover, social snobbery played its part. The popular enthusiasm aroused by the massed singing classes at Exeter Hall and elsewhere in London seemed to make simultaneous instruction in singing a pursuit appropriate only to the labouring classes. When music eventually came to be taught in the public schools, both the motivation for it and the form were quite different from music instruction in the elementary schools. The first move in that new direction was made at Uppingham in 1856.

When Edward Thring was appointed headmaster in 1853, Uppingham was an unremarkable rural grammar school of twenty-five boys. He left it thirty-five years later among the foremost of English public schools, transformed by a new attitude toward the curriculum which widened it beyond the Classics to embrace a range of pursuits designed to meet the needs and aptitudes of every pupil. Part of every day was devoted to French, German, chemistry, lathework, drawing, carpentry, or music; each boy was required to choose one or more of these besides the traditional range of classical studies.

One of Thring's biographers has emphasized the fact that though he was the first to introduce music teaching into a public school, he was himself quite unmusical:

> The importance of musical teaching was probably brought under his notice by his wife, who had brought from her German home a warm love of music and interest in it. The

[30] B. Rainbow, *The Choral Revival in the Anglican Church, 1839-1872* (London: Barrie and Jenkins, 1970), pp. 220-242.

refining and elevating influence of *serious* music on those who were able and trained to appreciate it could not escape Thring's rare powers of observation. An art which appealed at least as much to feeling and imagination as to the intellect, that bugbear of his, could not fail to attract him greatly. And furthermore, the power of vocal music to enhance and emphasise the meaning of words appeared to him of great value. It was with a view to their being set to music and sung, and thus brought forcibly home to a large number of performers and listeners, that he wrote his school songs. [31]

Yet the school songs which Thring introduced were not, as one might expect today, designed to be performed by the whole school. From an entry in his diary describing a school concert in 1873 we learn that a performance of the school song was encored "again and again, and all rose and stood while it was being sung." [32] It was performed by a trained group of singers whose attendance at rehearsals was made compulsory once they had joined the singing class, while Thring would often be present to demonstrate his support for the activity. The rest of the school did not join in.

Instead of basing music teaching in the classroom, as a discipline common to all and centering on vocal activity, Thring chose to foster an instrumental approach dependent on individual coaching and made available only to those who chose it. The school as a whole, however, was invited to share the experience as listeners by attending concerts given by the school choir and orchestra (stiffened by the instrumental coaches themselves) as well as by visiting soloists. To effect this policy Thring appointed Paul David, son of the eminent German violinist, Ferdinand David, to direct music teaching throughout the school.

The model presented at Uppingham was not immediately imitated elsewhere. But as former bias against musical performance as a time-wasting activity and sign of degeneracy gave way to a more balanced opinion among public school headmasters, Thring's policy was slowly adopted in other schools of similar calibre. The school song and the school concert both became generally accepted features of the life of a superior boarding school as the century progressed. Some part of the influence prompting their acceptance came also from Harrow, where the introduction of music teaching was not first instigated by the headmaster.

The circumstances of John Farmer's appointment to teach music at Harrow are not fully documented. Tradition has it that he was invited to teach the piano there by individual boys themselves in 1862; and that he was not made a formal member of staff for some years after that. However that may be, his influence upon the school during the next twenty years was indelible, involving a lasting tradition of house-singing and a collection of school songs which eventually came to enjoy immense circulation. At Harrow under

---

[31] G. R. Parkin, *Life and Letters of Edward Thring*, 2 vols. (London: Macmillan, 1898), II, 306-309.

[32] Quoted in P. A. Scholes, *The Mirror of Music* (London: Oxford University Press, 1947), p. 627.

Farmer's direction the whole school sang. Gradually his "wonderful power of making nearly everyone with whom he came into contact enthusiastic for music" turned many of the boys formerly brought up to scorn music into music-lovers (Scholes, p. 626).

That the admission of music to the curriculum of these two leading schools for boys took place at this particular time was a reflection of the changed attitude toward it in society generally. From an 1863 article in the *Cornhill Magazine* we find clear evidence of the broader acceptance of music at all social levels:

> The cultivation of music as a recreation is not now confined in England to one class. While striking its roots down lower in the social scale, its topmost branches have also widened and strengthened. The study is not alone more general, it is also better understood and more seriously undertaken. . . . A reaction set in some years ago; yet not so long since but Lady Blessington could venture in one of her books to pronounce openly against a man's occupying himself with music. . . . It is a great gain that all the barriers of prejudice against music have been broken down; that boys are permitted to be taught the art; and that it is now generally held to be a rational and humanising occupation for men of all conditions. [33]

The steady growth of music teaching in independent schools for boys fostered by this new tolerance owed its character to a combination of the methods adopted in the types of boarding schools already examined. In general the pattern adopted, and largely retained today, included the provision of music in the school chapel by both choir and congregation, the performance of works by a voluntary choral society, individual instrumental coaching for those who sought it, and the consequent establishment of a school orchestra. House-singing was allowed to develop into music competitions between houses where the spirit of rivalry found on the sports field might be brought into play. In general, music was not treated as a classroom discipline, no doubt partly because most boys lost their singing voices early in their secondary school career.

Hitherto the daughters of the well-to-do had received their education at home before going on to a "finishing school." But after mid-century a new pattern for their education was established with the foundation of Cheltenham Ladies' College and the North London School for Girls under the pioneer headmistresses, Dorothea Beale and Frances Buss. Modest musical proficiency had long been regarded as a desirable accomplishment in a young woman. In addition to the lessons in history, geography, grammar, writing, arithmetic, and needlework specified in the entrance rules for the girls' school attended by Charlotte Brontë in 1823, an additional charge of £3

---

[33] "Amateur Music," *Cornhill Magazine* 8 no. 43 (1863), 93-98.

a year was made for music or drawing. [34] What was provided under the heading of music was private tuition in playing the piano or harp, and singing. This was the usual pattern in similar schools at the time.

That this tradition was largely preserved in the new schools for girls as they came into being is evident from Dorothea Beale's account of music teaching at Cheltenham Ladies' College in 1865:

> Music is taught in the usual way, by private lessons; but there are also classes for the practice of concerted music, to which only advanced pupils are admitted. There may be from 4 to 12 performers, two to each piano; thus the pupils are enabled to obtain an intimate acquaintance with those works of the great masters (as Cherubini, Bach, Haydn, &c.) which are usually performed by an orchestra, and this promotes, also, decision, accuracy, and facility in reading. Twice a year we have a musical examination, i.e., each pupil is required to play some piece in the presence of her companions and as many parents as wish to attend; no strangers are admitted. [35]

Just how far instrumental teaching in the new schools fell short of thorough competence was emphasized at a meeting of the National Association for the Promotion of Social Sciences which took place in Cheltenham in 1878. During the discussion which followed a paper on music in schools, one speaker claimed that "the musical instruction in ladies' schools was in a most deficient state. He had often found ladies who could play a piece well, but when asked what key it was in were unable to give any answer" (*Transactions*, 1878, p. 675). The tendency in such schools, he claimed, was to concentrate on empty display. And it seems obvious today that the accepted image of the drawing-room pianist who dazzled suitors with empty technique or earned their affectionate indulgence with faltering execution obliged every young lady to learn to play the piano whether she had aptitude or not. The failure of many girls to benefit fully from their lessons must cause little surprise.

Yet this was a time of remarkable advance in the provision of educational resources for young women and girls. The foundation of Girton College, Cambridge in 1869, of Anne Clough's residential house for women students there in 1871, and of the first high school for girls in 1880 marked a decade of unprecedented progress. It was in the new high schools that class singing was first consistently developed. Maintained by the body later known as the Girls' Public Day School Trust (GPDST) and noted for its enlightened attitude toward music teaching, several of the schools appointed John Farmer to supervise this side of their activities, with results which earned the attention of the *Musical Times* in 1890: "Perhaps the Girls' High School Company does more to encourage the study of singing than other schools of this class. This Company has now nearly 4,000 pupils attending its numerous schools.

[34] Elizabeth Gaskell, *The Life of Charlotte Brontë* (1857); quoted in A. F. Scott, *An Age of Elegance* (Woking: Gresham Books, 1979), p. 97.

[35] Dorothea Beale in *Transactions of the National Association for the Promotion of Science* (London: n.p., 1866), p. 285.

To place themselves well in evidence before the public, they have arranged to hold a great demonstration at the Crystal Palace. . . . Mr John Farmer, who is to conduct, has decided to include only unison songs" (quoted in Scholes, pp. 627-628). A subsequent report of the occasion, published in the same paper, found the programme "decidedly monotonous" though the "sweetness and purity of tone of the voices" afforded a redeeming feature. Yet the editor doubted whether these high school girls would have been as successful as their board school counterparts in singing at sight.

The editor of the *Musical Times* was W. E. Barrett who also held a post as inspector of music in schools and training colleges between 1871 and 1891. As such he was unusually well placed to comment on existing standards. His comparison of the differing potential of high school and board school pupils in the field of sight-singing pinpoints what was perhaps the most remarkable and ambivalent aspect of popular musical education throughout Queen Victoria's long reign.

Among tokens of the class distinction which led Disraeli to speak of the queen's subjects as comprising Two Nations, none seems more bizarre than the opposing interpretations placed upon the content of the music lesson in schools catering for different classes. We have already noticed the "improving" benefits that music teaching was designed to bring to both old and young among the "lower orders" of Victorian society. Their social superiors, it seems, were not in need of singing lessons on this account. But as Sarah Glover pointed out in 1835, the reform of congregational singing — that other purpose of the singing class movement — required the participation of all branches of society:

> Amongst the superior orders of the community, singing is at present very rarely cultivated at all by gentlemen; and few ladies have such an acquaintance with intervals, as to venture to sing the simplest psalm tune, unprompted or unsupported by an instrument. Psalmody is therefore usually abandoned to the care of the illiterate . . . most of whom are accustomed, in their youth, to strengthen their vocal organs in various ways which would be deemed unseemly in nurseries and academies for the children of gentlefolk. . . . [But] let singing become a branch of national education, not only in schools for the children of labourers and mechanics, but in academies for young ladies and gentlemen, and the main point will be attained towards rendering psalmody truly congregational.
>
> (Glover, *Scheme*, pp. 5-6).

Her injunction, however, met with small response, though a few new boarding schools for boys began to encourage singing in their chapels a decade or so later. When a more general drive to introduce music teaching in similar schools took place toward the end of the century, it favoured instrumental activity.

That this choice was influenced by the occurrence of the boy's changing voice early in his secondary school career draws attention to another reason for the differences in music teaching in different types of schools: the widely differing ages of their pupils. The school-leaving age for elementary school pupils was fixed at ten years in 1880, rising to eleven in 1893 and twelve in 1899. Only in 1918 — as a new wave of reform began — was school attendance made compulsory between the ages of five and fourteen. The leaving age for a boy in an independent secondary boarding school, on the other hand, was normally eighteen.

An influence quite as great was the kind of musical training which the teachers in each of the two types of school had received. Music was taught in elementary schools by general class teachers whose musical knowledge and skill were commonly limited to basic matters included in a general teacher-training course. On the other hand, specialist teachers of music appointed in independent secondary schools (never in grammar schools for boys at this time) had generally received their training at a college of music or a university. Invariably instrumentalists — usually organists — they carried with them into their schools the unconscious bias of the instrumental performer.

The comparative weakness of secondary school pupils in the field of sight-singing, to which W. E. Barrett referred, was one consequence of their teachers' instrumental outlook. That this was a longstanding circumstance and not a by-product of the times is apparent from a discussion of music teaching published in France in 1818: "One thing that constantly puzzles observers is that among the vast number of those who have learned music, so few can sing at sight. Most of them have to consult their violin, their pianoforte, or their flute, in order to learn a new tune; and it is actually the instrument which does the reading for them. It is as if, in order to read books, one learned to operate a machine designed for the purpose instead of adopting the more direct medium of the words themselves. [36] In that passage from his *Exposition d'une nouvelle méthode pour l'enseignement de la musique* Pierre Galin laid bare, perhaps for the first time, a fundamental shortcoming in the average instrumental performer's musical equipment: an inability to "hear" a written melody before playing it. It was his contention that this skill had come to be regarded as rare only because teachers failed to concentrate on training the beginner's ear before training the eye to identify the symbols of music. Other, later teachers were to share his belief that by encouraging singing from sol-fa their pupils developed a more accurate sense of relative pitch than instrumental experience alone could afford.

Most of those who came to share Galin's belief also shared his amateur status. Few of the attempts to reform musical instruction which occurred dur-

---

[36] P. Galin, *Rationale for a New Way of Teaching Music* (1818), ed. and trans., B. Rainbow (Kilkenny: Boethius, 1983), pp. 41-42.

ing the nineteenth century were made by professional musicians; almost all were the work of amateurs with sufficient understanding of children to question traditional methods which presented obstacles to all but the talented. Foremost among such pioneers in England was John Curwen whose Tonic Sol-fa was designed specifically to ease the beginner's path.

But Curwen's amateur status, and his temerity in presuming to "interfere" in the jealously guarded field of music teaching, incensed professional musicians. The situation was not eased by his being a nonconformist minister of known radical sympathies whose massive popular following embraced the unfashionable, the teetotallers, and the poor. Above all, the ancillary notation of sol-fa initials used in Curwen's vocal scores was anathema to the orthodox; and the resulting combination of outrage and musical snobbery was enough to outlaw Tonic Sol-fa — even after the professors of music at Oxford and Cambridge both commended its usefulness (Scholes, p. 16). It is thus unsurprising that specialist teachers of music in independent schools were not anxious to introduce Tonic Sol-fa, or that general standards of sight-singing there were as relatively disappointing as Barrett had suggested.

In spite of such differences, the state of music teaching in schools at the close of Victoria's reign presented a very different picture from the desolation prevailing when the queen came to the throne. Then, it had proved necessary to justify music teaching to the nation and Parliament on other than purely musical grounds. Now, the choice of school songs no longer depended principally upon the message of their words, and a wide array of national and folk songs were being brought back into currency through children's participation. Then it had seemed politic to summon patriotic support by comparing native sloth with Prussian achievement. Just how far that situation had changed by the end of the century is shown by an article published in *Child Life* in 1899:

> It is the belief that only in Germany is there any musical education worth the name. This was true once upon a time, but nobody who knows anything about it could say that it is so today. "England," writes my German friend, "needs another twenty years of musical education before the teaching will be efficient." Most true! And when she has had it, Germany will need another twenty in which to catch her up. For during the past half-century England has been making strides, while Germany has been living on her reputation. [37]

Nor was this outspoken reproach just a reflection of the growing animosity between the two nations which marked those times. The "myth" of German supremacy in popular musical education had been under attack since the publication of Hullah's formal report on *Musical Instruction in Elementary Schools*

---

[37] A. J. Curwen, "Should All Children Be Taught Music, or only the Gifted?" *Child Life* (October 1899); rpt. in A. J. Curwen, *Music and Psychology* (London: J. Curwen & Sons, 1901), pp. 291-296.

*on the Continent* in 1880. After visiting schools in Württemberg, Bavaria, Austria, Bohemia, Saxony, and Prussia, Hullah dismissed the generality of the teachers' achievements as "the poorest conceivable."[38] Indeed, the decline of musical instruction in German schools was shamefacedly acknowledged by Hermann Kretzschmar in his *Musikalische Zeitfragen* (1903) and a policy of reform proposed.[39] At the same time, the two types of English school whose different interpretations of musical education had hitherto been so distinct now began to experience a process akin to cross-fertilization. The first example of the trend appeared when classes in violin-playing were introduced in a number of elementary schools in 1905. The venture was made possible by an astute London music firm which supplied instruments by hire-purchase at a low rate, boosting the enterprise by organizing the attendance of private teachers in urban schools throughout the country. By 1910 a massed "orchestra" of several thousand elementary school violinists trained in this way performed impressively at the Crystal Palace (Scholes, p. 623), and the beginnings of a new tradition of instrumental playing appeared in state schools which was to continue and develop to our own day.

That policy was first formally implemented by Stewart Macpherson, a teacher at the Royal Academy of Music, who obtained permission to try out the scheme at Streatham Hill High School (GPDST) with gratifying success. The school soon became virtually a normal school where would-be teachers

A movement also began in the same decade to improve aural training and sight-singing in secondary schools. The prime mover was Mary Agnes Langdale, whose challenging articles on "A Plea for Broader Treatment of Music in our Schools" appeared in a little-known Roman Catholic educational journal, *The Crucible*, in 1908.[40] Recommending that the teaching of music should more closely resemble the teaching of literature, Langdale urged the teaching of intelligent listening in addition to class singing. Piano and violin teaching would continue to rank with other optional studies, but obligatory lessons should be provided to "ensure to all pupils the benefits of a sound musical training." No amount of individual instrumental teaching or practice should be allowed to interfere with this regular class work so as to afford those who took up an instrument the general musical knowledge which was essential to intelligent performance. Lessons in musical rudiments and aural training for juniors would lead to the teaching of "Musical Appreciation" for seniors.

That policy was first formally implemented by Stewart Macpherson, a teacher at the Royal Academy of Music, who obtained permission to try out the scheme at Streatham Hill High School (GPDST) with gratifying success. The school soon became virtually a normal school where would-be teachers

---

[38] J. S. Curwen and J. Hullah, *School Music Abroad* (1880; rpt. ed. Kilkenny: Boethius, 1985), p. 18.

[39] Hermann Kretzschmar, *Musikalische Zeitfragen* (Leipzig: Peters, 1903), throughout.

[40] M. A. Langdale and S. Macpherson, *Early Essays in Musical Appreciation* (Kilkenny: Boethius, 1984), contains both articles in facsimile.

studying at the Royal Academy could practice teaching under Macpherson's supervision, while other girls' high schools were not slow to imitate the Streatham pattern. The creation of the Music Teachers' Association under Macpherson's leadership in 1908 "to promote progressive ideas upon the teaching of music, especially with a view to the more educational treatment of the subject in schools," accelerated the process.

As a result of these developments, by the first decade of the present century music had found a place in the curriculum of a wide variety of schools whether independent or maintained by the state. Only the academically slanted, examination haunted grammar schools for boys generally failed to admit music teaching. They continued to do so until the implementation of the Butler Education Act of 1944. Elsewhere syllabuses attempting broader treatment of the subject were consistently introduced to encourage greater musical understanding and wider familiarity with the masterpieces of the art than singing lessons alone could afford. Efforts of this kind were at first necessarily limited to the playing of pieces on the secondary school piano; the pianola, the gramophone, and the radio would enlarge the scope of this work in the future. But within the resources available at the time, well before Victorian self-confidence and earnestness had evaporated, a pattern of music teaching had been developed in schools nationally which was recognizably the fore-runner of the scheme existing today.

Mary Burgan

# HEROINES AT THE PIANO: WOMEN AND MUSIC IN NINETEENTH-CENTURY FICTION

OF ALL THE LUXURIES AVAILABLE TO THE MIDDLE CLASSES IN NINETEENTH-century England, the piano was perhaps the most significant in the lives of women; it was not only an emblem of social status, it provided a gauge of a woman's training in the required accomplishments of genteel society. Its presence or absence in the home could be a sign of social climbing, security of status, or loss of place. [1] And since the wife or daughter of the household usually presided over the piano, its presence afforded women a particular distinction within domestic culture. Accordingly, the sacrifice of her piano is one of the harshest elements of the woman's share in the economic disasters portrayed in nineteenth-century fiction. Without a piano, women with pretensions to gentility are deprived of the exercise of their special training, of any leading role in family recreation, and of one of their few legitimate channels for self-expression. And, in turn, the unexpected gift of a piano is one of the most effective sources of consolation for a young woman who has lost everything else. In Austen's *Emma* (1816), Jane Fairfax's narrow existence in cramped spinster quarters is enlarged through the gift of a small square pianoforte. In Thackeray's *Vanity Fair* (1847-48), Amelia Sedley's poor little piano is bought at auction by the faithful Dobbin and restored to its owner to soothe the cares of exile in Fulham Road. Without the piano to provide a field for her exertions in ascending the scale of class, Rosamond Vincy in George Eliot's *Middlemarch* (1871-72) could hardly entice Lydgate into her web. And

---

[1] The social history of the piano in Victorian England has been sketched by Arthur Loesser, *Men, Women, and Pianos: A Social History* (New York: Simon and Schuster, 1954), pp. 267-304. See also Cyril Ehrlich, *The Piano: A History* (London: Dent, 1976); Rosamond E. M. Harding, *The Piano-Forte: Its History Traced to the Great Exhibition of 1851* (1933; rpt. ed. New York: Da Capo, 1973); E. D. Mackerness, *A Social History of English Music* (London: Routledge, 1964); W. L. Sumner, *The Pianoforte* (London: Macdonald, 1966); and *The Romantic Age: 1800-1914*, ed. Nicholas Temperley, Vol. 5 of *The Athlone History of Music in Britain* (London: Athlone, 1981), especially the chapters by Temperley, "Ballroom and Drawing-Room Music," pp. 109-134 and "Piano Music: 1800-1870," pp. 400-423.

finally, in Gissing's *The Odd Women* (1893), Everard Barfoot can make no finer wedding gift to a friend in straitened circumstances than a cottage piano for his bride.

Nineteenth-century fiction thus pays continuing attention to the significance of the piano for women; indeed the linkage of music with women's role in domestic life was so pervasive that its manifestations in social history as well as fiction can provide a focus for the Victorian assessment of all feminine potential — not only in art but in the practical realm as well. In the beginning of the century, women at the piano tended to be objects of satire. But as the century progressed, the image became more complicated; women's aspirations for genuine education and high culture had to be taken more seriously. And as the issue of women's independence from the conventional round of family life became a feature of the "woman question" towards the end of the century, the possibility that woman's music could be a disruptive rather than a harmonizing force in the home became more insistent. In some novels — especially in the latter half of the century — feminine musicians were likely to exhibit gifts that were self-proclaiming and unsettling in their aggressive display of energy.

In this essay, I survey some nineteenth-century depictions of women and music in fiction, paying special attention to evolving attitudes about woman's capacity for original creative work. My subject is not music or musical history itself, but the image of music in Victorian fiction. To provide an adequate context for the fictional images, I will draw upon the economic, social, and musical history of a luxury which, by the start of the nineteenth century, seems to have become a necessity in many middle-class homes.

I

In Jane Austen's *Pride and Prejudice*, Lady Catherine DeBourgh lays down the rules of playing as tokens of the young gentlewoman's breeding, and intimates that the possession of an instrument is a privilege of domestic respectability limited to the upper ranks of the landed gentry. She is surprised to find that there is a piano in the Bennet household, but we learn elsewhere that there are others scattered about the minor households of Longbourn — in the Lucas house and in the Bingley's leased mansion, though not in the house of the less prosperous or reputable Uncle Phillips — where card-playing must take the place of music to while away a dull evening. Lady Catherine notes with self-satisfaction that Charlotte does not have "an instrument" in Mr. Collins's parsonage, and that Lady Catherine has two — the obscurest of which is offered to Elizabeth for that practice which would perfect her pretensions as the daughter of a gentleman and perhaps hone her skills for the inevitability of having to teach young children as a governess when the Bennet patrimony passes on to Mr. Collins. [2] That the piano was so ubiquitous at the period depicted in Pride and Prejudice indicates the phenomenal spread in England of a relatively new invention; pianos had been available for domestic use and display for only twenty-five years or so before Jane Austen completed the first version of her novel (1798). Historians have ascribed this growth not only to the affluence of an English middle class "eager to spend for prestige, enjoyment and self-improvement," but to the shrewdness of the major English piano makers in taking advantage of the market (Ehrlich, pp. 16-17). One measure of the rapid increase in popularity for the instrument is the publication of piano music in London between 1750 and 1800: whereas in 1750 there were over three hundred musical editions for the harpsichord, by 1785 editions designated for harpsichord rarely appeared, and by 1800 there were none at all (Sumner, pp. 50-51).

The piano got its name, "pianoforte," from its capacity to make sounds that could be "soft" or "loud." [3] Its dynamic qualities contrasted markedly with the limited dynamics of the harpsichord. The plucked strings of the harpsichord, which had been the domestic musical instrument of choice in the eighteenth century (in Fielding's Tom Jones [1749] Sophia Western quiets the fevered impulses of the Squire by playing old ballads on her spinet), could make a brilliant sound, but "could not produce subtle gradations of volume" (Ehrlich, p.11). The clavichord seems not to have been a functional substitute; although it could provide subtleties of effect, its tone was not powerful, and so it was primarily a private instrument. Thus in Italy and in Germany in the first half of the century, harpsichord makers experimented with an instrument that could allow for a stronger tone — striking rather than plucking the strings through intricately engineered "actions" that conveyed the pianist's touch from the key to a hammer to the string. Experiments in piano making moved forward on a number of fronts — allowing for freedom of vibration, damping, use of heavier strings at higher tensions, and later in the century the adaption of iron frames to allow for increased stress, more strings, and heavier hammers.

The pianoforte was thus the product of several technical advances; these led to the creation of an extremely versatile instrument — one which opened a number of possibilities for amateur players as well as for professional

[2] Jane Austen, Pride and Prejudice, Vol. 2 of The Works of Jane Austen, ed. R. W. Chapman, 5 vols. (London: Oxford University Press, 1940), bk. II, chap. 8.

[3] The technical details of the invention of the piano are best summarized by Edwin M. Good in Giraffes, Black Dragons, and Other Pianos: A Technical History from Cristofori to the Modern Concert Grand (Stanford: Stanford University Press, 1982), pp. 1-26. See also David Wainwright, Broadwood by Appointment: A History (London: Quiller Press, 1982).

musicians and composers. The pianoforte promised to give every home its own orchestra, as the well-known Victorian musical educator John Hullah noted (Mackerness, p. 173); it provided not only for individual pleasure but for collective family pleasure. Without the availability of the piano for dance music, the confrontations of Jane Austen's Elizabeth and Darcy could hardly have been staged. Jane Austen noted such a recreational use in a letter to her sister in 1808: "Yes, yes, we *will* have a pianoforte, as good a one as can be got for thirty guineas, and I will practise country dances, that we may have some amusement for our nephews and nieces, when we have the pleasure of their company."[4]

The piano's usurpation of the harpsichord's role was a commercial as well as a technical phenomenon. Utilizing some of the strategies of manufacture and merchandising that were to become standard later under industrialization, manufacturers like John Broadwood — who married into the family of one of the continental piano makers, immigrants to England in the eighteenth century — made London a center for the creation and perfection of pianos for concert and domestic use alike (Ehrlich, p. 19): "There were forty-five firms which manufactured pianos in London alone before 1800. Broadwood made 6,000 square and 1,000 grand pianos between 1780 and 1800, a large number when the size of the cultured population is taken into consideration" (Sumner, 51). Indeed, his is one of the few trade names mentioned in Jane Austen — Jane Fairfax's piano is from Broadwood's (see figure 1)[5] — and so is Amelia Sedley's in *Vanity Fair*; Becky Sharp remarks of the price it brings in auction, "Five-and-twenty guineas was monstrously dear for that little piano. We chose it at Broadwood's for Amelia, when she came from school. It only cost five-and-thirty then."[6] Later in the novel, Thackeray seems to have forgotten this piano's provenance and has Dobbin remember it as having been made by "Stothard," an allusion to Stodart, another London manufacturer.[7]

The number of pianos produced in London through the nineteenth century suggests a sizeable market, and that market was served by many manufacturers specializing in a variety of models and prices. From the beginning of the century a small piano was within reach of the middle classes, and towards the end of the century even workers could have pianos in their homes. Broadwood listed a single-action piano for as little as £17 6s. in 1815; the

[4] *Jane Austen's Letters to Her Sister Cassandra and Others*, ed. R. W. Chapman (2d. ed. Oxford: Oxford University Press, 1952), pp. 243-244.

[5] Jane Austen, *Emma*, Vol. 4 of *The Works of Jane Austen*, bk. II, chap. 8.

[6] William Thackeray, *Vanity Fair*, ed. J. I. M. Stewart (Harmondsworth: Penguin, 1968), chap. 18.

[7] *Vanity Fair*, chap. 56; Loesser has pointed out this inconsistency, p. 277.

(1) "Maternal Recreation" from *Emma* by Jane Austen, ed. R. W. Chapman (Oxford: Clarendon, 1923). The piano in the illustration is a Broadwood & Sons.

cheapest six-octave cottage model was listed at forty-four guineas in 1840. [8] In 1850, a cottage piano could be hired for a pound a month, though George Eliot — returning from Geneva to London in 1850 — asked a friend to see if she could rent her old piano for "16 s. per month which is quite enough." [9] Such prices were high but not prohibitive, and there seems to have been some trade in used and rehabilitated pianos. Thus a middle-class family could aspire to a good square piano, while a rich family could display a "grand." The modest "cottage" piano could be obtained through hire-purchase by the latter half of the century (Ehrlich, pp. 98-104). When Eliot's writing began to promise a life of some affluence, one of her first aspirations was to purchase a grand piano; she wrote to George Henry Lewes's son after the success of *Adam Bede* in 1859, "If I am able to go on working, I hope we shall afford to have a fine grand piano" (*Letters*, III, 125-126).

In the history of serious music, the invention of the piano had a major impact on musical composition. Mozart's playing of a German piano in 1777 seems almost to have been a conversion experience, leading to the composition of his great piano concertos. Haydn accepted the new instrument as well. Despite the heavier action of English pianos, Beethoven composed on a Broadwood given to him by the manufacturer. [10] And all piano manufacturers made efforts to supply the most famous virtuosi with their particular makes. Thus the conjunction of commerce and inspiration assured the creation of sublime concert music from the time the piano was first made available to composers. But on the domestic scene, the inspiration was not always sublime. Although Schubert's compositions for home musicales — Schubertiads, as they were called in the 1820s — combined a rare musical creativity with the pleasures and intimacies of domestic settings, the popularity of the piano as an instrument for the English home had less to do with such genius than with such matters as women's education, the upward mobility of the middle class, and the status of the bourgeois household as the locus for all legitimate general sociability.

Most of the young women who labored to learn the piano in the nineteenth century were not intent upon mastering the intricacies of Mozart, Haydn, or Beethoven. Though each of these composers wrote some music for the amateur, their compositions were rarely grist for amateur feminine art.

---

[8] Representative price lists are provided in Harding, Appendix F, pp. 378-384.

[9] *The George Eliot Letters*, ed. Gordon S. Haight, 9 vols. (New Haven: Yale University Press, 1954-78), III, 360.

[10] Many histories suggest that Broadwood's gift of a piano to Beethoven was a master stroke of public relations, but Wainwright makes a convincing case for the gift as a tribute to genius rather than a publicity move (pp. 114-119). In any case, the English piano was the only kind strong enough to withstand Beethoven's mistreatment as he sought for a more powerful sound to penetrate his encroaching deafness. He all but wrecked the Broadwood piano.

The expressive capacities of the new instrument promised effects that could make the amateur shine in the playing of showy "salon" music, simple ballads and sacred songs, or simplified transcriptions of more difficult pieces; such compositions did not demand a great deal of technical finish or musical intelligence. Simple chords and arpeggios could be made to sound as important as contrapuntal patterns (Ehrlich, p. 12); the slightest of accompaniments could embellish singing that would not have been pleasing without some amplification, or perhaps some masking; and touch could seem a proper substitute for dexterity. Dramatic effects could be easily obtained with the percussive aspects of the piano; indeed in performing one battle piece composition, a kind of programme music that became very popular in the early part of the century, one young lady used a special "swell" pedal to slam the lid of the piano so as to simulate the sound of a cannon explosion. [11]

Such drawing-room music attracted the scorn of early music critics like George Hogarth, Dickens's father-in-law, but its simple pleasures were not to be denied. Young Victorian women who played for show were more likely to bang through a piece like "The Battle of Prague" than to assay the subtleties of Schubert as Madame Merle does in James's *Portrait of a Lady* (1881) (see figure 2). For the discriminating, though, there were variations on ballad themes and airs — simple but expressive compositions like Mendelssohn's "Fantasia on an Ancient Irish Air" ("The Last Rose of Summer"). But even so musically sensitive a poet as Thomas Hardy could be nostalgic about old parlor standards such as the "Fall of Paris," "Battle of Prague," "Roving Minstrels," and "Elfin Call." [12] One historian of music has concluded that "no musical instrument (except the Spanish guitar) is more susceptible to insensitive usage than the pianoforte. This is reflected in the great mass of meretricious piano music produced throughout the nineteenth century" (Mackerness, p. 175). Mark Twain shared the general revulsion against this kind of programme music, working it into the genteel setting of the Grangerford parlor in *Huckleberry Finn* (1884): "There was a little old piano, too, that had tin pans in it, I reckon, and nothing was ever so lovely as to hear the young ladies sing, 'The Last Link is Broken' and play 'The Battle of Prague' on it." [13] In a letter written in 1878, Twain described hearing a young lady hammer out the battle piece in a Swiss hotel: "She turned on all the

---

[11] Harding, p. 113. Critics like Loesser have been quite severe about the limitations of such music, but Temperley takes a more balanced view: "It was often a pale reflection of the music of the great composers. . . . Nevertheless . . . it could often be the vehicle of strong emotion" (p. 119).

[12] "A Duettist to Her Pianoforte," in Thomas Hardy, *The Collected Poems* (London: Macmillan, 1930), pp. 555-556.

[13] Mark Twain, *Adventures of Huckleberry Finn*, ed. Henry Nash Smith (Boston: Riverside Press, 1958), p. 88.

**PUNCH'S PENCILLINGS.—N⁰. XLVIII.**

SOCIAL MISERIES.—No. 11.

## THE PLEASURES OF FOLDING DOORS.

Hearing "The Battle of Prague" played, with a running accompaniment of—One, and Two, and Three; —and One, and Two, and Three;——and

(2) "The Pleasures of Folding Doors," from *Punch* 3 (1842). The caption reads: "Hearing 'The Battle of Prague' played, with a running accompaniment of – One, and Two, and Three; — and One, and Two, and Three; —— and . . ."

horrors of *The Battle of Prague*, that venerable shivaree, and waded chin deep
in the blood of the slain." [14]


## II


If the piano became a fixture in parlors from London to backwoods
America, its impact on the education of young women was equally pervasive.
Though learning to play the piano was a requirement for middle-class girls,
tutelage in piano-playing seems to have had little place in the curriculum for
boys. Although there were fine professional male composers and performers
of music in nineteenth-century England, there seems to have been a bias
against educating middle-class males for amateur instrumental performance.
Perhaps this prejudice can be assigned to the spirit of John Locke, which
brooded over English education even in the Victorian period. In *Some
Thoughts Concerning Education* Locke had discounted musical training for
young men:

> *Musick* is thought to have some affinity with Dancing, and a good Hand, upon some In-
> struments, is by many People mightily valued. But it wastes so much of a young Man's
> time, to gain but a moderate Skill in it; and engages often in such odd Company, that
> many think it much better spared: And I have, amongst Men of Parts and Business, so
> seldom heard any one commended, or esteemed for having an Excellency in *Musick*, that
> amongst all those things, that ever came into the List of Accomplishment, I think I may
> give it the last place. [15]

Such a bias against music as a waste of the ordinary English gentleman's time
can be seen in nineteenth-century English fiction. The native Englishmen
who play instruments in British novels tend to be schoolmasters or clergymen, and in either case they tend to be seen as eccentric, though often admirable, examples of manhood. A number of Victorian memoirists have
commented on this British prejudice against amateur male musicians. Mrs.
C. S. Peel observed that "gentlemen also sang and duets were in high favour,
but play the piano gentlemen did not, that being considered a task only fit for
ladies and professional musicians." [16] And in his survey of music in Dickens's
work, James T. Lightwood recalls that in his own late Victorian experience,

---

[14] Quoted by Percy A. Scholes in *The Oxford Companion to Music*, ed. John Owen Ward (London:
Oxford University Press, 1970), p. 559. I have been unable to find this passage in Twain's collected
letters.

[15] John Locke, *The Educational Writing of John Locke*, ed. James L. Axtell (Cambridge: Cambridge
University Press, 1968), p. 311.

[16] Quoted in Wainwright, who notes that Prince Albert was an exception, though "he was foreign,
which no doubt accounted for it" (p. 147).

it was not considered "the correct thing for a gentleman to play the piano, though it might be all very well for the lower classes and the music teacher. Consequently we read of few male performers on the instrument."[17]

It is important to emphasize that Lightwood's generalization can apply only to amateur musicianship among the upper classes. Most professional pianists in Victorian England were male. But for amateur male musicians, instruments tended to have gender significance; thus gentlemen in Victorian novels tend to play instruments that, according to Nicholas Temperley, were generally considered masculine ("Ballroom and Drawing-Room Music," p. 120). Mr. Mell in *David Copperfield* (1849-50) plays the flute; Prince Turveydrop in *Bleak House* (1852-53) plays the "kit" or small violin for his dancing classes; and Mr. Harding in *The Warden* (1855) plays the cello. Despite such positive examples, Victorian society rejected piano playing for the gentleman, and as we shall see, this prejudice gave rise to some strange conventions in the presentation of male virtuosi in some of the late Victorian novels that broach the topic of masculine versus feminine musicianship.

It would be difficult to determine exactly how many girls labored and wept over the pianoforte during the nineteenth century, but a variety of sources suggest that at least one struggling female pianist was typical of every respectably prosperous family. The example of the untalented but ever ready Mary Bennet in *Pride and Prejudice* indicates the extent to which musical accomplishment could be part of the young woman's dowry and public identity. Maria Edgeworth sketches a picture of the forced labor behind such examples in her essay on "Female Accomplishments, Masters, and Governesses" in *Practical Education* (1798), when she urges the sensible mother to resist the temptation of turning her daughter into a musical "automaton for eight hours in every day for fifteen years, for the promise of hearing her, at the end of that time, pronounced the first private performer at the most fashionable and most crowded concert in London."[18] Edgeworth outlines the benefits of musical gifts — the "admission to fashionable company," the increase of "a young lady's chance of a prize in the matrimonial lottery," and their "value as resources against ennui" (p. 111), but, like Locke, she sees little intrinsic value in their pursuit. The best accomplishments are those that suit the young woman for her long and dismal servitude in the home:

> Women are peculiarly restrained in their situation, and in their employments, by the customs of society: to diminish the number of these employments, therefore, would be cruel; they should rather be encouraged, by all means, to cultivate those tastes which can attach them to their home, and which can preserve them from the miseries of dissipation. Every

[17] James T. Lightwood, *Charles Dickens and Music*, (1912; rpt. ed. New York: Haskell House, 1970), p. 33.

[18] Maria Edgeworth and Richard Lovel Edgeworth, *Practical Education* (Boston: Wait, 1815), p. 110.

sedentary occupation must be valuable to those who are to lead sedentary lives; and every
art, however trifling in itself, which tends to enliven and embellish domestic life, must be
advantageous, not only to the female sex, but to society in general.

                                                        (Edgeworth, p. 112).

Thus the ultimate rationale for musical training for young women was
the exercise of moral rather than aesthetic aptitudes: "Therefore the study of
the fine arts, considered as a part of female education, should be attended to
much less with a view to the acquisition of superior talents, than with a desire
to give women a taste for industry, the habit of application, and a greater variety of employments" (Edgeworth, pp. 117-118). Through the remainder of
the nineteenth century, advocacy of musical education for girls tended to
sanction one or the other of the uses advocated by Edgeworth: piano expertise was a commodity in the marriage market, a form of necessary self-discipline, or an innocent entertainment in an otherwise vacuous existence.

Some of the most vocal critics of such limited views and their attend-
ant coercion of female musicianship were the mid- and late Victorian music
critics and pedagogues (Mackerness, pp. 173-175). But criticism also came
from another, unexpected quarter. In the middle of the century, the science
of domestic economy began to evolve, and those experts who took to advising young women on their more mundane domestic duties found the contrast
between the useful work of cooking and the useless work of playing the piano
to be instructive. [19] William Kitchiner began his *Housekeeper's Oracle* (1829)
with an exhortation to the young woman to season her training in the graces
with training in household economy so that she "may learn the delectable
Arcana of Domestic Affairs in as little time as is usually devoted to directing
the position of her hands on a Piano-Forte . . . which will enable her to make
the Cage of Matrimony as comfortable as the Net of Courtship was charming." [20] And at the beginning of his treatise on *The Modern Housewife or
Ménagère* (1850), Alexis Soyer has a satisfied husband comment on the ways
in which his wife's genteel accomplishments have been augmented by training in home economics: "She speaks two or three different languages toler-
ably well, and, as an amateur, is rather proficient in music, but her parents,
very wisely considering household knowledge to be of greater importance,
made her first acquainted with the keys of the storeroom before those of the
piano." [21] According to a number of the Victorian treatises that advocated
the necessity of thorough training in domesticity, then, conventional femi-

[19] See Patricia Branca, *Silent Sisterhood: Middle Class Women in the Victorian Home* (London: Croom
Helm, 1975), p. 14, for an account of the rise of advice to housewives in the mid-Victorian period.

[20] William Kitchiner, *The Housekeeper's Oracle; or, the Art of Domestic Management . . .* (London:
Whittaker, Treacher, and Co., 1829), pp. 1-2.

[21] Alexis Soyer, *The Modern Housewife or Ménagère* (New York: Appleton, 1850), p. 4.

nine musicianship was a trivial pursuit, an unworthy distraction from the vocation of managing a home.

Commercial and social developments could thus send the aspiring
Victorian girl to music masters, but the philosophical, pedagogical, and practical oracles of the nineteenth century posed a dilemma for her. On the one
hand, she was to exert herself to attain accomplishments that would enrich
the home: on the other, she must remain a mere amateur — all her arts that
were not utilitarian were suspect.

Early Victorian fiction tended to portray the young woman's efforts at
the piano unsympathetically. In significant instances, early Victorian novelists could entertain the possibility that musical talent might have serious implications in women's lives, but in their predominant focus on the limitations
of social climbing, they were more likely to treat a female character's preten-
sion to musical achievement satirically. Although Thackeray was a lover of
music in his personal life, he presents piano playing as one of the more questionable successes of feminine education. [22] Amelia Sedley embodies the
slightness of talent and exertion required in the proper young lady's musical
education, and though her piano playing is a solace, it involves little more
than passive doodling on the keys: she sits "for long evening hours, touching,
to the best of her simple art, melancholy harmonies on the keys, and weeping
over them in silence" (Vanity Fair, chap. 59). No matter how inept, Amelia's
feeble artifice expresses the truth of her feeling. Becky Sharp's proficiency, on
the other hand, is heartless: singing the religious songs of Mozart to Lady
Steyne "with such sweetness and tenderness that the lady, lingering round
the piano, sate down by its side, and listened until the tears rolled down her
eyes" (Vanity Fair, chap. 50), Becky ruthlessly deploys the calculation in her
art.

In Charlotte Brontë's Jane Eyre, a similar distinction between art as
feeling and as artifice is set up by the contrast between Jane's piano playing
and that of Blanche Ingram. Jane plays the piano only as well as a governess
must, while Blanche exhibits her social superiority through a feverish virtuosity as she "seated herself with proud grace at the piano, spreading out her
snowy robes in queenly amplitude, [and] commenced a brilliant prelude; talk-
ing meantime." [23] Such brilliance is not only false but unseemly, and if it
evokes a certain censoriousness in Brontë, it causes even greater ambivalence
about feminine aggressiveness in other Victorian novelists.

Thackeray's attraction to the passivity of the feminine stereotype
makes his contrast between Amelia and Becky more anxious than Brontë's

---

[22] See Robert T. Bledsoe, "Vanity Fair and Singing," Studies in the Novel 13 (1981), 55-63.

[23] Charlotte Brontë, Jane Eyre, ed. Jane Jack and Margaret Smith (Oxford: Clarendon Press, 1969),
chap. 17.

pairing of Jane and Blanche. His treatment of women at the piano exhibits his characteristic problem in balancing the good woman against the wicked woman in *Vanity Fair*. Brontë can strike some balance by giving the unmusical Jane a living to earn and extraordinary expressive skill in another fine art, drawing. But in *Vanity Fair* and *Jane Eyre* alike the young woman who uses her artistic skill for social advancement is seen as nothing better than a schemer. Indeed those women who are depicted as conscious artists tend to be "performers" through and through, seeking an unseemly domination over their masculine audiences.

## III

Dickens's treatment of women and music presents a complex range of variations on the dilemma of whether feminine musical facility is a trifling emblem of marital eligibility or an achievement of talent and insight. In *David Copperfield*, Dora is so inept that she must play at the guitar rather than the more demanding piano (see figure 3). The impracticality of her cultivation of musical attainments at the expense of common sense calls forth a critique of the inadequacies of feminine education that Dickens reiterated often in his fiction and journalism. [24] David remarks on Dora's failure to think seriously about cooking, "We fell back on the guitar-case, and the flower-painting, and the songs about never leaving off dancing, ta ra la! and were as happy as the week was long. I occasionally wished I could venture to hint to Miss Lavinia, that she treated the darling of my heart a little too much like a plaything." [25]

Dickens often rattles the keys of the storeroom in his characterization of women, and nowhere is this more apparent than in his portrait of Esther Summerson as the epitome of the efficient housewife in *Bleak House*. Esther can appreciate the talents of others — she listens quietly when the gentle and impractical Ada plays and sings with Richard in their first days at Bleak House — but she is also aware that Harold Skimpole's musical facility is one more sign of the childishness of genteel people who use music to while away empty hours. [26]

Thus Dickens is apt to portray domestic piano playing as childish. Nevertheless, he had a genuine appreciation for music, and sought to master the accordion — an appropriately popular and cheerful instrument. [27] The

[24] See P. A. W. Collins, "Dickens and the Education of Girls," *Dickensian* 57 (1961), 86-96.

[25] Charles Dickens, *David Copperfield*, ed. Nina Burgis (Oxford: Clarendon Press, 1981), chap. 41.

[26] See Jane W. Stedman, "Child-Wives of Dickens," *Dickensian* 59 1963), 112-118.

[27] See Lillian M. Ruff, "How Musical Was Charles Dickens?" *Dickensian* 68 (1972), 31-42.

*My child-wife's old companion*

(3) "My Child-Wife's Old Companion" from *David Copperfield* by Charles Dickens, illustrations by H. K. Browne (1849-50).

nature of music's appeal to him can be seen in his depiction of hearty men who sing at pubs or clubs or who perform in music halls or circuses. And women's musicianship can be redeemed when associated with the active, practical running of affairs or the provision of communal entertainment. It seems likely that Dickens's toleration of some feminine efforts at the piano may have been influenced by his affection for his sister Fanny, who was remarkably well-trained as a pianist and vocalist. It was Fanny who received tuition at the Royal Academy of Music when Dickens went to the blacking warehouse. She studied under Ignaz Moscheles, one of the most famous of Victorian pianists, and she seems to have been able to earn her way through music — working as a "sub professor" and giving occasional concerts. She eventually married a fellow student and singer, and they made a joint career from music, moving to Manchester both to teach and to sing in a church. [28] Dickens's admiration for the bond of music in her marriage may be reflected in Caddy Jellyby's learning to play the piano in order to accompany children at her young husband's dancing school.

Thus in Dickens's fiction music as a practical endeavor, used in conjugal mutual support, differs from music as an ornament for lightheaded husband-hunters. Esther Summerson openly approves of Caddy's labors to master the pianoforte; music for her is, after all, a species of home economics: "I conscientiously believed, dancing-master's wife though she was, and dancing-mistress though in her limited ambition she aspired to be, she had struck out a natural, wholesome, loving course of industry and perseverance that was quite as good as a Mission." [29] But although Esther embodies the more acceptable mid-Victorian image of true female accomplishment in her efficient bustling about the house, her lack of any means of overt self-expression — of any music beyond the tinkling of Dame Durden's keys — may account for a lack of resonance in her characterization.

Dickens's depictions of women and music generally followed mid-Victorian prejudices about woman's place in society. But on occasion his fiction recognizes the deeper power of music under a woman's hand. His portrayal of Rosa Dartle in *David Copperfield* strikes a note that echoes in a number of later nineteenth-century novels. Rosa's performance on the harp dramatizes a capacity to feel that has been perverted by intense repression and suffering:

> I don't know what it was, in her touch or voice, that made that song the most unearthly I have ever heard in my life, or can imagine. There was something fearful in the reality of it. It was as if it had never been written, or set to music, but sprung out of the passion within her; which found imperfect utterance in the low sounds of her voice, and

---

[28] See William J. Carlton, "Fanny Dickens, Pianist and Vocalist," *Dickensian* 53 (1957), 133-143.

[29] Charles Dickens, *Bleak House*, ed. George Ford and Sylvère Monod (New York: Norton, 1977), chap. 38.

crouched again when all was still. I was dumb when she leaned beside the harp again, playing it, but not sounding it, with her right hand.

(chap. 29).

The great male virtuoso figures of the Victorian period were often de-picted in demonic terms, suggesting a sexual source for sublime musical rap-ture. For one thing, the popular Victorian heroes of music were thought to have obtained almost diabolical skill. Paganini, Mendelssohn, Liszt, Rubin-stein, and — later — Paderewski seemed inhumanly masterful during their concerts. Moreover, their allure seemed most potent for the females in their audiences. Even though the feminine adulation of Liszt and others gave rise to a number of cartoons in comic periodicals both in England and on the Continent, the sexual implications of their appeal could also be a serious concern (see figures 4 and 5). Thus the fictional treatment of women and the demonic in music suggests the fear that too powerful an inspiration can over-whelm impressionable female hearers, often in pathological ways.

In English literature, sublime rapture could sometimes originate in fe-male figures such as Coleridge's damsel with a dulcimer and Dickens's Rosa Dartle. In such cases, the demonic threat passes from female to male rather than from male to female: the damsel of "Kubla Khan" inspires an ecstatic vi-sion that gives rise to the warning to the rapt poet, "Beware! Beware!" And Rosa seems ready to tear Steerforth apart, even though she is the one who bears the scar of his childhood violence. Despite the threat of suppressed ani-mal energy in Rosa Dartle (her passion "crouched again when all was still"), Dickens honors its eloquence and pathos.

When he returns to the image of feminine musical passion again, however, he makes it less conscious and he places it under the control of a male master. In this permutation of the theme, the woman cannot manage her own talent and is therefore especially vulnerable to the unscrupulous male musician. She is an angel, too innocent to recognize the evil around her. Such depictions of extraordinary musical gifts provide additional evi-dence of the doubleness of the Victorian myth of woman as angel and devil. [30] In *The Mystery of Edwin Drood* (1870), John Jasper accompanies Rosa Bud with a hypnotic insistence on a single note which places her under his spell: "As Jasper watched the pretty lips, and ever and again hinted the one note, as though it were a low whisper from himself, the voice became less steady, until all at once the singer broke into a burst of tears, and shrieked out, with her hands over her eyes: 'I can't bear this! I am frightened! Take me away!' " [31] In *Drood* the countervailing musical impulse is found in Mr.

---

[30] See Nina Auerbach, *Woman and the Demon: The Life of a Victorian Myth* (Cambridge: Harvard University Press, 1982).

[31] Charles Dickens, *The Mystery of Edwin Drood*, ed. Margaret Cardwell (Oxford: Clarendon Press, 1972), chap. 7.

(4) "Liszt and his Sabre" from *La Vie Parisienne*, 3 April 1886.

(5) A Nineteenth-Century Cartoon of Paderewski.

Crisparkle, a valiant singer whose music is healthily communal, liberating, and English; nevertheless, the image of the wily male music master, seducing the woman through music mastered in some exotic birthplace, is the more insistent and compelling one.

It is this stereotype of the foreign musician that mirrors in Victorian fiction that bias against music on the part of middle- and upper-class males mentioned earlier. Images of powerful musicians from foreign lands can be found in a number of Victorian novels that treat woman's potentially demonic affinity with music as a susceptibility to corruption by an alien whose talent is likely to be unscrupulous. George DuMaurier's *Trilby* (1894) is, of course, the locus classicus for this motif (see figure 6). Musically gifted villains from such sinister places as "the East" and the Mediterranean also turn up in Bulwer-Lytton's *Strange Story* (1862) and Wilkie Collins's *Woman in White* (1860). Such sensational manipulators of music as an instrument for sexual domination illustrate an awakened recognition of its significance outside the drawing room. The increasing attribution of demonic musical power to Svengali-like figures perhaps involved a growing awareness that women's music might embody genuine power. The question of who was to wield that power became paramount in assessing the ability of women to take charge of their own lives.

Certain it is that images of men and women joined in making music together suggest a struggle for domination in many late-Victorian novels. Even when women's musicality is presented as an avenue for her autonomy in society, its depiction is strained and unconvincing. George Meredith, one of the most musically sophisticated of late Victorian novelists, tried to present an affirmative image of women's music in *Sandra Belloni* (1864), but although he wished to use the extraordinary musical gifts of his heroine as a foil for social criticism, he was incapable of keeping her in proportion. In reaction against her shallow English lover, the musically gifted heroine loses her voice. Her singing — a gift of her Italian heritage — is eventually allied with her heroic efforts in the liberation of her native land. But in the revolutionary conclusion of Meredith's complicated novel, the heroine becomes a figure more suitable for the opera stage than the boundaries of realist fiction. Though Meredith viewed women's music as a necessary antidote to the masculine British stolidity that was always the target of his comedy, he could portray its power only through posturings in a wildly improbable plot.

IV

The Victorian novelist who explored women's music most successfully within the confines of firm social observation and psychological realism was

" AU CLAIR DE LA LUNE "

(6) "Au Clair de la Lune" from *Trilby* by George Du Maurier, illustrations by George Du Maurier (1894).

George Eliot. She considered herself to be only an amateur musician, but her characterization of musical women negotiates a variety of possibilities beyond amateurism, mesmerism, or idealization.

George Eliot's biography and letters reveal a life-long attachment to playing the piano — as a source of inner recreation, as a goad to self-discipline, and as an expression of the deepest spiritual harmony. In many ways her notions about the uses of piano playing show her to be a daughter of Maria Edgeworth. The Edgeworthian motifs of recreation and self-discipline are always near when she talks of her own playing. Thus during her first stay in Geneva, she describes her regimen to Sarah Bray: "My want of health has obliged me to renounce all application. I take walks, play on the piano, read Voltaire, talk to my friends, and just take a dose of mathematics every day to prevent my brain from becoming quite soft" (*Letters*, I, 321).

But although Eliot shared Edgeworth's emphasis on recreation and discipline, she also appreciated the communal powers of musical performance. In 1850, she wrote to Charles Lewes in delighted anticipation of their playing duets together (*Letters*, III, 125-126), though she could not be content with her facility:

> I was a very idle practiser, and I often regret now that when I had abundant time and opportunity for hours of piano-playing, I used them so little. I have about eighteen sonatas and symphonies of Beethoven, I think, but I shall be delighted to find that you can play them better than I can. I wish Bertie could be exhorted to *work* at his music, since he appears to have a decided ear for it. I am very sensitive to blunders and wrong notes, and instruments out of tune, but I have never played much from ear, though I used to play from *memory* a great deal.
>
> (*Letters*, III, 177-178).

Thus the emphasis on discipline is always in counterpoint to George Eliot's emphasis on the delight of music. She could not resist linking the ideal of habitual exactitude — the only reliable stay against moral confusion — with an aspiration for emotional spontaneity. In her experience, music was the perfect arena for testing the relationships between these frequently conflicting values, for she was not only a rapt enthusiast, she was aware that piano-playing was one form of art in which her skill was incommensurate with the intensity of her feeling.

The result of the discrepancy between George Eliot's musical aspiration and achievement lends a note of poignant vanity to her biography. Frederick Lehmann, a friend with whom she often played violin duets, described her for the official record as a "very fair pianist, not gifted, but enthusiastic, and extremely painstaking" (*Letters*, VIII, 385). Off the record, Lehmann was much less kind. In her memoirs of literary life in mid-century London, L.

B. Walford quotes him to a quite different effect (she is recounting her observation of George Eliot at a private concert given by Rubinstein):

> His playing was glorious, and among the rest George Eliot gave herself up to it entirely.
> That it cast a spell over her was obvious. Her massive brow unbent, and a softened
> expression stole over her heavy features. She did not look the same woman as when last I
> saw her.
> Music, it was said, always had on her a great effect. "Indeed, she is a real lover of
> it," said Mr. Lehmann, sitting down beside us in an interval. "The pity is, that she rather
> prides herself on being a performer too, as I know to my cost. I play duets with her some-
> times. Well, they are odd performances, those duets. She has feeling, certainly she has
> feeling — but her execution is — erratic;" — and he laughed a little. "However," he con-
> tinued, "it gives pleasure to one auditor at any rate, for whenever we get through a whole
> page without a breakdown, Lewis [sic] claps his hands and cries 'Exquisite!' " [32]

No matter how deluded it may have seemed to outsiders, George
Eliot's pursuit of pianistic skill never slackened. Indeed, returning to the piano keyboard helped her overcome sorrow at the death of George Henry
Lewes, even while it strengthened her bond with John W. Cross. In his *Life*
of Eliot, Cross recalls the turning point in her grieving: "At the end of May
[1879] I induced her to play on the piano at Witley for the first time; and she
played regularly after that whenever I was there, which was generally once or
twice a-week." [33] We can reasonably surmise that she kept at it until she
died.

Given this biographical context, it is not surprising that George
Eliot's novels are rich in musical allusion. In *Mill on the Floss* (1860), for ex-
ample, music is a pervasive source of imagery, characterization, and plot. [34]
Eliot's other novels feature a number of case studies of women whose musical
responses indicate either great resources of character or total vacuity. Thus in
*Middlemarch*, Dorothea is gifted with a rich, low musical voice, while
Rosamond Vincy, who cannot sing very well, has a surface dexterity at the
piano, learned by rote from a good teacher at her country school:
"Rosamond, with the executant's instinct, had seized his manner of playing,
and gave forth his large rendering of noble music with the precision of an
echo. It was almost startling, heard for the first time." [35] And in *Felix Holt*
(1866), Mrs. Transome's girlhood accomplishments, which included singing
and playing "a little," have "become as valueless as old-fashioned stucco or-
naments, of which the substance was never worth anything, while the form is
no longer to the taste of any living mortal." [36]

---

[32] L. B. Walford, *Memories of Victorian London* (London: Edward Arnold, 1912), p. 142.

[33] J. W. Cross, *George Eliot's Life as Related in her Letters and Journals*, 3 vols. (New York: Harper, 1885), III, 259.

[34] William J. Sullivan, "Music and Musical Allusion in *The Mill on the Floss*," *Criticism* 16 (1974), p. 232.

[35] George Eliot, *Middlemarch* (Boston: Houghton Mifflin, 1956), chap. 16.

[36] George Eliot, *Felix Holt, the Radical*, ed. Fred C. Thomson (Oxford: Clarendon Press, 1980), chap. 1.

Thus in the tradition of Thackeray, Brontë, and Dickens, Eliot satirized conventional feminine musicianship. But even in satire her fiction measured more than the limits of musical education for girls in a culture that could not take women seriously; it also measured the frailty of consciences that have never been touched by the largeness of emotion that music could express.

While music is a recurrent motif in all of George Eliot's fiction, in *Daniel Deronda* (1874-76) her preoccupation with its implications for the development of woman's character becomes central to the structure and meaning of the novel. Here Eliot's main moral and sociological preoccupations come together in a definitive exploration of the varieties of musical experience available in late Victorian society. Albert R. Cirillo notes that George Eliot found in Feuerbach's notion of music as the disciplined "language of feeling" a philosophical foundation that informs her treatment of the positive values of music in the novel. [37] And Shirley F. Levenson further elaborates on George Eliot's perception that such a concept of music countered deeply ingrained English moral tone-deafness: "There is a formal, superficial quality about the English society which Eliot is describing that works against the development of music because music . . . is associated in [*Daniel Deronda*] with the expression of deep feeling." [38]

This conflict between the convention of music as a feminine social grace and Eliot's ideal of music as socially significant feeling animates the contrast between Gwendolen Harleth's ability to amuse through playing and singing in the drawing room and the transcendent musical gifts of Mirah Cohen — gifts that require a more natural amphitheater (indeed Daniel first hears her voice while he is rowing on the river). Although F. R. Leavis has divided *Deronda* between Gwendolen and Daniel, I am inclined to emphasize the narrative alternation between Gwendolen and Mirah. [39] In any case, as George Eliot shifts attention from Gwendolen's struggle to salvage her fortunes through music to Mirah's role in helping Daniel to find his musical heritage, there unfolds a complex analysis of the cultural and psychic situations of Victorian women who seek to control their destinies by exploiting their own talents.

Gwendolen is shown as almost irremediably shallow in her approach to music. Herr Klesmer, the benign Liszt/Rubinstein prototype in the novel, nearly destroys her self-esteem with his critique of her deficiencies in feeling

[37] Albert R. Cirillo, "Salvation in *Daniel Deronda*: The Fortunate Overthrow of Gwendolen Harleth," *Literary Monographs*, I, ed. Erick Rothstein and Thomas K. Dunseath (Madison: University of Wisconsin Press, 1967), p. 231.

[38] Shirley F. Levenson, "The Use of Music in *Daniel Deronda*," *Nineteenth-Century Fiction* 24 (1969), 318.

[39] F. R. Leavis, *The Great Tradition* (New York: New York University Press, 1967), p. 80.

and skill. [40] And Klesmer emphasizes the fact that Gwendolen's limitations are not simply the results of her nationality and class: Klesmer's student, Catherine Arrowpoint, has taken her musical education beyond the limitations of the conventional school-girl attainments. She has made herself a suitable partner for Klesmer in four-handed duets, and eventually in life. Her choice of such a mate, one with whom she will share a musical vocation, upsets the prejudices of her class against male musicians and, incidentally, provides one of George Eliot's rare depictions of an independent woman making a vocational decision that does not immure her in the home.

Although Gwendolen Harleth must be held accountable for her musical limitations, she escapes the moral failure of prototypes like Rosamond Vincy and Mrs. Transome by learning to value the kind of inspiration and skill that she will never have. She struggles for self-recognition after she has been told by Herr Klesmer that her musical ambitions are based upon too fragile a talent — and also too frail a concept of "what excellence is" — to achieve "more than mediocrity." [41] The images of the music room in which he leaves her after their interview impress into her consciousness a sense that up to now she has only been playing: "All the memories, all objects, the pieces of music displayed, the open piano — the very reflection of herself in the glass — seemed no better than the packed-up shows of a departing fair" (chap. 23). Despite the disintegration of her scheme to become a musician in order to escape marriage with Grandcourt, however, Gwendolen is still not without musical recourse. When she goes to Daniel for advice he urges her to take up her lessons again. [42] That duty, like the other duties which can give her life meaning, will put her in touch with the feelings of others, and with her own feelings as well.

But George Eliot is interested in the mystical as well as the moral aspects of women's music, embodying this interest in Mirah Cohen. In the contrast between Mirah and Gwendolen, she points to the relationships among the main factors in musical achievement — the habitual discipline required for artistic expression, the self-sacrifice necessary for the choice of music as a vocation, and the native genius that is somehow validated through suffering. The combination of these factors is, however, alien to native English soil, and the musicians of *Daniel Deronda*, like the musical villains in the Victorian sensation novels mentioned above, come from foreign places. Music in *Daniel Deronda* is specifically Jewish; "klesmer" is the Yiddish word for musician (Levenson, p. 137) and of course Mirah is Jewish.

---

[40] For an argument that Rubinstein is the proper model for Klesmer, see Gordon S. Haight, "George Eliot's Klesmer," in *Imagined Worlds*, ed. Maynard Mack and Ian Gregor (London: Methuen, 1968), pp. 205-214. I suggest that Klesmer combines characteristics of Liszt and Rubinstein alike.

[41] George Eliot, *Daniel Deronda*, ed. Graham Handley (Oxford: Clarendon, 1984), chap. 23.

[42] See Bonnie Zimmerman, "Gwendolen Harleth and 'The Girl of the Period,'" in *George Eliot Centenary Essays and an Unpublished Fragment*, ed. Anne Smith (London: Vision Press, 1980), p. 212.

In thus evoking the mysteries of music, George Eliot shares the late Victorian impulse to appeal to the exotic and demonic, but she sees this appeal as positive rather than pathological. As a matter of fact, she locates the power of song in a sort of racial consciousness that transcends the limitations of an English culture mired in commercialism and caste. To be sure, there is some narrative strain in the conception of Mirah as an innocent girl who happens to be possessed by a native talent that transports all hearers (her training with Klesmer involves strengthening her natural voice rather than the drudgery of practicing scales). And Mirah's last-chapter marriage to Daniel so that they can work together in the East holds less promise for her own independence than does Catherine Arrowpoint's marriage to Klesmer. With Mirah's story we are caught up in the book of romance; nevertheless, Eliot turns a new page by suggesting that Deronda's liberation must lie in his submission to the music of the women of a dispossessed race. His determination to treat music and its values as profound gifts, worthy of all his manly striving, marks an important innovation in Victorian fiction.

George Eliot's last novel reverses some of the stereotypes in the Victorian evocation of women and music even as it falters before the challenge of finding a fully satisfying resolution. Perhaps there was no resolution; perhaps the competing claims of domesticity, sexuality, isolated training, and communal cooperation must remain a cacophony in women's lives. But if Mirah's last act is impossibly hopeful, it follows close upon George Eliot's narrative of another woman's musical achievement that is more believable, if more tragic. The Princess Alcharisi, Daniel's mother, embodies the sad possibility that women might never be able to rise above their mundane circumstances on the wings of song without suffering drastic consequences. Alcharisi is a singer who has abandoned family ties to pursue her art, and the result is both exultant and forbidding. The epigraph to the chapter in which Daniel finally confronts his long-lost mother allegorizes the situation of most women who cannot indulge their impulse to sing:

> She held the spindle as she sat,
> Erinna, with the thick-coiled mat
> Of raven hair and deepest agate eyes,
> Gazing with a sad surprise
> At surging visions of her destiny —
> To spin the byssus drearily
> In insect-labour, while the throng
> Of gods and men wrought deeds that poets wrought in song.
>
> (chap. 51).

Daniel's mother has chosen to escape the "insect-labour" of the domestic round through singing her own song. [43] But the price she has paid is the loss of

---

[43] In the Penguin edition of *Deronda*, Barbara Hardy remarks: "George Eliot here seems to be playing on associations of feminine genius *and* domesticity" (Harmondsworth: 1967), p. 900.

her son; their reunion is not a triumph of love surviving separation but a dry recognition of separate and unalterable fates. If Alcharisi is not fulfilled as a woman, however, she possesses the dignity conferred by choosing her own destiny, and George Eliot is unwilling to soften the result. A woman artist, she seems to admit, must lead an uneasy life, but she will at least know who she is.

As the fictional preoccupation with women's potentialities became more imperative through the Victorian period, so did novelists' probing of music as one of the main areas in which the female sex might exercise initiative, expertise, and talent. In earlier explorations of women's experience, the piano had been used as a prop to illustrate the foibles of social climbing and feminine artifice. In later fictions, feminine aspirations for success in performance were likely to illustrate the meagerness of women's opportunities. And eventually the possibility that music might become an instrument for feminine rebellion presented itself to the Victorian imagination in terms that recall Coleridge's damsel "wailing for her demon-lover." In some ways the rapt female musicians of late-Victorian romance and melodrama — most of them untrained singers rather than players of sophisticated instruments like the piano — could be reassuring. Although their native woodnotes could be made to follow a sinister tune, their music could be found so eccentric as to pose no threat to the general social order. Or, like Jenny Lind, they could be assimilated into the myth of the ministering angel whose holy song signified undying spiritual passion. The image of women as conscious, trained musicians involved sacrificing home and safety for the risks of a difficult apprenticeship, unpredictable inspiration, and bohemian circumstances. Even George Eliot feared the disruptions of this kind of rebellion and placed it under the protection of a strong hero. Ultimately, then, the art of music could never be a reliable escape for women in Victorian fiction. Indeed, it may be best to conclude this survey with George Gissing's clear-eyed assessment of the limits of women's musical education in *The Odd Women*. There Rhoda Nunn inquires of a postulant in her typing school, "Did you ever have piano lessons?" When the answer is "No," Miss Nunn responds with sisterly sympathy. But her sympathy is not for the deprivation of a social grace or of the chance to indulge in passionate inspiration. It is for the economic handicap: "No more did I, and I was sorry for it when I went to typewriting. The fingers have to be light and supple and quick."[44]

---

[44] George Gissing, *The Odd Women* (London: Virago Press, 1980), chap. 4.

William J. Gatens

# JOHN RUSKIN AND MUSIC

THERE IS NO DISPUTING THE FACT THAT JOHN RUSKIN (1819-1900) IS A MAJOR figure in Victorian thought and letters, but to examine his career in relation to music may at first seem somewhat contrived and in need of justification. Some may be surprised to learn that Ruskin devoted serious attention to music in both its practical and philosophical aspects. He even composed several short songs which are extant. While it is undeniable that many other subjects predominate over music in Ruskin's voluminous writings, this should not obscure the importance that the mature Ruskin attached to music in its moral and metaphysical significance and in the crucial place he felt it should occupy in general education.

Ruskin's serious attention to music began rather late in life. His principal writings on the subject date from after 1860, the year of the fifth and final volume of *Modern Painters*, a year justly regarded as marking a turning point in Ruskin's career. The earliest of Ruskin's extant songs date from 1880. The only suggestion of earlier musical composition consists of a group of singing dances that Ruskin devised for the pupils of a rather progressive girls' school at Winnington Hall near Northwich in Cheshire, with which he was informally associated between 1859 and 1868. According to Edward Tyas Cook (1857-1919), a Ruskin biographer and co-editor of his collected works, some of the tunes for these dance songs may have been composed by Ruskin. [1]

In 1894 Augusta Mary Wakefield (1853-1910) published a book entitled *Ruskin on Music*. It is a compilation of passages about music from Ruskin's writings with some explanation and commentary supplied by Wakefield. The compilation, however attractive it may be, is far from exhaustive, and the commentary is not particularly penetrating. The book is so thoroughly suffused with an aura of hero-worship that it impresses the reader as more of a tribute to the still-living Ruskin than as a piece of critical examination. In any event, it can scarcely be regarded as the last word on its subject.

Ruskin's ideas about music could be, to say the least, peculiar. Certainly they were well outside the main stream of musical theory and practice of his own day. Even within the somewhat circumscribed world of Victorian

---

[1] See the introduction to Volume XXVII of *The Works of John Ruskin*, Library Edition, ed. by E. T. Cook and Alexander Wedderburn, 39 vols. (London: George Unwin, 1903-12), lxxiv.

English music, Ruskin cannot be regarded as a prominent figure. His general hostility towards so many of the prevailing trends in musical practice would have guaranteed as much. Against this, it may be argued that Ruskin is such as important figure in his own right that no significant aspect of his career is without interest.

I

Towards the end of his life, Ruskin left a candid self-assessment of his musical abilities and propensities. It was intended for Volume II of his unfinished autobiography, *Praeterita* (1886-87), but was deleted from the published version. The passage refers particularly to his childhood and adolescence up to 1841:

> I had . . . a sensual faculty of pleasure in sight, as far as I know, unparalleled. . . . I scarcely count my love of music as a separate and additional faculty, because it is merely the same sensitiveness in the ear to sound as in the eye to colour, joined with the architectural love of structure. But this faculty never had the same chance of cultivation as the others, for the simple reason that while I could see good painting or architecture whenever I chose, it was impossible at this period of my chrysalid existence to hear good music anywhere. The modern Italian school was represented by executants of the highest genius, with the result of such popularity throughout France and Italy, that the optional music of cathedral services continually was arranged from opera airs of that school, which also had as much power over my then temperament as Shelley's poetry, — and I never came across any one who could explain a single principle of music to me, nor had any opportunity of hearing music of a pure school in simplicity.
>
> Scientific German music — full of conceit of effort — I rightly abhorred then, as I abhor now; and rightly feeling besides that no energy would be enough to follow up painting and music together, I allowed the latter only such chance thought as I could spare — steadily progressive thought however — until I felt myself justified in speaking of its laws, as I have done lately, in their perceived relations to the laws of other arts. [2]

Clearly Ruskin had no illusions as to the limitations of his technical proficiency in music, but he felt that he could offer some significant philosophical insights. At the same time, some of the observations in this passage need to be taken with a grain of salt in the light of biographical information and opinions expressed in other writings. In particular, Ruskin's childhood seems not to have been quite as devoid of music as the passage might lead us to suspect.

Ruskin's early childhood was almost unbelievably sheltered, and music played no part in the strict scheme of education devised for him by his parents, both of whom came from a serious Scottish evangelical background. His mother was especially pious and never cultivated any musical talent she might have possessed. She had what Ruskin called "the strictest Puritan prejudice against the stage" (XXXV, 176). Ruskin's father seems to have been

---

[2] Ruskin, *Works*, XXXV, 619. Subsequent references are given by volume and page number.

less severe in this respect, and even Mrs. Ruskin did not object strenuously to her husband taking their son to the theater.

In *Praeterita* we get some glimpses of Ruskin's childhood musical experiences. In 1827, for instance, when he was eight years old, he went with his parents to a grand military dinner at Tunbridge Wells, where he was fascinated by the music of a wind band, though too shy to accept the invitation to try the drum which had captured his special attention. He reflected whimsically, "No one will ever know what I could then have brought out of that drum, or (if my father had perchance taken me to Spain) out of a tambourine" (XXXV, 170).

Sunday afternoons in the family home at Herne Hill were given to reading devotional books. "We none of us cared for singing hymns or psalms as such;" Ruskin reports, "and were too honest to amuse ourselves with them as sacred music, besides that we did not find their music amusing" (XXXV, 73). There was evidently a piano in the house, as Ruskin reports on the playing, which seems not to have been very accomplished, of Mrs. Richard Gray, a neighbor and the wife of one of the elder Ruskin's business associates. He also mentions that his cousin Mary from Perth, who was living with the Ruskins for a time, practiced "scales, and little more" (XXXV, 170).

Domestic music of greater proficiency was also to be heard at Herne Hill, namely the singing of Mr. Ruskin's chief clerk, Henry Watson, and his three sisters. They were frequent guests at the Ruskin home. Their repertory seems to have consisted primarily of German part-songs, which Ruskin found tedious, and Italian songs and arias, which he found pleasant but unworthy of serious attention. He would have preferred "English glees, or Scotch ballads, or British salt-water ones," but in retrospect he noted with appreciation that "from early childhood, I was accustomed to hear a great range of good music completely rightly rendered, without breakings down, missings out, affectations of manner, or vulgar prominence of execution" (XXXV, 174).

In 1835 Ruskin attended the Italian opera in Paris. This was not his first experience of the theater, though by his own admission, he could not remember distinctly his first visit to one. This is strange when one considers the vivid detail with which, in old age, he was able to recall events and places from early childhood. Be that as it may, Paris in 1835 seems the earliest documented instance of his hearing a professional musical performance, apart from the military band at Tunbridge Wells. The opera was *I Puritani*, the last work of the recently deceased Vincenzo Bellini (1801-35). This, the original production of the work, was the rage of Paris. The principal roles had been written for four of the greatest singers of the day: soprano Giulia Grisi (1811-69), basso Luigi Lablache (1794-1858), tenor Giovanni Battista Rubini (1795-1854), and baritone Antonio Tamburini (1800-76). Ruskin's response was mixed: "To be taken now at Paris to the feebly dramatic *Puritani* was no great joy to me; but I then heard, and it will always be a rare, and only once or twice in a century possible, thing to hear, four great musicians, all rightly to be called of genius, singing together, with sincere desire to assist each other, not eclipse; and to exhibit, not only their own power of singing, but the beauty of the music they sang" (XXXV, 175). Ruskin may have found the opera dramatically impeachable, but he surely admired Bellini's gift for lyrical melody, though he ranked it lower than that of Mozart or even Rossini, for whom he elsewhere expressed great admiration. He relished the leisurely performances by the great singers of the 1830s in contrast with the faster tempi that became fashionable later, citing with particular disapproval a performance involving Adelina Patti as Zerlina in the duet "La ci darem" from Mozart's *Don Giovanni* (XXXV, 176).

In 1837 Ruskin entered Christ Church, Oxford, as an undergraduate. He joined the college's musical society and had lessons in singing and piano from William Marshall, the cathedral organist. He reports that he learned to sing the Florentine canzonetta "Come mai posso vivere se Rosina non m'ascolta" and to play at least the introduction to the aria "A te o cara" from the aforementioned *Puritani* as well as "what notes I could manage to read of the accompaniments to other songs of similarly tender purport, in which, though never even getting so far as to read with ease, I nevertheless, between my fine rhythmic ear, and true lover's sentiment, got to understand some principles of musical art" (XXXV, 177).

These pieces of biographical information furnish some background for an event of 1838 that brought forth Ruskin's first serious writing on music. In that year Charlotte Withers, the daughter of a widowed coal merchant whose wife had been a pious friend and neighbor of Mrs. Ruskin, was a houseguest at Herne Hill. Withers disputed with John Ruskin on the relative merits of music and painting, she favoring the former. Feeling obliged to demolish her arguments, according to what he called "my usual manner of paying court to my mistresses" — one suspects that being a houseguest of the Ruskins could be something of an ordeal — he produced An *Essay on the Relative Dignity of the Studies of Painting and Music and the Advantages to be Derived from Their Pursuit.* [3] Withers was apparently flattered by such attention, and she carried off the essay as something of a prize. It was not published until 1903, though William Gershom Collingwood had given a summary of its arguments in his 1893 Ruskin biography, and A. M. Wakefield had included a few extracts in her book.

---

[3] *Works*, XXXV, 222. The *Essay*, hereafter to be called *Essay on Painting and Music*, is found in *Works*, I.

In the essay, Ruskin proceeds on the assumption that the appreciation of music does not depend on a cultivated and educated taste, while the appreciation of painting does. He distinguishes two dimensions of human consciousness which may be addressed by art: first, the feelings or "life" with its abode in the heart, and second, thoughts, intellect, or "soul" with its abode in the brain. Music operates only on the first of these, or not even quite that, since music is at best "a mere sensual gratification," depending on extraneous circumstances to influence the feelings. The most it can do is enhance the reception of other influences which are more sublime and meaningful. Music is not meaningful in itself, but only by association. Painting, on the other hand, operates on both dimensions of consciousness, involving the pleasures of the intellect, which are distinctly higher and greater than those of the feelings. As for the qualifications of a musician, Ruskin's opinion could hardly be lower:

> Let us consider what is necessary to form a musician, and even one who can not only execute, but compose. It requires talent, distinguished talent — but of what description? A musical ear? — that is not intellect; and a something else, we do not know what to call it, which involves neither thought nor feeling, — a sensual power, a corporeal property. A musician may be also a great man, and yet I doubt it: for the habit of sensuality in the ear must gradually embrace and swallow up the other faculties, but on the other hand a musician *may* be what he has been, — a brute in habits, and a bear in manners; an epicure in palate as in ear, a glutton in eating as in hearing; a man of vulgar mind, of mean thought, of debased intellect, — of no principle. All this a man may be, and yet may be a great musician. What splendid talent! what lofty character! In order to add the weight of example to that of argument, compare the character of Handel with that of Raphael.
> (I, 279).

Ruskin restricts the sphere of the intellect to those distinct thoughts and images that can be represented by words and pictures, but not well by musical sounds. Since he is unwilling to grant intellectual value to the more abstract expressiveness of musical language and to the operation of musical forms, he concludes that music is a purely sensual experience. It follows, then, that the study and practice of music is intellectually far inferior to the study and practice of drawing and painting.

Without going into greater detail, one may characterize the essay as manifestly an immature and shallow effort. Ruskin's argumentation is flawed and his evidence weak. Furthermore, one must allow for the fact that the essay was written with a specifically polemical purpose in mind; he was "arguing for victory" rather than for truth. [4] Never in any of his later writings will Ruskin be so harsh in his references to music in general, though he will inveigh harshly against specific composers, styles, and genres. On the contrary, most of his references to music, even in writings dating from before 1860, clearly indicate that he found music at least enjoyable and attractive.

[4] E. T. Cook, *The Life of John Ruskin*, 2 vols. (London: Macmillan, 1911), I, 94.

A case in point occurs in a letter from Rome in December 1841, describing an impressive religious ceremony he had recently witnessed at the Church of *Il Gesù*. Ruskin makes it clear that he was deeply moved by the event, and he gives the music a major share of credit for producing this effect (I, 385). Even so, the music was but one element in a mixture with ritual, architecture, and decoration that provided the associations to help make the music meaningful and deeply moving.

Another noteworthy incident was his meeting on 30 January 1849 with Jenny Lind, at an intimate dinner party given by a family friend. After coffee, the singer went to the piano and sang first some Swedish songs and then Bellini's "Qui la voce." Describing the performance in a letter to his father, Ruskin said that she sang the Bellini aria "very gloriously, prolonging the low notes exactly like soft wind among trees — the higher ones were a little too powerful for the room, but the lowest were heard dying away as if in extreme distance for at least half a minute, and then melted into silence. It was in sound exactly what the last rose of Alpine sunset is in colour" (XXXVI, 92-93).

Ruskin's spontaneous response to music was generally favorable, though he did have his likes and dislikes. Such early instances, however, demonstrate a great difference between this spontaneous response and Ruskin's first attempt to deal with music in a deliberately intellectual or philosophical manner.

II

W. G. Collingwood wrote that Ruskin, despite his delight in certain kinds of music and his periodic study of singing, piano, and the rudiments of theory, "has no ear for the higher efforts of the art; is not what we call musical."[5] In later life, Ruskin would have been greatly offended at being called unmusical, and he could have discoursed learnedly for hours to refute the allegation. Whatever his conscious attitude might have been at the time of the Charlotte Withers episode, after 1860 his serious regard for music increased immensely. As early as 1867, in his Robert Rede Lecture at Cambridge, he ranked music above painting in the hierarchy of the arts, placing it second only to poetry. But this heightened regard had little or nothing to do with any gain in understanding or appreciation of music as an autonomous art.

A. M. Wakefield claimed that the sentiments expressed in the 1838 *Essay on Painting and Music* are incompatible with Ruskin's later high regard

---

[5] W. G. Collingwood, *The Life and Work of John Ruskin*, 2 vols. (2d. ed., London: Methuen, 1893), I, 93.

for music, but strange to say, they are quite compatible. Ruskin remained essentially deaf to the vitality of purely musical expression, unwilling to admit any independent significance of musical form, and insistent that there is no intellectual content whatsoever in music apart from its association with a verbal text. Ruskin's opinion of music's value and dignity changed because he came to recognize a powerful relationship between music and words, an insight derived largely from his study of the Greek classics, especially Plato. Nevertheless, the prejudices so openly displayed in the 1838 *Essay* are still discernible in his mature writings on music.

Nowhere is this better illustrated than in an interchange of correspondence given as a lengthy footnote in Ruskin's preface to *Rock Honeycomb* (1877), an edition of psalm paraphrases by Sir Philip Sidney. The unnamed correspondent, whom Ruskin describes as "a man of the highest scientific attainments, and of great general sensitive faculty and intellectual power," challenges Ruskin's contention that in a musical setting the music must be subordinate to the words:

> MY DEAR RUSKIN, — "Subordinate" is not the right word, though I think you mean right. "Co-ordinate" would be more correct. Both words and music should express as far as possible the idea intended to be conveyed; but music can convey emotion more powerfully than words, and independently of them. Mozart in his Masses only thought of the words as syllables for hanging notes on, and so wrote music quite profane. Bach, on the contrary, wrote, as it were, on his knees, when he wrote church music. For instance, the "Dona nobis" was set by Mozart to noise and triumph; by J. S. Bach is made a solemn, gentle, and tender prayer, preparing the congregation for the rest of the service. There, no repetition of the words "dona nobis pacem" would give calm to the mind of the listener or reader, but the musical repetition, with variation, extends and enhances the calm both in listener and singer; but it would be quite incorrect to say Bach had "subordinated" the music to the words, for, to a musician, no words could express so much as his music does. Like painting and poetry, music has its own special power, and its own field; it is vague compared with poetry in description, but more exact in expressing feeling.

He goes on to bemoan the misunderstandings attending preparations for the first performance in England of Bach's B Minor Mass, which was given by the London Bach Choir under Otto Goldschmidt on 26 April 1876 at St. James's Hall. Perhaps it was indiscreet of the writer to exalt Bach at the expense of Ruskin's favorite composer, Mozart, especially as Ruskin was known to abhor "scientific German music." The correspondent ends on a note of resignation, that the incomprehension of Bach's greatness "must ever be — during our days, at any rate." Ruskin's reply was merciless, and highly revealing:

> I hope better, dear friend; thinking in truth, more highly of music in its true function than you do; but replying to your over-estimate of its independent strength, simply that music gives emotions stronger than words only to persons who do not completely understand words, but do completely enjoy sensations. A great part of the energy of the wars of the world is indeed attributable to the excitement produced by military bands; but a single word will move a good soldier more than an entire day of the most artistic piping

and drumming. The Dead March in Saul may be more impressive than words, to people who don't know what Death is; but to those who do, no growling in brass can make it gloomier; and Othello's one cry, "O, Desdemona, Desdemona — dead!" will go to their hearts, when a whole cathedral choir, in the richest and most harmonious of whines, would be no more to them than a dog's howling, — not half so much, if the dog loved the dead person. In the instance given by my friend, the music of Bach would assuredly put any disagreeable piece of business out of his head, and prepare him to listen with edification to the sermon, better than the mere *repetition* of the words "dona nobis pacem." [We may take the point without quibbling over liturgical order.] But if he ever had needed peace, and had gone into church really to ask for it, the plain voices of the congregation, uttering the prayer but once, and meaning it, would have been more precious to him than all the quills and trills that ever musician touched or music trembled in.

(XXXI, 111n-112n).

One might never guess that this exchange occurs as a note to an introductory essay in which Ruskin insists that music must be an integral part of general elementary education. Certainly his instincts were not those of a musician. Ruskin's correspondent was asserting a commonplace of musical practice. There is nothing extraordinary in the idea of a composer producing a large-scale setting of a brief text, like Bach's setting of the *Agnus Dei*, deriving the expressive element from the meaning of the text, but expressing it in musical terms, thus producing a piece of purely musical design that stands firmly and makes sense entirely as such. The music is structurally independent of the words, yet intimately related to them. This relationship of words and music, the "co-ordination" of which his correspondent wrote, was a concept that Ruskin never grasped, however undeniable his genius.

While Ruskin found music attractive, he evidently felt an ambivalence towards it, being persuaded that the art was in need of intellectual and moral justification. In this he reflected an attitude that was prominent in English culture during most of the nineteenth century, especially in the first half. Music might be regarded as a pleasant diversion, socially useful as an "accomplishment" (particularly for young ladies), but to take it really seriously showed a distinct misplacement of values if one were a member of respectable society. A number of nineteenth-century writers met this attitude head-on, producing books, tracts, and articles addressing the moral dimension of music and presenting the art as a worthy object of serious cultivation, one capable of conferring valuable intellectual and moral benefits on practitioners and listeners alike, and one that should be an indispensable part of general education. Closely related to such lines of thought were the efforts of other writers to promote and defend the use of music, especially elaborate choral music, in Christian worship. [6]

---

[6] See W. J. Gatens, *Victorian Cathedral Music in Theory and Practice* (Cambridge: Cambridge University Press, 1986), chaps. 1 and 2, for a more detailed discussion of this subject in both the secular and sacred aspects. Among the nineteenth-century writings that deal with the moral aspect of music are John Hullah, *The Duty and Advantage of Learning to Sing* (London: John W. Parker, 1846);

Ruskin's case presents a fascinating variant in both the secular and sacred categories. While he became a self-proclaimed champion of music and musical education, his ambivalence led him to impose an array of qualifications and restrictions so severe and eccentric as to separate him effectively from the main musical practice of his day. Meanwhile he expressed vehement disapproval of elaborate church music.

One may readily perceive in Ruskin's attitude towards music a manifestation of values instilled as part of his strict evangelical upbringing in a self-consciously upper middle class setting. Indeed, the influence of evangelicalism — the earnestness and high sense of moral duty — has often been credited with contributing greatly to the distinctive cultural flavor of Victorian society at large, of which the aforementioned attitude towards music is a characteristic aspect. In the Ruskin home, as we have seen, amateur music making was welcomed, though certainly not over-indulged. When, however, in 1849 Ruskin wanted to invite Jenny Lind to the family home to see his collection of Turner drawings, his mother reacted in horror, looking upon the great singer "just as on an ordinary actress."[7] Although Ruskin had decisively abandoned the doctrinal tenets of evangelical Christianity by the time he began his mature thinking and writing about music, he seems to have retained much of its temperamental predisposition.


III


Ruskin's main writings on music date from after 1860. It is worth noting, however, that his earlier books on the visual arts contain numerous musical references. Most often, they are analogies which help to reinforce or clarify a theoretical point on such matters as composition or coloring, but it

Joseph Mainzer, *Music and Education* (London: Longman, Brown, Green, and Longmans, 1848); Adolf Bernhard Marx, *General Music Instruction* (1839; English trans. London: J. Alfred Novello, 1854); Hugh Reginald Haweis, *Music and Morals* (London: W. H. Allen, 1871); and Edmund Gurney, *The Power of Sound* (London: Smith, Elder & Co., 1880). Most of these seek to promote music as a vital part of general education, as did Ruskin, and to encourage amateur music making, especially choral singing. Among the writings which specifically defend and encourage elaborate choral music as a part of Christian worship are John Antes Latrobe, *The Music of the Church* (London: R. B. Seely and W. Burnside, 1831); Edward Hodges, *An Apology for Church Music* (London: Rivingtons, 1834); John Jebb, *Three Lectures on the Cathedral Service* (2d. ed., London: F. & J. Rivington, 1845), *Dialogue on the Choral Service* (London: Rivingtons, Burns, Houlston, & Storeman, 1842), and *The Choral Service* (London: John H. Parker, 1843); and Robert Druitt, *A Popular Tract on Church Music* (London: Francis & John Rivington, 1845) and *Conversations on the Choral Service* (London: Thomas Harrison, 1853). To these may be added many nineteenth-century articles, pamphlets, published sermons, and lectures, of which numerous specimens are cited in Gatens's book.

[7] *Works*, XXXVI, 92-93. A. M. Wakefield attributes the incident to "a moment of youthful enthusiasm," though Ruskin was nearly thirty at the time (*Ruskin on Music*, p. 9). E. T. Cook then cites Wakefield's passage in connection with the Charlotte Withers episode, which took place in 1838, nearly eleven years before Ruskin met Jenny Lind (Introduction to *Works*, I, xlvii).

seems significant that Ruskin should deliberately have chosen musical analogies for the purpose. Thus, for example, in *Modern Painters* II (1846), *The Seven Lamps of Architecture* (1849), and *The Elements of Drawing* (1857), he compares visual proportion and composition with melodic contour and balance, maintaining that neither the visual nor the aural varieties are completely reducible to rule (IV, 102, 108; VIII, 163; XV, 162-165). In the second of his *Addresses on Decorative Colour* (25 November 1854), Ruskin makes a series of analogies between drawing and painting on the one hand and music on the other, in an ascending order of elaboration: from drawing in outline, which he likens to clear speaking; then drawing in outline with addition of color, which is like clear articulation in singing; all the way to the complete mastery of light and shade in painting, which is like the skillful management of the full orchestra (XII, 490). In *Modern Painters* IV (1856) and *The Two Paths* (1859) Ruskin likens intensity of color to dynamic levels in music (VI, 327; XVI, 424).

If there was one purely musical element to which Ruskin was sensitive, this was melody, and his references to melody in these pre-1860 works come as near as he ever did to acknowledging an autonomous power of music. In the third volume of *The Stones of Venice* (1852), for instance, he says, "It is at our choice whether we will accompany a poem with Music or not; but if we do the Music *must* be right and neither discordant nor inexpressive. The goodness and sweetness of the poem cannot save it, if the Music be false; but if the Music be right the poem may be insipid and inharmonious and still saved by the notes to which it is wedded" (XI, 218-219). He goes even farther than this in *The Elements of Drawing* (1857), as he follows an analogy between color and melody: "If the colour is wrong, everything is wrong: just as, if you are singing, and sing false notes, it does not matter how true the words are. If you sing at all, you must sing sweetly; and if you colour at all, you must colour rightly. Give up all the form, rather than the slightest part of the colour: just as, if you felt yourself in danger of a false note, you would give up the word, and sing a meaningless sound, if you felt that so you could save the note" (XV, 135). Perhaps such passages as these tell us as much about Ruskin's thoughts on music as does the essay of 1838.

The year 1860 marks a dividing line in Ruskin's life and career. In his writings on art, Ruskin had always been ready to see and proclaim a moral lesson, but his main concern had been for art. After 1860 the horizon of his intellectual activity broadened, and while he continued to write about art, his main concern was for society. Collingwood noted that "since then, art has sometimes been his text, rarely his theme. He has used it as the opportunity, the vehicle, so to say, for teachings of far wider range and deeper import; teachings about life as a whole, conclusions in ethics and economics and reli-

gion, to which he seeks to lead others, as he was led, by the way of art"
(Collingwood, *Life*, II, 3).

In the years prior to 1860 there are distinct foreshadowings of Ruskin's
change of perspective. Pre-echoes of his social and economic writings appear
in *The Seven Lamps of Architecture, The Stones of Venice,* and *The Political
Economy of Art* (1857, later renamed *A Joy For Ever*). His evangelical religious beliefs had been eroding since the mid-1840s, and "a morbid sense of
the evil of the world, a horror of great darkness" came into decidedly sharper
focus at this critical period than heretofore (Collingwood, *Life*, II, 7). He
perceived that the institutions of society were producing and perpetuating
conditions of misery that he so abhorred. He began to feel that mere philan-
thropy was futile to correct these conditions, "that no tinkering at social
breakages was really worth while; that far more extensive repairs were needed
to make the old ship seaworthy" (Collingwood, *Life*, II, 6). Ruskin seemed
conscious that the publication in 1867 of the fifth and final volume of *Modern
Painters* marked an epoch in his life. He thus accomplished the mission he
had set for himself in 1842, and turned to follow a new vocation. Renouncing
the old orthodoxies of religion, art, politics, economics, and education, he
became a prophet of reproach, hurling verbal thunderbolts against the institutions of society that he regarded as guilty of mortal offense. He also became
the self-appointed architect of a new order of social justice and human fulfillment. Music was to be an integral part of that new order.

The most noticeable feature of musical references in the writings after
1860, even in works that are not primarily about music, is the great prominence given to the ethical element. Even when Ruskin's remarks, taken at
face value, pertain to the actual practice of music, there is the unmistakable
feeling that his intention is far broader in application than to mere technique, as in this passage from *Sesame and Lilies* (1865):

> From the beginning, consider your accomplishments as means of assistance to others.
> . . . In music especially you will soon find what personal benefit there is in being service-
> able: it is probable that, however limited your powers, you have voice and ear enough to
> sustain a note of moderate compass in a concerted piece; — that, then, is the first thing
> to make sure you can do. Get your voice disciplined and clear, and think only of accu-
> racy; never of effect or expression: if you have any soul worth expressing, it will show it-
> self in your singing; but most likely there are very few feelings in you, at present, needing
> any particular expression; and the one thing you have to do is to make a clear-voiced
> little instrument of yourself, which other people can entirely depend upon for the note
> wanted.
>
> (XVIII, 38-39).

Another tendency in these writings is to go beyond mere analogy and exhortation to recondite etymological and mythological interpretations. Consider,
for example, this passage from *Munera Pulveris* (1862-63): "As Charis becomes Charitas on the one side, she becomes — better still — Chara, Joy, on

the other; or rather this is her very mother's milk and the beauty of her child-hood; for God brings no enduring Love nor any other good, out of pain; nor out of contention; but out of joy and harmony. And in this sense, human and divine, music and gladness, and the measures of both, come into her name; and Cher becomes full-vowelled Cheer, and Cheerful; and Chara opens into Choir and Choral" (XVII, 227). After a passage like this, one may need to be reminded that Ruskin intends his thoughts to have a practical application in real choral music, not to be a mere metaphor or ethical symbol.

E. T. Cook has noted that Ruskin, in making such interpretations, tended to rely more on imagination than on scholarship: "In plunging, per-haps with inadequate equipment, into the perilous sea of etymological deriva-tion, it may be that fancy, or *prima facie* impressions, sometimes led him astray." While Ruskin was at this period a keen student of the texts of the Greek and Latin classics, "he troubled himself with little *apparatus classicus*," and hardly ever used scholarly commentaries, but "noted carefully any allu-sion, suggestion, or usage which fitted in with his own line of thought."[8] One should keep this in mind when pondering the lessons Ruskin purported to extract from mythology or ancient authors.

On 24 May 1867 at the Senate House in Cambridge, Ruskin delivered his Robert Rede Lecture *On the Relation of National Ethics to National Arts*. In it he presented his theories of the relationship of art to morality, inspired pri-marily by Plato, and devoted considerable attention specifically to music. A portion of this lecture was later elaborated and incorporated into another course of lectures, delivered in part at University College, London, and pub-lished under the title *The Queen of the Air: Being a Study of the Greek Myths of Cloud and Storm* (1869). Since his interpretation of the imagery of Greek myth helps to illuminate many of the allusions and principles discussed more abstractly in the Rede Lecture, it will be helpful to consider the slightly later work first.

The lecture which most concerns music is the first of the course, enti-tled *Athena Chalinitis* (literally "Athena the Restrainer," but subtitled by Ruskin "Athena in the Heavens"), in which the goddess represents the air as a medium for communicating the pulsations of sound. She thus represents the physical dimension of music. Apollo, on the other hand, represents the order and measure of music. His instrument, the lyre, is a device for measurement. The tortoiseshell body of the lyre is the vault of heaven. The sun — Apollo being the sun god — is the master of all time and rhythm. In this intellectual and mathematical side of music, Apollo is aided by the Muses, who are god-desses of instruction. When the balance is proper, Athena's province of the

---

[8] E. T. Cook, I, 535. See Cook's introduction to *Works*, XIX, lxv-lxx.

physical, impulsive, and passionate complements the measure, order, and design of Apollo and the Muses. When, however, the inspiration is degraded in its passion, the nobility of the Doric flute sinks into the pipe of Pan and the double reed-pipe of Marsyas, the adversary of Apollo, and is then rejected by Athena. In the myth, Athena saw her reflection in the river while she was playing the double pipe, and was so appalled at the distortion it produced in her face that she cast it away, whereupon Marsyas took it up, and it was corrupted.

The distinction is thus between music which is disciplined and ordered, pure in its expression, chastened by its being wedded to the nobility of morally beautiful words, and music which abandons all discipline to the sensual pleasure and promiscuity of empty sounds; between measured, orderly music, "in which the words and thought lead" and "brutal, meaningless 'music' in which the words are lost, and the wind or impulse leads." This distinction was the subject of the musical meditations of the Greek philosophers, for whom "true music is the natural expression of a lofty passion for a right cause" (XIX, 343).

Art must necessarily reflect the ethical state of its creators, and at the same time it tends to communicate and reproduce the ethical condition which gave rise to it. Art is thus a powerful instrument of moral instruction, and no art more so than music, "which of all the arts is most directly ethical in origin, [and] is also the most direct in power of discipline; the first, the simplest, the most effective of all instruments of moral instruction; while in the failure and betrayal of its functions, it becomes the subtlest aid of moral degradation. Music is thus, in her health, the teacher of perfect order, and is the voice of the obedience of angels, and the companion of the course of the spheres of heaven; and in her depravity she is also the teacher of perfect disorder and disobedience, and the Gloria in Excelsis becomes the Marseillaise" (XIX, 343). The great danger in failing to use music as an agent in the promotion of good is that its great powers can then be appropriated for the promotion of evil, or rather, when music is not inspired by ethical motivation, all that is left is sensuality.


IV


In his Rede Lecture, Ruskin discussed the role of art as a reflection of and influence on the national morality. He maintained that the arts spring from the whole of one's humanity, not just from an isolated part of it, and certainly not from the mere mechanical skills involved, important as these might be. All human energies must be healthy for any of them to be healthy, for perfect ethical humanity is a harmonious blending and balance of all the virtues without exaggeration. Ruskin describes this as the ideal "Ethos" of man, the acquisition of which is the object of education. The artistic faculty, moreover, is "a visible sign of a national virtue," the state of the national ethos having a decisive influence on the formation of the individual's ethos: "All art being the Formative or directing Action of a Spirit, whatever charac-ter the spirit itself has must be manifested in the Energy or Deed of it, and makes the deed itself Bad or Good." Ruskin seems to be saying here that, apart from the question of purely technical competence, only a good person can produce good art. A bad person can produce only bad art, or at most, a mock imitation of good art. A good person cannot produce bad art, "but inas-much as the being of man is mixed of good and evil inextricably, the art which it produces is inextricably mixed also" (XIX, 164-165). A bad person may, of course, succeed in mastering the mechanics of an art form, and pro-duce works which are technically accomplished, but nonetheless bad as art. Similarly, the lack of attention to technical details can be vicious to the artis-tic productions of a good person.

In this lecture, Ruskin's distinctions between morally good and mor-ally bad music run along lines of thought similar to those developed in *The Queen of the Air*: "There is a kind of music which is balanced, reserved, con-structive, inventive, complete, pure, and lovely. There is, on the other hand, a kind of music which is unsymmetrical, intemperate, unconstructive, unimaginative, incomplete, sensual, undelightful. Every one of the words by which I express these absolute merits and demerits attaches itself justly also to the quality of soul by which they are produced, and by which they are will-ingly received. To the order of mind from which they spring they are also ac-ceptable, and the temper by which they have been produced they have also a tendency to reproduce" (XIX, 165). Such principles, especially the capacity for music to reproduce moral atmospheres, occurs in the works of several other Victorian writers, particularly the Reverend Hugh Reginald Haweis. [9] According to such lines of thought, music may have an actively pernicious ef-fect, depending on the moral state of the producer and recipient. The worst corruption possible in music is the degradation of emotional expression, the separation of it from a worthy object:

> In good music, the pleasure received by the ear is wholly subordinated to the purpose of expression; . . . but when the emotion is lower, or more common, the bodily sense, though that is always degraded together with it, yet maintains a higher relative position, and the moment this bodily sense of pleasure leads, the music is base and corrupting. . . . The worst corruption of music in modern days is not in, as it might at first be supposed, the exhaltation of a dangerous sentiment by faithful sound, as in the hymn of the Marseil-

[9] H. R. Haweis, *Music and Morals*, bk. 1, "Music, Emotion, and Morals." See also note 6 above.

> laise, but it is the idle and sensual seeking for pleasure in sound only, without any true
> purpose of sentiment at all, and often without the slightest effort to discern the com-
> poser's intention, or understand the relation in a master's work between the syllable and
> the note.
>
> (XIX, 177-178).

Under such circumstances, the listener wallows in the sensuality of musical
emotionalism, being "excited by the Sirens, who are Goddesses of Desire,
instead of by the Muses, who are Goddesses of Instruction" (XIX, 178).

This temptation to musical sensuality and all its moral evils is more
pernicious in relation to sacred music. Few are the souls who can hear elaborate church music in the proper devotional way,

> But between these and the common hunter after pleasure in pathetic sensation, for whom
> the strain of the cathedral organ is made an interlude to the music of the ballet that he
> may excite his palled sensation by the alternate taste of sacred and profane, there is an
> infinite range of gradually lowered faculty and sincerity, receiving in proportion to the
> abasement of its temper injury from what, to the highest, brings only good. . . . It is not a
> good thing for a weak and wicked person to be momentarily touched or charmed by sa-
> cred art. It is a deadly thing for them to indulge in the habitual enjoyment of it. The
> *Miserere* of the Sistine sends every one home a degree hardened who did not come there
> to ask for mercy; and the daily chanted praise of the cathedral choir leaves every one who
> comes not to adore daily less capable of adoration. And as it is with the religious feelings,
> so in all others capable of being expressed by sound. If you have them, and desire truly to
> utter them, music becomes the most perfect utterance, . . . but if we seek only the pleas-
> ure of the sense, then the music searches for the dregs of good in our spiritual being, and
> wrings them forth, and drinks them; and thus the modern opera, with its painted smiles
> and feverous tears, is only the modulated libation of the last drops of our debased blood
> into the dust.
>
> (XIX, 179-180).

In connection with this, one may mention some contemptuously sarcastic remarks about Mendelssohn included in a set of notes dating from 1875 for a
course of lectures at Oxford on the *Discourses* of Joshua Reynolds. Ruskin
depicts Mendelssohn as a shallow trifler, "a man with the heart of a lark" who
"sees no more . . . than a migrating butterfly might, understands no more."
He singles out the oratorios *St. Paul* and *Elijah* and the anthem "Hear my
prayer" (based on Psalm 55) for special vituperation, on the ground that
Mendelssohn has trivialized their profound subject matter by clothing it in
music of meretricious prettiness: "The Psalms of David talk of matters of life
and death. If you don't believe them, or don't want them, let them alone;
deny them, defy them, if you will, but don't play with them like piping
bullfinches play[ing] with their mistresses' hair" (XXII, 497).

As noted earlier, Ruskin's attitude, especially his attitude towards sacred music, seems to manifest a survival of instincts implanted during his
evangelical upbringing, particularly the evangelical uneasiness about the aesthetic element in worship. In *Fors Clavigera* no. 83 (1877), however, he combined this paradoxically with an attack on philistine puritanism, as it was

popularly conceived, for suppressing morally good music, thus creating a void which has been filled with morally pernicious music. In discussing Scott's *The Heart of Midlothian* (1818), Ruskin condemns the Presbyterian banishment of music and dancing for creating just such a void to be filled with "satyric dance and sirenic song, accomplished, both, with all the finish of science, and used in mimicry of every noble emotion towards God and man, become the uttermost, and worst — because the most traitorous — of blasphemies against the Master who gave motion and voice submissive to other laws than of the elements" (XXIX, 269). This, of course, is not mere literary criticism, but the interpretation of a prophetic parable, intended by Ruskin for his own day, and one that he related to the teachings of Plato:

And this cry of the wild beasts of the islands, or sirenic blasphemy, has in modern days become twofold; consisting first in the mimicry of *devotion* for pleasure, in the oratorio, withering the life of religion into dead bones on the siren-sands; and secondly, the mimicry of *compassion*, for pleasure, in the opera, wasting the pity and love which should overflow in active life, on the ghastliest visions of fictitious grief and horriblest decoration of simulated death. But these two blasphemies had become one, in the Greek religious service of Plato's time. "For, indeed, this had come to pass in nearly all our cities, that when any public sacrifice is made to the Gods, not one chorus only, but many choruses, and standing, not reverently far from the altars, but beside them" (yes, in the very cathedrals themselves), "pour forth blasphemies of sacred things" (not mockeries, observe, but songs precisely corresponding to our oratorios — that is to say, turning dramatic prayer into a solemn sensual pleasure), "both with word and rhythm, and the most wailing harmonies, racking the souls of the hearers; and whosoever can make the sacrificing people weep the most, to him is the victory."

(XXIX, 269-270).

In dealing with medieval sources, Ruskin translated essentially the same lessons — the dignified order of carefully defined musical categories, the intimate and necessary relationship of true music to moral rectitude and the spirit of worship — into Christian terms. In *The Pleasures of England* (1884), for example, Ruskin comments on a miniature of St. Cecilia in a late thirteenth-century illuminated antiphonaire from the convent of Beau Pré, which shows the saint seated silently at a banquet, while surrounded by musicians. The miniature is part of the initial to the antiphon:

Cantantibus organis Cecilia virgo in corde suo soli Domino decantabat, dicens, Fiat Domine cor meum et corpus meum immaculatum ut non confundar.

(Whilst the instruments played, Cecilia the Virgin sang in her heart only to the Lord, saying, O Lord, be my heart and body made stainless that I be not confounded.)

(XXXIII, 489).

Of the lesson to be derived, Ruskin is unequivocal: "I need not point out to you how the law, not of sacred Music only so called but of all Music, is determined by this sentence, which means in effect that unless Music exalt and purify it is not under St. Cecilia's ordinance, and is not virtually Music at all"

(XXXIII, 489-490). In a similar vein, in the second part of *Fiction, Fair and Foul* (1880), Ruskin writes that "the pure chant of the Christian ages . . . is always at heart joyful," and citing his own *Laws of Fésole* (1877-88), declares that "all great Art is Praise, of which the contrary is also true, all foul or miscreant Art is accusation, . . . 'She gave me of the tree and I did eat' being an entirely museless expression on Adam's part, the briefly essential contrary of Love-song" (XXXIV, 310-311).

All of this was not intended to be mere theory. Like Plato, Ruskin felt that music is an indispensable part of education, as essential to the health of the soul and the development of the intellect and passions as physical exercise to the health of the body. The important thing is participation in music, specifically choral music, the communal act of devotion as opposed to soloistic vanity. As for those persons incapable of singing, who are content to be amused by the performances of professionals, Ruskin likens them to the degraded crowds in the Roman amphitheater being amused by the fighting of gladiators (XXIX, 239). So important is singing that Ruskin says in the preface to *Rock Honeycomb* that "not to be able to sing should be more disgraceful than not being able to read or write," since it is possible to be virtuous and happy though illiterate (XXXI, 108). According to Ruskin's Platonic ideal, the separation of music from poetry constitutes a distortion, since "all perfectly rhythmic poetry is meant to be sung to music, and all entirely noble music is the illustration of noble words. The arts of word and note, separate from each other, become degraded; and the museless sayings, or senseless melodies harden the intellect, or demoralize the ear" (XXXI, 107). Although Ruskin does not endorse instrumental music, he regards it as a lesser evil than the abuse of the noble and the holy: "Yet better — and manifoldly better — unvocal word and idle note, than the degradation of the most fateful truths of God to be the subjects of scientific piping for our musical pastime. There is excuse, among our uneducated classes, for the Christmas Pantomime, but none, among our educated classes, for the Easter Oratorio" (XXXI, 107). In his scheme for education, however, Ruskin was intent to describe the ideal. Musical education in his view is synonymous with learning to sing, and like Plato, Ruskin sets out the conditions which govern the music to be sung. He does this in the form of seven "Laws of Song" given in the preface to *Rock Honeycomb*. They may be summarized as follows: First, "none but beautiful and true words are to be set to music at all." Songs must be noble and temperate, with no excess of grief, pathos, or morbidity. Second, accompaniment is to be subordinate to the voice or choir. Third, the greatest music is vocal. Independent instrumental music is necessarily inferior. Fourth, words must be set without distortion: no prolongation of syllables or roulades, no word repetition or fragmentation of the verse. In other words, the structure of the verse must completely determine the structure of the music. Fifth, music should never be used for words other than those for which it was composed, except on authority of the composer. Sixth, music without words is incapable of expressing feelings definitely, as is proved by strophic ballads, in which "the merry and melancholy parts of the story may be with entire propriety and satisfaction sung to precisely the same melody." Finally, comic songs are subject to the same laws as play and jesting: "No vulgar person can be taught how to play, or to jest, like a gentleman; and, for the most part, comic songs are for the vulgar only. Their higher standard is fixed, in note and word, by Mozart and Rossini; but I cannot at present judge how far even these men may have lowered the true function of the joyful muse" (XXXI, 108-112).

V

Devising a set of dogmatic regulations is one thing, but Ruskin went further by attempting to put his laws into practice through musical composition. As noted earlier, he had taken music lessons at various times in his life, from his undergraduate days onward. In a letter of 1869 to Charles Eliot Norton he reported, for instance, "I am learning how to play musical scales quite rightly, and have a real Music-master twice a week, and practice always half an hour a day" (XXXVI, 314). Collingwood claims that lessons in singing probably helped his speaking voice, very important to him as a lecturer, as he always had a delicate chest and was subject to periodic spells of a mild consumption. [10] Around 1880, Ruskin engaged the services of George Frederick West as music master for lessons which included the rudiments of musical composition. Ruskin was evidently a difficult student, who wanted to know the reason for every prescription of musical grammar and was unwilling to accept anything on mere authority. In 1880 he began to write songs.

The fact that Ruskin's primary instincts were not those of a musician helps to explain the difficulty he had in assimilating elements of musical grammar that must have seemed self-evident to a trained musician such as West. There are some crudities of harmony and part-writing in Ruskin's songs, but it is in the realm of rhythm and meter that the greatest conflicts arise between a natural sense of poetic meter and the subtly different characteristics of musical meter. This is dramatized in a booklet that Ruskin produced in 1880 entitled *Elements of English Prosody*, intended as a companion to *Rock Honeycomb* (see *Works*, XXXI). The booklet is liberally illustrated with musical notation which to the musician is often eccentric to the point of

---

[10] W. G. Collingwood, *Ruskin Relics* (London: Isbister & Co., 1903), pp. 151ff.

nonsensicality. Ruskin thinks instinctively in terms of poetic feet, but a musical bar does not always behave in quite the same way. The first syllable of a poetic foot is not always the long or accented one. The iamb and the anapest, for example, begin with short or unstressed syllables, unlike the trochee or dactyl in this respect. The first beat of a bar of music, on the other hand, is by definition a downbeat and receives an accent, except in the case of such devices as the hemiola or other syncopations which in any event are exceptional and momentary, depending for their effect on a regular musical meter with accented downbeats to establish the normal context. Thus when Ruskin attempts to illustrate iambic or anapestic meter in musical notation, he puts bar lines between the poetic feet, producing the musical anomaly of a series of unaccented downbeats (see figure 1).

(1) One of Ruskin's attempts to render poetic meter in musical notation, from *Elements of English Prosody* (1880).

One of Ruskin's happier attempts to render strict poetic meter musically is his setting of a lyric by Horace, "Faune Nympharum." Some of the turns of melody are unexpected, and perhaps not grateful vocally; Ruskin often seems to lose sight of the exigencies of specific vocal ranges. In this case, the melody spans nearly two octaves. At the same time, there is a certain freshness that results from Ruskin's approach to the meter. Most of the phrases consist of two bars of common time plus one bar of two-four time. Many a trained musician of the period would undoubtedly have prolonged certain of the stressed syllables, perhaps setting some of them to several slurred notes in order to adapt the text to a series of regular four-bar musical phrases. The end result might be more technically polished and professional, but far less interesting than Ruskin's unorthodox effort.

West assisted Ruskin with his compositional projects. A letter of 1882 suggests, however, that there were sometimes conflicts of opinion arising, no doubt, from the clash of Ruskin's poetic sense with West's musical sense: "Mrs. West sang me my 'Come unto these yellow sands' and 'Old Ægina' — very prettily — but Mr. West's alterations always take out exactly the points I've been driving at, and leave the things just like everything else! But he's so good and eager to help me that he's quite a delight" (XXXVII, 401-402). The two songs mentioned in the letter are among the most problematic from an editorial point of view. Judging from the manuscripts, it appears that Ruskin began by outlining his melodies using solid note-heads, and afterwards went back to work out the exact durations of the notes and their arrangement into bars. [11] Careful examination reveals that certain of the solid note-heads have been modified, some of them very faintly, to form half notes and whole notes. Faint bar lines are inserted at various points, but these by no means guarantee metrical regularity.

"Come unto these yellow sands" is of particular interest, since in part of the preface to *Rock Honeycomb*, Ruskin discusses how this should not be set to music, using letter type graphically to represent a despised roulade (XXXI, 109; see figure 2). It is fortunate that we can know something of how he

---

(IV.) All songs are to be sung to their accompaniment, straight forward, as they would be read, or naturally chanted. You must never sing

```
                          aw                          a-
                    aw    aw                    a-   a-
"Scots whaw-aw              aw-hae wi' Wa-         a-

              a-      a-  a-
        a-  a-a-  a-  a-
                        al-lace bled,"
```

nor "Welcome, welcome, welcome to your go — to your go — to your go-oo-ooo-ory bed"; but sing it as you would say it. Neither, even if a song is too short, may you ever extend it by such expedients. You must sing "Come unto these yellow sands" clear through, and be sorry when it is done; but never

```
                        a-        a-
                  a-  a-  a-  a-
"Come unto these ya-      a-      a, etc., low sands."
```

(2) Ruskin's explanations of how words should not be sung, from the preface to *Rock Honeycomb* (1877).

[11] See the MS facsimiles in the appendix to *Works*, XXXI, 515, 520.

thought this Shakespeare text ought to be set to music, even if the melody, with its many leaps and twists, is one of his oddest creations.

"At Marmion's Grave" (1881), to a text by Walter Scott, was published by W. G. Collingwood in his book *Ruskin Relics* (1903) and reprinted in the appendix to Volume XXXI of the collected *Works*. The unpretentious but elegantly figured piano accompaniment is more polished than those of the other Ruskin songs, and one suspects that West may have had a lot to do with the final version. The song unfolds in short, recitative-like phrases. The simple rhythmic and melodic motif that opens the voice part recurs throughout the song, imparting a feeling of unity in a composition that otherwise does not move in regularly balanced phrases.

Although Ruskin decided in 1842 that he would not become a poet, he did occasionally write verses later in life. Among them are a group of short "Rhymes to Music," one of which, "A Note of Welcome," was composed for his cousin, Mrs. Arthur Severn. Ruskin would often sing it on her arrivals at his home in Brantwood. Another of his later poems is the tender lyric, "Trust thou thy love," which he set to music in 1881. The song consists of four two-bar phrases in common time, each in an identical rhythmic pattern incorporating gently flowing triplets. In contrast with the quirkiness of "Old Ægina" and "Come unto these yellow sands," "Trust thou thy love" has a shapely melody which reaches an understated but touching climax at the beginning of the final phrase.

Ruskin's ideas about music, despite the element of paradox, are largely coherent, though one can find individual instances of direct contradiction. But this is hardly surprising in a man who advocated a radical restructuring of society along lines that sound overtly socialistic, but who was assuredly not an egalitarian, and in the first sentence of *Praeterita* described himself as "a violent Tory of the old school." He was, after all, a man who once said, "I am never satisfied that I have handled a subject properly till I have contradicted myself at least three times" (Cook, I, 1). Certainly his meditations upon the moral, social, religious, and educational aspects of music are of a piece with his utopian vision. Peculiar and eccentric as many of Ruskin's ideas may be, they do represent a highly individual manifestation, perhaps at times an exaggeration, of notions that were more generally current in Victorian England, even if they were not always as passionately held or as elaborately developed as they are in his writings.

*Peter Horton*

# SAMUEL SEBASTIAN WESLEY AT LEEDS: A VICTORIAN CHURCH MUSICIAN REFLECTS ON HIS CRAFT

"I HAVE MUCH PLEASURE IN WRITING THIS, THOUGH MY OPINION CAN ADD but little weight to the universal consent of all musicians in England, that Dr. W. is the first among us, both for extraordinary talent, and for unwearied diligence in improving that talent to the utmost. He is not only the finest organ-player that we have, but also a most accomplished musician."[1] With these words (written in November 1841), Thomas Attwood Walmisley, professor of Music in the University of Cambridge, extolled the merits of his fellow organist and composer, Samuel Sebastian Wesley. Wesley was then 31, having been born in London as the first of seven children of an irregular union between Samuel Wesley, a composer and organist, and his housekeeper Sarah Suter. Named after his father's musical idol, Johann Sebastian Bach, he received his early musical training as a chorister in the Chapel Royal, leaving in 1826 when his voice broke to embark upon a career as a professional musician. During the next six years he held several organists' posts in the capital, besides assisting with the musical direction of the English Opera Company and trying his hand at composition, so that by the time he received his first major appointment — as cathedral organist at Hereford in 1832 — he had acquired a thorough knowledge of music. Until his death in 1876 he pursued the career of a provincial cathedral organist, and he gained an enviable reputation as the country's foremost organist and church composer.[2]

---

[1] J. T. Lightwood, "S. S. Wesley — A Sad Story," *Choir and Musical Journal*, 32 (1941), 117.

[2] For biographical information on Wesley, readers should consult Paul Chappell's full-length study *Dr. S. S. Wesley, 1810-1876: Portrait of a Victorian Musician* (Great Wakering: Mayhew-McCrimmon, 1977), or Betty Matthews's brief survey, *Samuel Sebastian Wesley 1810-1876: A Centenary Memoir* (Bournemouth: Kenneth Mummery, 1976). Nicholas Temperley has provided a critical assessment of the composer in *The New Grove Dictionary of Music and Musicians*, 20 vols. (London: Macmillan, 1980) and of his church music in the chapter "Cathedral Music" in *The Romantic Age 1800-1914*, ed. Nicholas Temperley, Vol. 5 of *The Athlone History of Music in Britain* (London: Athlone Press, 1981). Watkins Shaw writes perceptively of Wesley's character and achievement in "Samuel Sebastian Wesley (d. 19 April 1876): Prolegomenon to an Imagined Book" (*English Church Music*, 1976, 22-30). The history of English church music is covered by J. S. Bumpus in *A History of English Cathedral Music*, 2 vols. (London: T. Werner Laurie, 1908; rpt. ed., Farnborough: Gregg international, 1972) and, more critically, by E. H. Fellowes in *English Cathedral Music*, 5th ed. rev. by J. A. Westrup (London: Methuen, 1969).

Despite the success he achieved, Wesley never found life easy. Born into a family in which the "one consistent thing . . . was mentality, often rising to genius,"[3] he could be extremely difficult to deal with, although capable of showing great kindness to pupils and close friends. Both at Hereford and later Exeter (where he moved in 1835) he was often at loggerheads with the cathedral authorities and by the early 1840s was anxious both to escape from the cloistered environment of a cathedral close and to bring public attention to bear upon the poor state of music in the cathedrals. Such an opportunity appeared upon the death in May 1841 of John Thomson, leaving vacant the Reid Professorship of Music in the University of Edinburgh. Wesley applied for the post, supported by an array of testimonials, including Walmisley's glowing reference. His application was unsuccessful, but another opportunity had already arisen: the offer of the post of organist at the newly rebuilt parish church in Leeds where, only a few weeks earlier (on 18 October), he had "opened" the new organ. As Wesley's pupil William Spark recorded, "he was so much impressed with the wealth of Leeds, and delighted to be asked by two rich merchants to select grand Broadwood pianofortes for them, that bearing in mind his disagreement with Dean Lowe at Exeter, he forthwith accepted from the vicar and church wardens the offer of organist at £200 per annum, guaranteed for ten years."[4]

Wesley's problems at Hereford and Exeter had undoubtedly been partly of his own making, and his own often fractious behaviour was ill calculated to endear him to his superiors. Nevertheless, as he wrote later, the cathedral authorities were themselves not blameless:[5]

> Painful and dangerous is the position of a young musician who, after acquiring great knowledge of his art in the Metropolis, joins a country Cathedral. At first he can scarcely believe that the mass of error and inferiority in which he has to participate is habitual and irremediable. He thinks he will reform matters, gently, and without giving offence; but he soon discovers that it is his approbation and not his advice that is needed. The Choir is "the best in England," (such being the belief at most Cathedrals,) and if he give trouble in his attempts at improvement, he would be, by some Chapters, at once voted a person with whom they "cannot go on smoothly," and "a bore." The old man knows how to tolerate error, and even profit by it; but in youth, the love of truth is innate and absorbing.[6]

Having now escaped from such circumstances he was able to criticize them without immediately jeopardizing his own career, and during his stay in Leeds

[3] Ernest Ford, "The Wesleys," *Monthly Musical Record*, 47 (1917), 152.

[4] William Spark, *Musical Reminiscences* (London: Simpkin, Marshall, Hamilton, Kent & Co., 1892), p. 166.

[5] For a discussion on the general state of cathedral choirs readers should consult Paul Barrett's article "English Cathedral Choirs in the Nineteenth Century," *Journal of Ecclesiastical History*, 25 (1974), 15-37. *The Organists and Composers of S. Paul's Cathedral* (London: Bowden, Hudson, 1891) by J. S. Bumpus also contains much of general interest as the situation at St. Paul's was by no means atypical.

[6] S. S. Wesley, *A Few Words on Cathedral Music and the Musical System of the Church* (London: F. & J. Rivington, 1849), pp. 11-12.

he published two essays and an extended pamphlet on the reform of cathedral music, besides giving a series of lectures on Choral Music which covered much of the same ground. [7] The notes used in the preparation of the last also give a fascinating insight into his thoughts on the role of music in the church service and the form it should take. [8] Before proceeding to examine these writings, and in particular the vision of the cathedral service that inspired his work, a glance at the unique choral establishment at Leeds Parish Church and the man responsible for it, Walter Farquhar Hook, will help to set the scene.

Hook had been appointed vicar of Leeds in 1837 and on arrival found himself in charge of a vast parish encompassing both the town and much of the suburbs, and served by fifteen churches. The population had risen from 53,162 in 1801 to 123,393 in 1831 and was still increasing. [9] During the course of his ministry he was responsible for a large church-building programme and the subdivision of the parish, but his initial concern was with the Parish Church — a much altered medieval building — and in particular with the improvement of its internal arrangements to accord with his own moderate High Church views. Work started in 1838 but the whole structure was soon found to be unsafe and the obvious course was to demolish it and re-build. Demolition began immediately and the new church was consecrated on 2 September 1841.

It was not only the building that Hook had found to be in poor condition. The choir (one of the earliest to be robed in the North of England) was equally run down, "the surplices in rags, and the service books in tatters" (DNB, IX, 1171). Determined that this state of affairs should be improved, he campaigned for — and against vigorous opposition achieved — the increase in the church rate needed to maintain the choir. A far more important development, however, took place early in 1841 as the new church neared completion: "A number of Churchmen [now] waited upon the Vicar (Dr. Hook), and requested that he would permit Choral Service to be daily performed after its consecration. This was gladly acceded to by the Vicar, who promised

---

[7] Wesley prefaced both the second edition of A Selection of Psalm Tunes (London: R. Cocks & Co., 1842) and A Morning & Evening Cathedral Service (London: Chappell, 1845, henceforth referred to as the Service in E) with essays on the reform of cathedral music, while A Few Words on Cathedral Music and the Musical System of the Church is devoted to the subject. In the early months of 1844 he gave a series of lectures on Choral Music at the Liverpool Collegiate Institution.

[8] Although A Few Words has been the subject of critical comment, less attention has been paid to the two prefaces and none to the lecture notes (preserved in Royal College of Music [Lcm] MS 2141f). Neither has any attempt hitherto been made to relate changes of style in Wesley's music to his written views on the subject.

[9] Dictionary of National Biography, 22 vols. (London: Smith, Elder & Co., 1903), IX, 1171.

his utmost support, so long as funds could be provided to sustain the choir in such a state of efficiency that the services should be performed complete in all their perfection and beauty." [10] Hook recorded his progress in February 1841: "I am now fully occupied in preparing to form a choir, a subject on which I am profoundly ignorant; but John Jebb has kindly assisted me. . . . How I shall raise the money I know not; but this I know, a good choir must be formed. . . . My whole heart is set on this business." [11]

The Reverend John Jebb to whom he had turned for advice was a nephew of his former mentor, Bishop Jebb of Limerick, and himself a prebendary of the cathedral there. He was also one of the foremost advocates of the "cathedral" service. Its alternative, the model established by Frederick Oakeley at All Saints', Margaret Street (and favoured by the Tractarians) was based on the idea of congregational participation in the musical portions; Jebb would have none of this and the "cathedral" model was therefore adopted at Leeds. By way of preparing the ground, Hook also commissioned Jebb to give a series of *Three Lectures on the Choral Service of the Church of England* at the Leeds Church Institute. [12] These were subsequently published and, according to the *Parish Choir*, circulated widely and "greatly contributed to promote a strong feeling in favour of the Choral Service" ("Church Music," 3, 148).

On Jebb's advice Hook had appointed a new choir master, James Hill, to superintend the establishment of choral services, but the organist at the old church, Henry Smith, initially continued in office and played at the consecration. For the inauguration of the new organ, however, a better-known player was wanted and, probably at the instigation of Martin Cawood (a wealthy ironmaster and amateur musician), Wesley was engaged. His subsequent appointment marked the final achievements of Hook's ambition: not only had he succeeded in establishing a choir which was already the equal of most cathedral ones, but he had also attracted the country's leading organist and church musician. The general satisfaction felt at this achievement is evident from reports in the local press: "We have hitherto abstained from mentioning that Samuel Sebastian Wesley, Esq., Mus. Doc., and now organist of the Cathedral, Exeter, had accepted the situation of organist and composer of this splendid church . . . [and] we cannot but congratulate our readers on the high acquisition which music will receive from having so distinguished a professional gentleman to reside in our town." [13]

---

[10] Anon., "Church Music in Leeds," *Parish Choir*, 3 (1850), 148.

[11] W. R. W. Stephens, *The Life and Letters of Walter Farquhar Hook*, 2 vols. (London: Richard Bentley & Son, 1878), II, 125.

[12] John Jebb, *Three Lectures on the Choral Service of the Church of England* (London: J. G. F. & J. Rivington, 1841).

[13] *Leeds Intelligencer*, 1 January 1842, p. 5.

Wesley's move to Leeds was a major turning point in his career. The attractions were obvious: only one daily service, no clerical interference (from a precentor) in directing the music, and a very generous salary. The choir, too, was well-trained and clearly left a favourable impression (as Hook reported): "Dr. Wesley says that our service is most sublime: beyond anything he ever heard in any cathedral" (Stephens, II, 134-135). Indeed, the realization that a higher standard of music could be achieved in a new church in a Northern industrial town than in one of the time-hallowed cathedrals must have strengthened Wesley's determination to draw public attention to the fact that, as he wrote, "the musical arrangements at cathedrals are susceptible of infinite improvement" (Wesley, *Selection*, p. 2).

Two recent developments — the rise of the Oxford Movement and the establishment of the Ecclesiastical Commissioners — had both served to bring ecclesiastical matters before a much wider public than hitherto. Established in 1835 in the wake of the Reform Bill, the Commissioners were specifically instructed "to consider the state of the several Cathedral and Collegiate Churches in England and Wales with reference to ecclesiastical duties and revenues," a task which naturally included a review of their musical arrangements. [14] They found that the relative positions (and salaries) of the cathedral clergy and other officers had changed radically since the time of their foundation. The dean of St. Paul's was also bishop of Llandaff and had a total income of £8624; the minor canons and lay clerks who formed the choir received an average of £32 and £21 respectively, plus a share of the "Cupola money" paid by the public to see the building. [15] St. Paul's was by no means atypical. At many other cathedrals endowments originally intended for supporting the choir and music had been diverted to the chapter coffers. Where "Cupola" (or "Tomb money" as it was called at Westminster Abbey) was not available, another solution was to offer the minor canons livings near the cathedral and free them from their statutory duty to be present at all services. Neither the low salaries nor the absenteeism of the minor canons promoted efficiency: at Hereford Cathedral (where all the adult members of the choir were in holy orders) there arose the situation for which Wesley wrote his well known anthem "Blessed be the God and Father": "This Anthem was written for an occasion (Easter day) when only Trebles and a single Bass Voice were available." [16]

In those cathedrals where the choir was composed of both minor canons and lay clerks, the former had frequently ceased to take an active part in

[14] [Edward Taylor], *The English Cathedral Service, its Glory, — its Decline, and its Designed Extinction* (London: Simpkin, Marshall, 1845), p. 37.

[15] H. J. Gauntlett, "The Musical Profession; and the Means of its Advancement Considered," *Musical World*, 3 (1836), 211-212.

[16] S. S. Wesley, *Blessed be the God and Father* (London: Hall, Virtue and Co., 1862), p. 1.

the singing and merely intoned the responses and collects. Such a situation inevitably led from bad to worse. Not only was the choir now depleted, but as the minor canons came to do less, so less was expected of them, and it was by no means unknown for totally unmusical persons to be appointed to vacancies.

This state of affairs had developed gradually over the past two centuries. Now, with reform in the air, it was finally judged to be intolerable. The Commissioners' proposals, however, met with little favour from musicians because their effect was to legalize many existing abuses. Thus it was that the bishop of London could state: "It is not our intention to tax the musical powers of the Minor Canons," and thereby officially sanction their present nonchoral role ([Taylor], p. 60). Endowments were not to be returned to choirs but included in the general redistribution of income. As Wesley himself wrote, "a very strong probability exists, that Cathedral property will be taken away for objects in which Cathedral localities have but a remote, if any, interest, such as the building of Clergymen's houses, and the erection of school buildings, in far distant places" (Wesley, *A Few Words*, p. 76).

The publication of the Commissioners' first four reports the following year immediately prompted one musician, H. J. Gauntlett, to enter the debate with a series of trenchant articles which highlighted the poor treatment accorded to cathedral music and musicians as well as the unsatisfactory nature of their proposals. [17] The time was clearly ripe for a concerted attack on the attitudes (largely clerical) which had led to such a state of affairs.

It is clear from his notes that Wesley knew Gauntlett's articles and was influenced by these and the similar publications of Edward Taylor and Jebb. [18] Although approaching it from different positions — Taylor as a professional (but not church) musician and Jebb as a cathedral dignitary — both stressed the historical aspect of the subject and went to considerable lengths to underpin their arguments with documentary evidence. Indeed, both devoted considerable space to an attack on what they saw as the spoliation of the cathedrals by the Ecclesiastical Commissioners. After referring to cathedral statutes Taylor continues: "These tell us what Cathedral Music was designed to be, and what it was, — the evidence of our own senses will tell us what it is, — and the Ecclesiastical Commissioners' Reports, and above all their Bill, clearly indicate its future fate" ([Taylor], p. iv).

Like Jebb and Taylor, Wesley based his argument for the improvement of cathedral music on a comparison of what it was intended to be and

---

[17] H. J. Gauntlett, "The Musical Profession; and the Means of its Advancement Considered," *Musical World*, 3 (1836), 129-135, 161-167, 193-198, 209-213; 4 (1837), 33-40.

[18] In addition to *Three Lectures* Jebb also published *The Choral Service of the United Church of England and Ireland* (London: John W. Parker, 1843).

what it actually was. Because he was a composer, however, historical matters were much less important to him than an appeal to the emotions. This appeal is expressed most clearly in the notes he prepared for his lectures:

> Now should we not say if it is decidedly that music *should* be employed in our worship of the Divinity, that it *is* our duty to see that the best efforts and those alone, are devoted to an object which is perhaps among the most important it ever falls to the task [of] humanity to execute, must we not agree in the principle that whatever forms a part of our National worship should be the best of its kind. That our Architecture, our music and all the details of religious establishments as well as the more important matters of our liturgy itself should possess a degree of merit and excellence unattained to in things designed merely for our own uses and gratifications, that they should be the most cared for, the objects of our highest and wisest and most enduring [endeavour].
>
> (Lcm MS 2141f, f. 48).

Indeed, his thoughts on the subject center in his vision of the Anglican cathedral service as the pinnacle of an art form:

> That I prefer the Choral Service of the church to any other public mode of worship whatever . . . I do most [blank] assert. I admire its pervading feature that of separating in its offices everything which might tend to remind the congregation of the earthiness of its ministering servants, all of whom appear in garments unlike those of their common use, while almost everything uttered is unlike the ordinary language of mankind. Language, and that only of the most exalted character and connected with music of the most simple and I do not hesitate to say . . . of the most sublime character, [means that] the individuality of the ministering servants scarcely anywhere appears. Its object had been to command the attention of congregations to heavenly things, the sermon is an innovation — originally it formed no part of the Choral Service but was delivered outside the Choir, sometimes indeed outside the Church, the views of it projectors being of a higher character than to sanction man's individuality as an integral part of the creature's worship of the Creator. . . . The object of man's assembling thus was to address God, not to be addressed by man, to have their thoughts by the magnificent effects of architecture and music more effectively wrested from common pursuits bringing all heaven before their eyes to use the words of Milton.
>
> (Lcm MS, 2141f, f.7).

Something of the same idea is to be found in Jebb's lectures: "In the constitution of her Choirs, the Church of England has made the nearest possible approach to a primitive and heavenly pattern. Her white robed companies of men and boys, stationed at each side of her Chancels, midway between the Porch and the Altar, stand daily ministering the service of prayer and thanksgiving. The whole idea and arrangement is beautiful and holy" (Jebb, *Three Lectures*, p. 18).

There can be little doubt that Wesley's surroundings at Leeds Parish Church played a part in shaping his vision of the ideal choral service. The combination of a handsome gothic building, a service conducted with a degree of reverence and solemnity unknown in most cathedrals, and an eloquent sermon certainly produced a strong effect on a contemporary visitor:

> The service was conducted according to the strict letter of the rubric, and with a fervor and solemnity of manner, which gave it a proud pre-eminence over those similar estab-

lishments where the pure and beautiful language and formularies of the Protestant church are sacrificed to the rapid and careless manner of the officiating priests, who seem not to feel what they utter; who appear to discharge their duty for a salary, and are indifferent how it be done, so it be got through. . . . The prayer for the church militant, the absolution, the consecration of the sacred elements, and the administration of the Holy Sacrament, were all said and performed with becoming solemnity. . . . We had never previously seen or heard the services of the English Church so impressively conducted; and we left that house of God fully impressed with the conviction, that the influence of the example here set would rapidly effect wondrous changes in the manners, habits, and religious opinions of British society, from which manifold blessings, spiritual and temporal, will inevitably follow.

(*Leeds Intelligencer*, 14 October 1843, p. 7).

To Wesley the choral service lay outside the sphere of everyday things, thereby allowing one to escape from the harsh realities of the world. In so conceiving it he revealed one of the most important facets of his personality, a strong attachment to the ideals of Romanticism. Church music, he wrote, "bends the mind to devotion, removes all impression of mere sublunary things, and brings home to man an overwhelming sense of his own insignificance and the majesty of the Eternal" (Wesley, *A Few Words*, p. 45). This union between the music, language, and architecture in the service of religion is a theme which recurs many times in his writings. Yet as he was only too painfully aware, the weak link in this partnership was invariably music. Choirs were depleted, inefficient, and even more importantly lacked good music — especially contemporary — to sing. Having therefore described the ideal choral service, he now proceeded to outline his views on the types of music, both ancient and modern, that should be employed. His words here have an especial interest because they not only reflect his interest as a composer in the contributions of past generations, but they can also be compared directly with the music known to have been in use at Leeds.

Like most contemporary musicians he subscribed to the belief that music was steadily moving towards a state of perfection, and in consequence he viewed condescendingly the works of earlier periods as the products of composers "fettered . . . by the deficiencies of imperfect art" (Wesley, *Service in E*, p. iii). Antiquity alone was insufficient to commend a work; it must also possess that feature which to him mattered above all others, expression. Certain short late sixteenth or early seventeenth century anthems passed the test, among them Richard Farrant's "Call to remembrance" and "Hide not thou thy face from us," but few service settings were worthy of performance. Most suffered from the "same jog-trot emphasis . . . from the first word to the last, let the sentiment be what it may" (Wesley, *Service in E*, p. iv). Among later composers Wesley praised Henry Purcell, Maurice Greene, and William Boyce, and anthems by all three regularly appeared in the service lists at the Parish Church. [19] Contemporary English composers, however, receive no

[19] From 1846 the *Leeds Intelligencer* published the weekly service lists.

mention in his writings and the only recent works known to have been in use at Leeds are three anthems by Thomas Attwood (d.1838), two by William Crotch (d.1847) and the *Evening Service in B flat* by Walmisley (1845). In contrast the Leeds anthem book contained at least six works by Mozart, Beethoven and "the pure and beautiful SPOHR," his favourite composer (Wesley, *Service in E*, p. vii). It was to them that he looked for musical salvation, and his own works certainly reflect the qualities he sought; many years later he referred to "the manner in which the words are expressed" as being one of his main achievements:[20] "Since the greatest works of the best German writers — Bach, Handel, Mozart, and others, have dawned upon us, no musician of eminence has devoted his time to the preparation of church music which might to some extent embody and exhibit the finest qualities observable in the works of these great and immortal men, particularly as regards that most important feature in vocal composition, *expression*, fashioned, of course, in a *church* garb" (Wesley, *Selection*, p. 2).

Words had always meant a great deal to Wesley, and it was his fortune to be able to marry them to music which enhanced their power. Much thought clearly went into the preparation of his texts. Verses from many different sources — the Old and New Testaments, the Book of Common Prayer and *Paradise Lost* — are frequently juxtaposed and then rearranged to give the exact meaning he wanted. Small changes — often no more than the omission of a word or two — abound, but invariably improve the verbal rhythm or correct the accentuation and by so doing help create that blend of words and music so important to him. Indeed, much of the success of Wesley's music lies in the fact that he possessed such an instinctive feel for word setting, and this, coupled with his strong religious bent, gives his most inspired passages their exceptional emotional power. His thoughts on the subject are clearly expressed in the preface to the *Service in E*: "The subjects to be treated are so various, of such grand and universal application, — as necessarily to divest composition of its ordinary features; rendering almost every species of amplification of a particular subject either difficult or impossible; and this, too, in connection with words which seem, in the musician's judgement, to demand of him the most exalted efforts of which his art is capable" (p. i).

Word painting as such held little appeal for him, but the relationship between words and music had clearly exercised his thoughts: "Purcell and Handel [were] wrong about to thee all angels. My Father also (to some little extent) about He hath put down the mighty; it is our business to sing of his praise of his having done these things not to describe by music our own little notions of the means employed by God in doing them. . . . Father's service

---

[20] British Museum MS Add. 35019, f. 124.

exalted the humble, (novel and charming)."[21] Through the resources of melody, harmony, and vocal and instrumental scoring, music was the ultimate means of expressing his emotions, and it is always the musical, not the verbal, element which is dominant. Within a few years of Wesley's writing these words, however, his music underwent substantial changes of both form and style, changes which are also reflected in his writings.

Hitherto Wesley had concentrated almost exclusively on verse or full-with-verse anthems consisting of a succession of separate movements (or sections) scored for full choir, various combinations of verse (solo) ensemble, and solo voices, and lasting for up to twenty minutes in performance.[22] All had included substantial solo arias — movements which rank among the finest of their type — and in many cases obbligato organ parts as well, and each had been written in a thoroughly contemporary idiom. From henceforth arias are most notable by their absence and the organ parts much less independent. What prompted this change of heart is not clear, but when taken in conjunction with Wesley's own words on the subject, it becomes clear that a significant change had taken place:

> Solo singing in the Church, I confess, I do [not] think should be much encouraged. I do not think it should be absolutely prohibited, but the portions of the service set apart for music are meant to be the voice of the people, and altho' perhaps our music should not altogether be restricted to chorus, still I think the Solo should be a rare exception, and in almost every instance so mixed with chorus that the individuality of the singer may not attract that attention to himself which belongs to the sense of the words, and for a higher purpose.[23]

It is perhaps not entirely coincidental that Jebb held similar views: "And besides, [in the performance of full anthems] . . . there is less room for that personal exhibition to which the more modern compositions so largely administer. Disregard of self is one of the chief moral characteristics of Catholic Christianity: and the sinking of the individual in the ministerial office should always be borne in mind in Christian worship" (Jebb, *Three Lectures*, p. 27). Nor should it be forgotten that Hook, too, would probably have supported this view and might have discouraged the use of solo anthems.

---

[21] Lcm MS 2141f, f. 2. The works by Henry Purcell and G. F. Handel here referred to are settings of the Te Deum. While their precise identification is impossible, it is probable that Wesley had in mind Purcell's festal *Te Deum in D major*, and Handel's *Utrecht Te Deum*. In the latter work the words "To thee all angels cry aloud" are allocated to a pair of alto voices in an obvious attempt at simple word-painting. The reference to Samuel Wesley is to the Magnificat from his *Service in F* in which word-painting is again employed: that Samuel Sebastian had himself done the same in his *Service in E* (around 1843-44) reveals the extent to which his views on the subject had changed.

[22] The terms full, full-with-verse and verse anthem are here used as follows: a full anthem is scored for full choir throughout; a full-with-verse anthem opens and closes with movements for full choir but includes movements for solo voices or verse ensemble; a verse anthem opens with a movement for solo voice or verse ensemble.

[23] Lcm MS 2141f, f. 18 v. 25 r. Wesley's omission of 'not' from the first sentence is apparent from his original wording: "Solo singing in the Church I confess, I am not desirous to see promoted."

Of one thing, however, there can be no doubt: the most important anthems written at Leeds ("Cast me not away" and "The face of the Lord") are both in a radically different style from their predecessors. The contrast becomes even more apparent when it is remembered that they were written in 1848, only four years after the completion of the other major work of the Leeds years, the *Service in E*. Completed at the instigation of Martin Cawood (who paid Wesley for the copyright), the *Service in E* is in the composer's most expansive style and includes an important organ part. Its combination of dramatic choral writing, a vivid, up-to-date harmonic vocabulary, and an independent accompaniment make it one of the landmarks in the development of the form.

The anthems (and the evening canticles of the *Chant Service in F* written two or three years earlier) are far more restrained. In all three the organ does little more than double the voice parts or provide harmonic support for a unison vocal line. The change in musical style is even more pronounced. Largely turning his back on those influences which had coloured his earlier works, Wesley now revealed a new debt to Gregorian chant (in the *Chant Service*) and the vocal works of the late Renaissance. It is surely not coincidental that this transition took place around 1844-46, the period in which he was most actively involved in the study of earlier music, particularly for his Liverpool lectures.

Despite his deliberate use of an archaically inspired idiom, Wesley never allowed his own voice to become submerged, and thereby avoided the artistically dead pseudo-antique style he had earlier condemned. Indeed, by combining contemporary harmony with "word-setting and vocal texture . . . not inferior to some of the best work of Byrd or Morley,"[24] he achieved in "Cast me not away" a wholly satisfying synthesis of ancient and modern. The style of the anthems, however, was destined to be short lived. Within a year of their first performances Wesley had left Leeds for the more traditional surroundings of Winchester Cathedral where, two years later, he returned to a form he had neglected for the past decade, the extended full-with-verse anthem.[25] "Ascribe unto the Lord" (1851) and its successors, "By the word of the Lord" (1854), "Praise the Lord, O my soul" (1861), and "Give the King thy judgements" (1863), inhabit a different world from "Cast me not away," a world as different as Winchester Cathedral is from Leeds Parish Church.

Why Wesley should have done this remains a mystery, and one can only assume that he considered the two Leeds anthems to be experimental works and chose not to pursue that line of development further. The musical

---

[24] Arthur Hutchings, *Church Music in the Nineteenth Century* (London: Herbert Jenkins, 1967), p. 103.

[25] For an account of Wesley's time at Winchester see Alan Rannie, *The Story of Music at Winchester College 1349-1969* (Winchester: P. and G. Wells, 1970).

language of "Ascribe unto the Lord" and the other later anthems sits firmly in the mid-nineteenth century tradition he had previously cultivated, although two Leeds features did have a lasting influence: the abandonment of the solo aria and (with a few exceptions) the avoidance of elaborate organ parts. All in all there is no reason to doubt that his views on these two subjects had undergone a fundamental change.

In retrospect, therefore, the years Wesley had spent at Leeds can be seen to form a watershed in his career. He had gone there full of energy and enthusiasm, glad to escape from Exeter; he left seven-and-a-half-years later regretting his move. Paradoxically he was then even more securely established as the country's leading church musician, but his career as composer had already passed its peak: "I was earning a fine income [at Exeter] & loved the County of Devon but I packt up, I gave up *all* — & much it was — & went to *Leeds*. There — attached as I am to *nature*, to Scenery, fine Air, & all the advantages of the *Country*, & disappointed as I was with Dr. Hook & his powers to either aid his Church Music or me — I soon bitterly repented of leaving Exeter & when *this* place was vacant I offered for it & was elected." [26] Perhaps his most important achievement, however, was to set down his views on church music and, by bringing them before a wider public, at least partly achieve his goal:

> Let us indulge a hope that the claims of this subject will find support, and that its merits will be better understood. Amongst the dignitaries of the Church are several distinguished persons who are fully alive to the high interests of music, and who do not forget that whatever is offered to God should be as faultless as man can make it. Music should not be compelled to bring her worst gift to the altar! Is it too much to ask of them some public effort in support of Cathedral Music? . . .
> 
> If the effect of these pages should happily be, in any way, to contribute to so desirable a result, the writer will have cause to rejoice.
> 
> (Wesley, *A Few Words*, p. 75).

Several factors had contributed to this achievement. Wesley had gone to Leeds dissatisfied with the state of music in cathedrals and already turning his attention to its reform. By a happy quirk of fate, the writings of Jebb and Taylor appeared shortly after this and provided an additional stimulus, while the invitation to lecture at Liverpool gave a further outlet for his thoughts. Above all, however, the practical experience of working in Leeds Parish Church had shown him what could be achieved given a good choir and music. From an amalgam of all these influences Wesley's own vision of the choral service, the practical proposals for its improvement, gradually emerged. [27]

---

[26] Royal School of Church Music manuscript album of autograph letters, f. 40.

[27] In the course of this article no attempt has been made to examine the practical proposals that Wesley made for the improvement of choirs and the training of musicians. A discussion of these may be found in Peter Horton, "The Music of Samuel Sebastian Wesley (1810-1876)" (D. Phil. thesis, Magdalen College, Oxford, 1983).

Behind these lay his guiding principle that music was an art of equal value and importance to the visual arts, and that the church musician was first and foremost an artist in the service of religion: "The principles of Music are of no narrow and limited application: they belong not merely to one country or nation, or even to one world, but are universal and natural: surely then we are warranted in affirming that the good which might here be done should be done for Music's own sake, and in humble imitation of that example of perfect accuracy and order displayed in all His works, by the incomprehensibly Great Author of all things." [28]

---

[28] S. S. Wesley, *Reply to the Inquiries of the Cathedral Commissioners, Relative to Improvements in the Music of Divine Worship* (London: Piper, Stephenson and Spence, 1854), p. 8.

Linda K. Hughes

# FROM PARLOR TO CONCERT HALL: ARTHUR SOMERVELL'S SONG-CYCLE ON TENNYSON'S *MAUD*[1]

ARTHUR SOMERVELL'S NAME IS HARDLY A HOUSEHOLD WORD TODAY, EVEN among Victorian specialists; nor, within the framework of music history, can Somervell be said to have broken new ground in his compositions. Yet his song-cycles are certainly worth knowing, not as historical footnotes or curiosities, but as works which approach major and demanding poetic texts with extraordinary sensitivity and verve. His *Cycle of Songs from Maud*, for example, achieves independent life while also respecting the integrity of Tennyson's text: the relationship between music and text is symbiotic rather than parasitic or predatory. Beyond his gift of enabling the sister arts of music and poetry to meet without subordinating the claims of either form, Somervell also claims interest as a transitional figure from the Victorian to the modern era.

Somervell was born in mid-Victorian England at Windermere in 1863, six years after the birth of Edward Elgar. He was educated at Uppingham and King's College, Cambridge, and went abroad to study for two years at the Berlin *Hochschüle für Musik*. He returned to England and spent two more years as a student at the Royal College of Music, where he joined the teaching staff in 1894. During his life he was best known as a music educator and as a composer of choral cantatas suitable for competition festivals. For his achievements he was knighted in 1929. He returned to his native Lake District in his retirement, where he died in 1937.

[1] This essay was originally part of a session initiated and organized by Nicholas Temperley and presented at the 1985 meeting of the Midwest Victorian Studies Association (MVSA) in Chicago. I wish to thank Professor Temperley for first suggesting this project to me, and for graciously allowing me to draw from his own MVSA presentation the biographical facts of Somervell's life and the details of the cycle's public performance in 1901.

I also wish to thank Boosey and Hawkes for permission to publish excerpts from Somervell's *Cycle of Songs from Maud.*

Finally, I wish to thank Margaret D. Hughes, Organist Emeritus of the First Christian Church, Topeka, Kansas, without whose performance and recording of Somervell's song-cycle I could not have begun work on this study.

Today most critics regard Somervell's five song-cycles, all based on poems published during Queen Victoria's reign, as his most important work. *Maud*, his first song-cycle, was published in 1898, six years after Tennyson's death. The *Maud* cycle was followed by *Love in Springtime* in 1901, based on poems by Tennyson, Dante Gabriel Rossetti, and Charles Kingsley; *The Shropshire Lad* — Somervell's best-known work — in 1904, based on A. E. Housman's 1896 poem; and two cycles based on Robert Browning's poetry, *James Lee's Wife* in 1907 and *A Broken Arc* in 1923. All Somervell's song-cycles, then, were based on well-known Victorian poems, but except for *A Shropshire Lad* all were composed after the poets' deaths — suggesting at once Somervell's strong attachment to Victorian poetry and his distance from it.

Somervell's *Maud* was first published as a collection of twelve songs "designed for continuous performance"; and a thirteenth song was added in 1907.[2] (See the Appendix for a complete listing of songs in the cycle, and the passages of Tennyson's poem to which the songs correspond.) The title page of the cycle says that it was "sung by Mr. Plunket Greene [a leading baritone at the turn of the century particularly known for his interpretations of Elgar and Charles Parry] and Mr. Keith Falkner." The earliest performance date is not known, but the 7 March 1901 performance at St. James's Hall in London, sung by Harry Plunket Greene and accompanied by Somervell himself, was reviewed by the *Musical Times* on 1 April 1901. The reviewer observed that "most music-lovers are now agreed that [the] union of musicianship, elegance, and the higher qualities of passion is found in a greater degree in Mr. Somervell's cycle of twelve songs from 'Maud' than in any of his other work." I am particularly interested in how Somervell's "musicianship" and "passion" combined to serve as an interpretation of Tennyson's poem, and the degree to which this interpretation represents Victorian and post-Victorian attitudes that reflect Somervell's status as a mediating figure between the two eras.

Appearing in 1855, only five years after Tennyson published *In Memoriam* and became poet laureate, *Maud* was his only major mature work to meet hostility from the reading public. The poem's title, it was said, had one too many vowels: the poem was attacked both for its obscurity ("Mud") and the untempered ravings of its speaker ("Mad").[3] Even Gladstone, generally an ardent supporter of Tennyson, publicly criticized the poem's apparent glorification of the Crimean War.[4] In response Tennyson added additional

---

[2] Ernest Walker, *A History of Music in England*, 3d ed., rev. by J. A. Westrup (Oxford: Clarendon Press, 1952), p. 341.

[3] Cited by R. J. Mann in his *Maud Vindicated*, selections reprinted in *Tennyson: The Critical Heritage*, ed. John D. Jump (London: Routledge and Kegan Paul, 1967), pp. 197-198.

[4] [William Gladstone], "Tennyson's Poems," *Quarterly Review*, 106 (October 1859), 454-485. Portions of this essay are reprinted in *Tennyson: The Critical Heritage*, pp. 241-266.

lines to later editions of the poem to clarify narrative links — just as Somervell, interestingly, published twelve songs in his *Maud* cycle in 1898 and then added "Maud has a garden" (Song 6) in 1907 to provide an additional narrative link between the cycle's beginning and end.

But the 1855 poem had its defenders, most notably R. J. Mann, whose *Maud Vindicated* in 1856 was personally endorsed by Tennyson. Mann stressed that *Maud* was dramatic, not the personal effusions of the laureate, and praised the poem's psychological acuity and metrical virtuosity. [5] Still, the poem continued to be a stumbling block for many Tennysonians, even while a growing number acknowledged the beauty and subtlety of its lyrics. Nor had the state of critical opinion changed much by the 1890s, the decade in which Somervell composed his song-cycle on *Maud*. The poem's advocates followed the line taken by Mann, and the poem's critics continued to object to the war theme and the hero's hysteria. Stopford A. Brooke's remarks are representative of the climate of critical opinion contemporary with Somervell's composition. In *Tennyson: His Art and Relation to Modern Life*, first published in 1894 and reprinted thereafter for over a decade, Brooke praises the artistry of the poem but censures its handling of war, calling the poem's subject "artistically unfortunate, for the Crimean war was the most foolish . . . of all our wars." [6] And as for the poem's hero, his "physical irritability transfers itself to his moral world, and becomes a weak anger with man and God without one effort to meet the evils at which he screams. His first utterance in the poem is a long shriek in a high falsetto note against the wrongs and curses which come of a vile peace" (Brooke, p. 235).

Unlike Brooke, Somervell presumably neither heard a falsetto note in the poem's opening lines (since his song-cycle is written for baritone voice) nor faced serious obstacles to his admiration of *Maud*. His song-cycle is in many ways a tribute to the poem, translating into musical terms what Tennyson achieves with poetic devices such as meter and alliteration. [7] Somervell's scoring of the poem's mad section (II, 239-342), for example, effectively suggests horses' hooves beating the pavement — or a brain throbbing (S.41.9-12, 42.1); while his setting of "Come into the garden, Maud" (S.30.1ff.) employs the rhythms of the dance that Tennyson's early readers detected in his lyrics' meters (I, 850ff.). More subtly, Somervell parallels in musical terms

---

[5] Portions of Mann's book are reprinted in *Tennyson: The Critical Heritage*, pp. 197-211.

[6] Stopford A. Brooke, *Tennyson: His Art and Relation to Modern Life* (London: Sir Isaac Pitman & Sons, 1894), p. 230.

[7] References are to Alfred Tennyson, *Maud*, in *The Poems of Tennyson*, ed. Christopher Ricks (1969; rpt. ed. New York: Norton, 1972), pp. 1037-93; and Arthur Somervell, *Cycle of Songs from Maud by Alfred Tennyson* (London: Boosey & Co., 1898, 1907). Citations of the song-cycle are by page number and then measure number(s) on individual pages (preceded by an "S" to distinguish the song-cycle from the poem).

Tennyson's verbal devices in "She came to the village church" (Song 3). Tennyson indicates the increasing intensity of the hero's emotions by expanding the number of metrical feet from three to four when Maud lifts her eyes and meets those of the speaker:

> An ángel wátching an úrn
> Wept óver her, cárved in stóne;
> And ónce, but ónce, she lífted her éyes,
> And súddenly, swéetly, strángely blúshed.

(I, 303-306)

Somervell maintains a constant 4/4 time, but at the word "suddenly" shifts from the minor to the major mode to embody the sweetness of that blush and the hero's response.

* (1) Somervell, "She came to the village church" (*All musical examples are by permission of Boosey and Hawkes.*)

But a song-cycle is never identical with the poem that inspires it. Lawrence Kramer, in *Music and Poetry*, in fact argues that the relationship of poetry and music is "implicitly agonic." "A poem," he says, "is never really assimilated into a composition; it is *incorporated*, and it retains its own life, its own 'body,' within the body of the music. . . . A song . . . does not *use* a reading; it *is* a reading, in the critical as well as the performative sense of the term: an activity of interpretation that works through a text without being bound by authorial intentions. . . . The song is a 'new creation' only because it is also a de-creation."[8] It is equally interesting, then, to see how Somervell's *Maud* is truly a "new creation," if one clearly related to Tennyson's poem. In this context we can say that Somervell removed *Maud* from Tennyson's parlor, where the poet in his many famous readings controlled the poem's interpretation, and placed the poem in new guise in the concert hall.

The first point of interest is Somervell's selection of Tennyson's text. He used only 234 of Tennyson's 1,324 lines, and in the sections he used he retained the exact wording of the poem.[9] But significant reinterpretation occurs in Somervell's prefatory notes to the cycle, and in one case in his altered sequencing of Tennyson's sections (see Appendix). Somervell's published notes summarize the entire plot of Tennyson's poem and explain how each song in the cycle furthers the plot. Because of those notes, Somervell can both establish the context he desired for the cycle and omit those sections of the poem which serve primarily to develop the plot (for example, I, 285-300).

Yet the effect of the prefatory notes is to alter Tennyson's text substantially. Somervell flatly asserts that "at the time of Maud's birth [the fathers] planned a match between the two children who grew up as intimate playmates" (see Appendix); while in the poem the betrothal is presented as a nebulous memory of the speaker's, and in fact readers have grounds for viewing the betrothal as a figment of the speaker's troubled imagination, a form of wish fulfillment.[10] Somervell better retains the ambiguities of Tennyson's

[8] Lawrence Kramer, *Music and Poetry: The Nineteenth Century and After* (Berkeley: University of California Press, 1984), p. 127.

[9] Only two minor departures exist. In Song 11 Somervell changes Tennyson's "And here beneath it is all as bad" (II, 252) to "And here in the grave it is just as bad" (S.42.10-13), since Somervell omits the preceding lines of Tennyson's text establishing the antecedent of "here" as the grave. In the same song Somervell also alters "O me, why have they not buried me deep enough? / Is it kind to have made me a grave so rough?" (II, 334-335) to "Ah me, why have they not buried me deep enough? / Is it kind to give me a grave so rough?" (S.44.16-18, 45.1-3). The "give" is perhaps more ironic than "have made," but the changes are so minor that they do not bear significantly on interpretive issues.

[10] Marilyn J. Kurata points out that none of the hero's characterizations of Maud or of their relationship can be assumed true; the inner life he posits in Maud could from start to finish be mere projection or fantasy. See Kurata, " 'A Juggle Born of the Brain': A New Reading of *Maud*," *Victorian Poetry* 21 (1983), 369-378.

text in his notes to the Epilogue, which teasingly quotes lines from Tennyson's text instead of proffering an interpretation of the ending. Similarly, his notes assert only that the circumstances in which the hero's dead father was found "pointed to suicide" (unlike the betrothal, the suicide is merely suggested). But Somervell does give explicit directions on how to read the significance of this death: "The effect of this on his son, still a boy, is shown again and again throughout the poem, specially in the songs Nos. 1 and 6." Tennyson's poem precipitates the reader directly into the restless flow of the speaker's consciousness, leaving the reader to grasp and construct, perceive and half-create all narrative links. Indeed, though Gladstone recanted his charge against the poem's stance on the Crimean War in 1879, he, like so many readers of twentieth-century texts, wondered "whether it is to be desired that a poem should require from common men a good deal of effort in order to comprehend it." [11] Somervell's preface makes the plot concrete and delivers it whole to an audience which had largely wanted such a prologue to Tennyson's "muddy" poem all along. By providing the prefatory notes, Somervell trims a difficult poetic text into acceptable shape for Victorian audiences. [12]

The most striking alteration of Tennyson's poem is Somervell's inverting the sequence of the germ of *Maud* ("O that 'twere possible," II, 141-144) and the mad scene. In the poem the hero feels great guilt after the duel. But only after learning of Maud's death, then yearning for the presence of the remembered lover rather than the wraith that haunts his mind, does the hero collapse into the raving insanity of Part II's closing section. In Somervell the mad scene follows the expression of guilt ("The fault was mine," Song 10) and precedes "O that 'twere possible" (Song 12). The effect is to tie madness more closely to guilt than to grief, perhaps anticipating Freudian more than Victorian interpretive patterns. The poem's ending, problematical for Victorians and modern readers alike, is also transformed by the altered order. Tennyson's hero moves directly from the mad scenes to his avowal of recovery and his departure for the Crimean battlefield; Somervell's moves directly from yearning for the arms of the dead Maud to the battlefield. If Somervell seems to align desire for Maud with recovery from madness, he more strongly suggests that going to battle is the hero's means for reunion with Maud in death. That is, the hero's mission seems more overtly suicidal in Somervell's text than in Tennyson's — in the poem many readers see a nonironic affirmation of patriotism as the transcendence of (or at least consolation for) his individual sufferings and loss of his beloved.

[11] Hallam Tennyson, *Alfred Lord Tennyson: A Memoir*, 2 vols. (London: Macmillan, 1897), I, 399.

[12] Interestingly, in the *Memoir*, Hallam Tennyson also provides a plot outline of the poem, noting that many readers desired such an outline (I, 402-405).

Music is not well suited for conveying ideas or facts, and so it was natural for Somervell to exclude from his song-cycle two plot strands that figure importantly in Tennyson's poem: the hero's rivalry with a nouveau-riche lord seeking the hand of Maud with her brother's encouragement, and Tennyson's social criticism, his attack on the materialism that creates in society a state of "Civil war, as I think, and that of a kind / The viler, as underhand, not openly bearing the sword" (I, 27-28). But it is interesting to see what kind of poetic text emerges in the cycle as a result. Deleting the hero's rival creates a far more attractive, accessible hero than Tennyson's text did: in the songs we do not encounter a speaker who calls Maud's brother an "oiled and curled Assyrian Bull" (I, 233), or brands the rival "a padded shape, . . . a waxen face, / A rabbit mouth that is ever agape" (I, 358-360). Just as Somervell's prefatory notes provided a clearly articulated plot that eliminated what for some was the poem's murkiness, so his deleting the rivalry theme created a more acceptable surface for the hero. In the concert hall, Somervell gave listeners a hero fit to appear in parlors.

And by deleting the poem's social criticism and religious doubt — "the yell of the trampled wife," "chalk and alum and plaster . . . sold to the poor for bread" (I, 38-39), a "nature . . . one with rapine" (I, 123), and a world in which "the drift of the Maker is dark, an Isis hid by the veil" (I, 144) — Somervell in effect anticipated Harold Nicolson's 1923 study, which marked a major turning point in Tennyson criticism. Nicolson argues that Tennyson suffered from being born in the Victorian age, forced to become "inevitably less and less the lyric poet, and more and more the civic prophet. . . . For whereas Tennyson was an extremely good emotional poet, he was, unfortunately, but a very second-rate instructional bard."[13] Nicolson's book helped sustain interest in Tennyson during the anti-Victorian reaction of the 1920s and thereafter by positing two Tennysons, the authentic lyric poet and the sincere but misguided — and mediocre — public prophet. He invited readers to slough off the dross of instruction and concentrate on the lyric gems that remained. This is essentially what Somervell had done: he focused on the private psyche of the hero's quest of love and death, and obliterated the social and metaphysical framework that had been an essential part of the 1855 poem.

Somervell also anticipated more recent criticism of Tennyson's poem in the text and musical score that comprise the song-cycle. As Kramer observes, "a piece of vocal music based on a well-known poem necessarily risks a comparison that may make it seem expressively inferior. A composer . . . will have to grapple with the accumulated force of meaning lodged in the poem.

---

[13] Harold Nicolson, *Tennyson: Aspects of His Life, Character and Poetry* (London: Constable, 1923), p. 5.

. . . A song that masters a significant text, then, does so by suggesting a new interpretation — specifically a skeptical interpretation, one that rewrites the text in some essential way. In other words — slightly exaggerated but only slightly — the music becomes a deconstruction of the poem" (pp. 145-146).

Somervell composed his song-cycle amidst a reasonable consensus about what the poem meant. When Victorian audiences responded favorably to *Maud*, its ending was typically read in the affirmative terms Tennyson's own note to the poem suggested:

> This poem of *Maud or the Madness* is a little *Hamlet*, the history of a morbid, poetic soul, under the blighting influence of a recklessly speculative age. He is the heir of madness, an egoist with the makings of a cynic, raised to a pure and holy love which elevates his whole nature, passing from the height of triumph to the lowest depth of misery, driven into madness by the loss of her whom he has loved, and, when he has at length passed through the fiery furnace, and has recovered his reason, giving himself up to work for the good of mankind through the unselfishness born of a great passion.
>
> (*Poems*, p. 1039).

The reading public would have encountered this note in Hallam Tennyson's *Memoir* of his father, published in 1897. [14] The next year, the public was presented with Somervell's song-cycle, which becomes the story of a morbid, poetic soul who passes from love of Maud to love of death, and whose recourse to war is a private act of suicide rather than an unselfish act of service. Somervell creates this interpretation through both textual and musical means.

Because Somervell has deleted the social criticism from all earlier sections, the singer's assertion of patriotism in the Epilogue ("We have proved we have hearts in a cause, we are noble still, / I have felt with my native land, I am one with my kind") has absolutely no frame of reference. Unsupported by earlier references to the materialist civil war of exploitation for profit's sake, the assertion floats in a vacuum and invites an ironic response. The only frame of reference for the lines is Maud's military ballad (musically echoed in the Epilogue), which first aroused the hero from his torpor, and the dream of Maud following his madness. This hero seems to pursue not a public cause but a private vision:

> I saw the dreary phantom arise and fly
> Far into the North and battle, and seas of death . . . .
> The blood red blossom of war with a heart of fire.
>
> (S.50.9-20).

The "blood red blossom" passage, moreover, musically echoes the passage from "A voice by the cedar tree" (Song 2) in which the hero says Maud's

---

[14] In the *Memoir*, the passage has slightly different punctuation than in the passage cited in Ricks's edition; in the *Memoir*, the opening phrase through "Hamlet" is enclosed in quotation marks, implying that the succeeding words are Hallam Tennyson's, if based on his father's words.

sweet voice leaves him no choice "But to move to the meadow and fall before /
Her feet on the meadow grass, and adore" (S.10.8-11; see figures 2a and 2b).

(2a) Somervell, Epilogue

(2b) Somervell, "A voice by the cedar tree"

The hero, this musical link or echo implies, adores war as an extension of Maud and embraces "the purpose of God" (S.51.12-14) as a surrogate for arms that can enfold him — in death. True, his avowal of a noble cause also echoes in musical terms Maud's earlier singing of "honour that cannot die," and the music's vigor, energy, and emphatic cadences in the cycle's closing measures make the end sound glorious and triumphant. But the links forged within the cycle as a whole suggest that the closing's swelling music, which invites auditors' hearts to swell in unison, is a kind of patriotic and musical cliché, resting on nothing — or rather, on one man's sad, perhaps mad, vision.

This reading of the ending is reinforced by the textual motifs embedded in Somervell's lyrics, and by musical motifs. The two patterns that remain in Somervell's adaptation of Tennyson's poem are the blood/red/rose/purple cluster of images, and the death/horror/madness theme. The opening song introduces the "blood-red heath" and "red ribbed ledges drip[ping] with the silent horror of blood" in the "dreadful hollow." As the hero falls in love, positive images of the red rose of love appear in Songs 5, 6, and 7, the last suffused by the rose of passion and optimism. The cycle as a whole, then, oscillates (as does Tennyson's poem) between the red/rose of love and death, and finally merges them in the "blood red blossom of war."

The motif of death is even more interesting. The cycle opens with the hero obsessed with the dreadful hollow where his father died, and the frenetic piano interludes suggest frenzied emotions just barely kept under control in the sustained, slow notes of the sung text. The text concludes with the line, "And Echo there, whatever is ask'd her, answers 'Death' "; the word "Death," sung on a dissonant E-flat, and the uncadenced ending bespeak hysteria and loss of control (figure 3a).

And E-cho there, what-ev-er is ask'd her, answers

(3a) Somervell, "I hate the dreadful hollow"

The second song, "A voice by the cedar tree," is antiphonal, presenting the sweetness, energy, and beauty associated with Maud that counter the hero's morbid melancholy. The hero participates in her music; but as he sings her song about men "Ready in heart, . . . and ready in hand, / [To] March with banner and bugle and fife / To the death," something odd happens on the note on which "death" is sung. As opposed to the emphatically major-key, harmonious phrases up to that point, the word "death" is pitched on a similarly dissonant E-flat, briefly sustained (figure 3b).

(3b) Somervell, "A voice by the cedar tree"

Hence, when the second song continues, the hero singing that "Maud in . . . her youth and her grace, [is] Singing of Death, and of Honour that cannot die," the reference to "death" is charged with the residual darkness of the first song, however innocent and lyrically sweet the immediate context in which the word is lodged.

Similarly, "O let the solid ground," the fourth song, brims with quiet energy and hope; but the sustained notes held on "mad" and "sad" (S.13.2-3; 14.6-8) highlight these words and suggest that all is not so solid as it seems. Song 5 is the first wholly affirmative song, in which even nature joins in the lover's joy, as we see in the "bird" twitterings of the accompaniment. But it is succeeded by a song ("Maud has a garden," Song 6) which begins brightly and ends in horror, as the hero sees the "death-white curtain drawn" round Maud's house. One can hear the hero trying to resist his own morbidity when he sings he knew the curtains "meant but sleep" (S.23.3-4), because the music here almost recovers the major key with which the song began. But the hero's own dark thought is too entrenched, and the song culminates in the word "death," as did the opening song; and here the word is also sung on a sustained minor pitch.

"Go not, happy day" (Song 7) is even happier than "Birds in the high Hall-garden" (Song 5), sweet and so confidently serene that it is even playful, especially in the song's closing measures. "I have led her home" (Song 8) sustains the warmth of "Go not, happy day" in its opening phrase, but the eighth song twice sounds darker notes as well. When the hero proclaims he has achieved his "wished-for end," auditors are invited to respond to the word "end" in the sense of death. For not only have the accumulated meanings of the song-cycle thus far prepared listeners for this association, but the accompaniment, which has been sweetly flowing on like the hero's surging blood, suddenly halts, taking the form of half-note chords that suggest not only calm but a somber finality. And in a passage which also functions to foreshadow Maud's death, the pattern is repeated later in Song 8 when Maud closes the door and is gone. Indeed, here the accompaniment's ponderous half notes bring to mind a death march, suggesting that the hero reacts to Maud's momentary departure as if it were her death itself.

The accompaniment absorbs the dark thoughts and transforms them, at least on the surface, to sweetness by the song's end, so that we are led smoothly into "Come into the garden, Maud" (Song 9). This central song and tour de force of the cycle is remarkable for absorbing and resolving any dissonant notes almost as quickly as they are sounded (as, for example, at "To faint in his light, and to die"). But though it is joyously articulated, the song ends on the highly charged image of the dead heart blossoming in purple and red, and the emphatic repetition and closure of this song seal off the lover's last moment of intense joy. Up to now, love and beauty have been set against death, madness, and horror, the former expressed in plangent harmonies and rippling notes, the latter in dissonant, dark, minor notes, and either almost immobilized or else frenetic rhythms.

In the wake of the duel, however, the pattern begins to reverse itself; life and consciousness are now the source of distress, and death and obliteration a sweet haven. "The fault was mine" (Song 10) begins by echoing the melody and darkness of "I hate the dreadful hollow" (Song 1), and the darkness and dissonance are sustained until the final two measures. [15] The hero sings that he will hear Maud's passionate cry "till I die," and as he reconsiders, rethinks, and repeats "till I die," the music resolves into a cadence on the phrase in a major key — suggesting both that the final resolution of the hero's fate will be death, and that the hero recognizes death as a resolution of his sorrows. Similarly, in the marvelous "Dead, long dead" (Song 11), we gradually realize amidst the whirling fury of a disordered mind that the hero's dilemma is being alive. For when he imagines quiet, peaceful death — actual, not living death — the music expresses a lyric yearning for this state, and it prepares for the singer's recognition that he is "but half dead." He ends pleading for more emphatic burial, and the close does not resolve but rather remains suspended: until the hero is dead and buried indeed, he cannot attain resolution.

In this context the succeeding lyric cry for the lost Maud in "O that 'twere possible" (Song 12) is a cry for union that will heal the "long grief and pain" of madness and guilt at any cost. With all these accumulated links, we then move into the complex Epilogue, which deliberately echoes the various strands of the cycle now established. The opening, dark octaves of the accompaniment echo similar passages in "The fault was mine" and "Dead, long dead" (for example, S.38.15-19; 44.13-18ff.), establishing the speaker's guilt and madness as starting points. And when the music shifts to a sweeter tone as the speaker declares his mood has changed, telling how Maud "seemed to divide in a dream from a band of the blest," (S.48.6-10; figure 4a), we hear an echo of "Maud has a garden" (S.19.4-8: "And thither I climbed at dawn / And stood by her garden gate"; figure 4b), a song which began sweetly but ended with a vision of death. [16]

---

[15] This musical echo parallels Tennyson's verbal echoes. Part II of the poem opens as the hero recounts the duel and remembers that "a million horrible bellowing echoes broke / From the redribbed hollow behind the wood" (II, 24-25). Tennyson, in other words, verbally echoes his poem's opening sections, as Somervell musically echoes his opening song.

[16] The echo is clearly deliberate. Somervell wrote the Epilogue first, in 1898, then composed "Maud has a garden" in 1907 and incorporated into the later song a short melodic passage from the Epilogue. To listeners, the Epilogue appears to echo Song 6 rather than vice versa.

(4a) Somervell, Epilogue

(4b) Somervell, "Maud has a garden"

The hero's dream of Maud which yielded such delight is sung to the tune of "O that 'twere possible," and the echo suggests, as the text alone could not, a

longing for union with the dead Maud of the dream. True, the echo could sig-
nify that the dream brought momentary union with Maud, yielding renewed
energy that shores up the hero's psyche. But the accumulated associations, especially the pattern of death as sweet resolution (from Song 10 onward), suggest the darker interpretation. Thus, Somervell's ending gives us a hero
speeding towards death. If he is heroic at all, it is only, perhaps, in a desire for
love so strong that he will have union by death with Maud and her military
fervor rather than life and sanity without her.

   Somervell's song-cycle on *Maud*, then, is a fascinating cross section of
Victorian and modernist elements. In many ways it is strikingly faithful to
Tennyson's mid-Victorian text; Somervell's ability to capture the swings and
shifts, the despairs and exultations of Tennyson's hero is an impressive
achievement in its own right. Moreover, by eliminating the least attractive
utterances of Tennyson's hero (especially his vituperations against others)
and by providing a plot summary at the outset, Somervell revised Tennyson's
poem in ways wished for by so many of the laureate's contemporaries.
Somervell's selection of the text thus provides a Victorian compromise.
   But in his wholesale elimination of social prophecy and his re-crea-
tion of a poem focused squarely on a lonely, melancholy hero who pursues a
private vision and a private voice, Somervell adumbrates by more than a decade the critical approach to Tennyson undertaken by Nicolson and a generation to whom poets as social prophets were laughable at best, intolerable at
worst. Most interesting of all, Somervell anticipates the interpretation which
our current skeptical, Freudian, and deconstructive generation finds congen-
ial, whereby the hero's departure for the Crimean War is no victory over
madness but an expression of it, and perhaps a self-willed suicide. [17] So far as I
am aware, no one at the time of Somervell's composition had proffered such
an interpretation; if readers did not endorse Tennyson's interpretive notes to
the poem, they refrained from doing so because they understood the poem to
offer war as affirmation, not because they viewed the ending ironically. As
Kramer claims that successful song-cycle composers always do, Somervell
achieves a new creation independent of Tennyson's by pursuing the darkest
threads of meaning embedded in Tennyson's text. In doing so Somervell
gives us a song-cycle striking in its own right and returns us, as the best criticism always does, to the poem with fresh insight. Having heard Somervell's
*Maud* in the concert hall, listeners can go back to their own parlors to read
Tennyson anew.

[17] See, for example, the reading of the poem given by James R. Bennett in "*Maud*, Part III: Maud's
Battle-Song," *Victorian Poetry* 18 (1980), 35-49.

## APPENDIX
## SOMERVELL'S PREFATORY NOTES

The prefatory notes are given in their entirety below. I have indicated in brackets the title assigned to each song by Somervell, and the lines of Tennyson's poem which are sung in each song.

(*This Cycle of Songs being designed for continuous performance, no pause should be made between the numbers*).

The fathers of Maud and of the singer (the "I" of the songs) were close friends while the singer was a little boy — so close in fact that at the time of Maud's birth they planned a match between the two children who grew up as intimate playmates, until a crash came. "A vast speculation" failed; the boy's father was beggared, while Maud's father, his supposed friend, became a millionaire. Shortly afterwards the body of the ruined and desperate man was found in the "dreadful hollow behind the little wood," in circumstances that pointed to suicide. The effect of this on his son, still a boy, is shown again and again throughout the poem, specially in the songs Nos. 1 and 6. At the beginning of the poem, Maud, who is now 16, has returned to the Hall after an absence of several years.

### THE CYCLE

1. The singer expresses the horror he feels for the "dreadful hollow" where his father's body was found. ["I hate the dreadful hollow"; Tennyson, I, 1-4]

2. He hears Maud singing a battle song in the Hall garden. He tries to shut out the sound, but in the end is fascinated by the beauty of the voice. ["A voice by the cedar tree"; Tennyson, I, 162-189]

3. He sees Maud in church; their eyes meet, and she blushes. ["She came to the village church"; Tennyson, I, 301-307]

4. From that moment he is on fire for love of her. ["O let the solid ground"; Tennyson, I, 398-411]

5. They meet in the wood. ["Birds in the high Hall-garden"; Tennyson, I, 412-427, 432-435]

6. He goes out at dawn to Maud's garden. The curtained house where she is sleeping suggests to his haunted mind the house of death. ["Maud has a garden"; Tennyson, I, 489-494, 516-526]

7 and 8. Young love. ["Go not, happy day"; Tennyson, I, 571-598. "I have led her home"; Tennyson, I, 599-610]

9. There is a dance at the Hall to which the lover is not invited. He stands in the garden listening to the music, and his excitement rises to ecstasy when he hears her coming to the appointed meeting place. (They are surprised by her brother who hates the lover, and strikes him in their quarrel. There follows a duel in the "dreadful hollow," in which Maud's brother is killed). ["Come into the Garden, Maud"; Tennyson, I, 850-867, 902-923]

10. The lover flies the country, and during his absence ["The fault was mine"; Tennyson, II, 1-5, 34-35]

11. he goes temporarily mad, and Maud dies. ["Dead, long dead"; Tennyson, II, 239-258, 334-342]

12. He sings of his longing to hold her once more in his arms. ["O that 'twere possible"; Tennyson, II, 141-144]

EPILOGUE. He sees her in a vision, when she speaks of "a hope for the world in the coming wars" (in the Crimea). The song ends with self-dedication to his country. He "embraces the purpose of God, and the doom assigned." [Tennyson, III, 1-5, 9-11, 15-17, 34-37, 53-55, 58-59]

A.S.

*Robert Bledsoe*

# HENRY FOTHERGILL CHORLEY AND THE RECEPTION OF VERDI'S EARLY OPERAS IN ENGLAND

HENRY FOTHERGILL CHORLEY (1808–1872) WAS ENGLAND'S MOST INFLUENTIAL
music critic for almost three decades.[1] Known and respected on the Continent mainly as the author of *Music and Manners in France and Germany*
(1841; new edition 1854),[2] in England Chorley was famous for being the
chief arbiter of musical matters for the widely circulated *Athenaeum*.[3] Writing
in it almost every week, he reported to English readers about new performances and he influenced their views about new compositions. Chorley's
criticism is an especially valuable cultural record because he directed it not
toward professional musicians but toward the lay people who patronized the
Italian Opera during the last glittering years of the undisputed pre-eminence
of Her Majesty's Theatre in the Haymarket. By examining it in some detail,
we can better understand what seemed unusual and sometimes startling about
Giuseppe Verdi's early operas to a generation of English audiences nourished
on the dramatic genius of Gioacchino Rossini. No other author gives us such
a vivid idea of what caused conservative ears to resist the operas and what

---

[1] The best general account of Chorley's career is still *Henry Fothergill Chorley: Autobiography, Memoir, and
Letters*, compiled by Henry C. Hewlett, 2 vols. (London: Richard Bentley and Son, 1873). See also E. D.
Mackerness, "Henry Fothergill Chorley (1808–1872)," *Monthly Musical Record* (1957), Part I, pp. 134–
140 and Part II, pp. 181–188; and Robert Bledsoe, "Arbiter," *Opera News*, 13 February 1982, pp. 16–18.

[2] François Fétis in *Biographie universelle des musiciens* remarks that "Un jugement juste en ce qui concerne
l'art, et des observations originales exprimées avec esprit, distinguent cet ouvrage de beaucoup de publications de même genre" (2d ed., 8 vols. [Paris: Fermin-Didot, 1875–83], II, 286).

[3] A comprehensive study of the importance of this journal, emphasizing its function as a literary review, is
Leslie Marchand's *The Athenaeum: A Mirror of Victorian Culture* (Chapel Hill: University of North Carolina Press, 1941). Later in the century, specialized musical journals developed a readership overlapping
that of the general reviews, but during the period discussed in this essay, there were few and their influence
was slight. For a general survey of the musical press, see Stephen Banfield, "Aesthetics and Criticism" in
*The Romantic Age: 1800–1914*, ed. Nicholas Temperley (London: Athlone, 1981), pp. 455–473, and
Leanne Langley, "The English Musical Journal in the Early Nineteenth Century," Ph.D. dissertation, University of North Carolina, 1983.

caused general audiences to find them increasingly exciting. A discussion of Chorley's criticism in the light of Verdi's early career in general and of the conditions of English operatic performance practice in particular thus contributes to our understanding of an important aspect of the cultural life of early Victorian London.

I

After the first performance of *Macbeth* (at La Pergola, Florence) in March 1847, Verdi turned his full attention to Andrea Maffei's libretto, *I Masnadieri*, an adaptation of Friedrich Schiller's 1781 play, *Die Raüber*. Verdi's journey to England in the summer of 1847 for the premiere of this new opera came at an important stage in his career. He had already achieved real Italian success five years earlier with the production of his third opera, *Nabucco*, at La Scala in 1842, and his international success was beginning to reach remarkable proportions. Even more significant in the long run than his burgeoning popularity was the internal evolution of Verdi's image of himself as a serious artist.[4] One manifestation of this evolution was Verdi's crusade for guarantees that his operas would be performed exactly as he wrote them—no cuts, no changes in the orchestration, and no transpositions.[5] Of course, he could not get these guarantees—but from this time on, Verdi, with increasing success, applied pressure in order to get impresarios and singers to serve the requirements of the composer, not the other way around.

Looking back on Verdi's early operas today, we find it easy to see their dramatic energy and melodic inventiveness. Things are not necessarily the same, however, if we consider these early operas from the point of view of English audiences hearing them for the first time.

Verdi came to London in the summer of 1847, accompanied by his friend and student, Emanuele Muzio.[6] In one sense, the trip was a brilliant success. Muzio's letters to Barezzi tell at length of the tremendous ovations for

---

[4] This new self-esteem can be sensed in the dedication to *Macbeth* (1847) to Antonio Barezzi: "Florence, 25 March 1847 . . . Here is *Macbeth*, which I love more than my other works and which therefore I consider more worthy to be presented to you" (my translation) (*I Copialettere di Giuseppe Verdi*, eds. Gaetano Cesari and Alessandro Luzio [1913; rpt. ed., Bologna: Forni, 1968], p. 451). Subsequently cited as *Copialettere.*

[5] Letter to Giovanni Ricordi, 20 May 1847, *Copialettere*, pp. 37–39.

[6] Luigi Agostino Garibaldi, ed., *Giuseppe Verdi nelle lettere di Emanuele Muzio ad Antonio Barezzi* (Milan: Fratelli Treves, 1931), pp. 321–322. Subsequently cited as Garibaldi. The significance of the correspondence is discussed later in this article.

the work, the performers, and the composer. But in another sense, the journey was a failure: *I Masnadieri* was given a few performances but was not revived. The contract Verdi expected to be offered for more operas never materialized (*Copialettere*, pp. 42–44).

The apparently contradictory aspects of this situation illuminate important aspects of the mid-century operatic world in England. In many ways, this was a very small world, centering almost entirely on Her Majesty's Theatre in London. Covent Garden Theatre had fallen on hard times and was accurately termed by one journalist "this happless establishment."[7] Although Carl Maria von Weber's *Oberon* had been given its first performance there in 1826, since that time opera had played a secondary role. (By the mid-1840s there were "Masked Balls, Corn Law Meetings, Unending Concerts, Fancy Fairs," in other words, "anything but what ought to be.")[8] At the Lyceum and at Drury Lane, some operas were presented, but those theaters too were generally acknowledged to be of secondary importance.[9]

Her Majesty's Theatre in the Haymarket reigned supreme.[10] Benjamin Lumley was its manager, having taken over in 1842 on the death of the previous manager, Pierre Laporte, whose assistant Lumley had been since 1835. Lumley had decided views about what an opera house should represent: the "resort and 'rendezvous' of the *élite* of rank and fashion."[11] Accordingly, we find that newspaper accounts of the operas presented during the 1840s often discuss not only the singers and the operas, but also the social position and fashionable appearance of the audience. Was the Queen there? Prince Albert? The Duke of Wellington? How brilliantly dressed did the audience appear when everyone stood to sing "God Save the Queen" at the end of the performance? In one section of the house, "Fop's Alley," Lumley tells us that "during various portions of the performance," the "exquisite" young men gathered and chattered, making a general spectacle of themselves (Lumley, *Reminiscences*, p. 63). Both in the theatre and at his annual summer "fête" at his villa on the Thames, Lumley found that cultivating the aristocracy was "among

---

[7] *Illustrated London News*, 18 April 1846, p. 258. Covent Garden's history is narrated by Henry Saxe Wyndham in *The Annals of Covent Garden Theatre from 1732 to 1897*, 2 vols. (London: Chatto and Windus, 1906) and—from a better informed point of view musically—by Harold Rosenthal in *Two Centuries of Opera at Covent Garden* (London: Putnam, 1958).

[8] *Illustrated London News*, 18 April 1846, p. 258.

[9] Michael Balfe's *Bohemian Girl* was first performed at Drury Lane (1845) but the house was never primarily an opera house. A case has been made for the importance of English opera at the Lyceum: Nicholas Temperley, "The English Romantic Opera," *Victorian Studies*, 9 (March 1966), 293–301.

[10] There are no histories of Her Majesty's Theatre as thorough as those of Covent Garden by Saxe Wyndham and Rosenthal. A useful short history is Daniel Nalbach, *The King's Theatre 1704–1867* (London: Society for Theatre Research, 1972).

[11] Benjamin Lumley, *Reminiscences of the Opera* (London: Hurst and Blackett, 1864), p. vii.

the most pleasing of compensations for the anxieties and vexations to which a director is necessarily subjected." [12]

The artistic standards of Lumley's theatre should have been as high as the social standards for two reasons: the high quality of the orchestra under Michael Costa's direction, and the high ensemble level maintained by the principal singers. Sutherland Edwards, in a discussion of London opera companies published in 1862, tells us that "the same singers for nearly half a century past have for the most part sung alternately at the Italian operas of Paris and London." [13] In the 1830s and 1840s, these were the most celebrated in Europe: among them, Giuditta Pasta, María Felicia Malibran, Fanny Persiani, Giulia Grisi, Giovanni Rubini, Giuseppe Mario, Antonio Tamburini, and Luigi Lablache. And yet, looking back on the period from a mid-twentieth century perspective, Harold Rosenthal asserts that "by reading between the lines [of Lumley's *Reminiscences*], and taking into account the views expressed by Chorley in his criticism both in the *Athenaeum* and elsewhere, it is fairly easy to see just how artistically bankrupt Italian Opera in London was in the 1840s" (*Two Centuries*, p. 66).

To call Her Majesty's "artistically bankrupt" is surely an overstatement, but it is an accurate summary of Chorley's position. Coming to London from Lancashire in the early 1830s to work for the newly established weekly review of arts and letters, the *Athenaeum*, Chorley was by the mid-1840s a major power as a shaper of opinion. Though he reviewed many novels, his specialty was always reviews of musical performances. His odd appearance ("the missing link between the chimpanzee and the cockatoo") [14] and squeaky voice were laughed at, but his knowledge of music and singing was impressive, and his gift to be able to articulate his reactions vividly caused him to be taken seriously. His fortunes prospered with those of the *Athenaeum*, which established a high reputation for critical integrity (not a characteristic of many journals in the first half of the century). [15] One of Chorley's contemporaries, Charles Hallé of Manchester, recognized that Chorley was a "man of strong views, fearless in his criticism, perfectly honest," and yet Hallé cited as

---

[12] Lumley, Reminiscences, p. 30 and following. Lumley's social attentions were not confined to the aristocracy: Dickens and Thackeray were considered useful enough to be cultivated. See *The Letters and Private Papers of William Makepeace Thackeray*, ed. Gordon N. Ray, 4 vols. (Cambridge: Harvard University Press, 1945–46), II, 165, 269, 666; and *The Letters of Charles Dickens*, volume IV, ed. Kathleen Tillotson (Oxford: Clarendon Press, 1977), 672, and volume V, ed. Graham Storey and K. J. Fielding (Oxford: Clarendon Press, 1981), 78–79.

[13] Sutherland Edwards, *History of the Opera from Monteverde* [sic] *to Donizetti*, 2d ed., 2 vols. (London: Wm. H. Allen & Co., 1862), II, 224.

[14] *Memories of Half a Century: A Record of Friendships*, compiled and edited by R. C. Lehmann (London: Smith, Elder and Co., 1908), p. 228.

[15] Marchand, *The Athenaeum*, pp. 97–165. Also see Charles Wentworth Dilke, *The Papers of a Critic: Selected from the Writings of the Late Charles Wentworth Dilke*, 2 vols. (London: John Murray, 1875), "Memoir," (by his son), I, 1–91 and following.

Chorley's weak point the fact that he was "often and unconsciously swayed by personal antipathies or sympathies."[16]

Chorley's taste was for Felix Mendelssohn in the concert hall and Rossini on the stage.[17] Therefore, to later generations, he may seem strikingly conservative. We must remind ourselves, however, that all generations of music critics seem conservative to succeeding generations. By way of comparison, consider the Second Earl of Mount Edgcumbe, a distinguished and respected amateur, who lamented in 1828 that for the past twenty years he had seldom brought himself to attend the opera because of the changing style of composition and the decline in the singers' standards, which deviated "more and more from what I had been accustomed to in the *golden age* of the Opera."[18] And ten years after Mount Edgcumbe's complaint, George Hogarth asserted that the decline of singing had been caused by the operas of Rossini and his followers. In *Semiramide*, "the ear is absolutely stunned by the unremitting noise of the orchestra." The new approaches to writing operas "consist in a mere accession of *noise*."[19] Singers in general can no longer sing Mozart well because of Rossini's heavy orchestration:

> This species of accompaniment, the vices of which have been aggravated by Rossini's successors, has greatly injured the Italian style of singing. It has lost much of the sweetness and smoothness for which it has so long been pre-eminent. Forced to contend incessantly with such a mass of sound, the females are compelled to scream, and the males to shout; and the incorrect and slovenly harmony which they are accustomed to hear from the orchestra renders them by no means fastidious as to the purity of their roulades and embellishments.[20]

---

[16] *The Autobiography of Charles Hallé: With Correspondence and Diaries*, ed. Michael Kennedy (New York: Barnes and Noble, 1979), p. 118.

[17] During Chorley's first decade of opera-going, Rossini was the mainstay of the repertory at the King's Theatre (renamed Her Majesty's in 1837). See Henry Fothergill Chorley, *Thirty Years' Musical Recollections*, 2 vols. (London: Hurst and Blackett, 1862). This edition has been reissued by Da Capo (1984). A widely circulated version of the work is Ernest Newman's one-volume edition (New York: Alfred A. Knopf, 1926). Newman's introduction is important, but his decision to make several cuts and to regularize Chorley's punctuation makes the edition less useful than it might have been. Subsequent references will be to Chorley, *Thirty Years'*, 1862. For Chorley's reactions to operas and concerts on the Continent, see his reports in *Music and Manners in France and Germany: A Series of Travelling Sketches of Art and Society*, 3 vols. (1844; rpt. ed., New York: Da Capo, 1983). For Chorley's friendship with Mendelssohn, see Ignaz Moscheles, *Recent Music and Musicians as Described in the Diaries and Correspondence of Ignatz Moscheles*, tr. A. D. Coleridge (1873; rpt. ed., New York: Da Capo, 1970), p. 177 and following.

[18] Richard Edgcumbe, *Musical Reminiscences Chiefly Respecting the Italian Opera in England from the Year 1773 to the Present Times*, 3d ed. (London: George Clarke, 1828), p. xii.

[19] George Hogarth, *Musical History*, 2d ed., 2 vols. (London: John W. Parker, 1838), II, 214, 186.

[20] Hogarth, *Musical History*, II, 207. As an example of the "incorrect and slovenly harmony," Hogarth specifies the *Otello* trio, "Ah, vieni," which "contains within the compass of four bars, and in the vocal parts, a series of *five perfect fifths in succession*, besides *three discords of the seventh resolved upwards*; and the passage is twice repeated" (II, 208, italics in original). At the bottom of the page of the autograph score, next to the passage where these fifths occur, Rossini wrote "Queste cinque quinte sono per li Signori Coglioni" ["These five fifths are for the 'Signori Blockheads;'" "coglioni" are blockheads or, literally, testicles] (*Otello* [facsimile], ed. Philip Gossett [New York: Garland, 1979], II, 67. See also Gossett's comment on the passage "Introduction," I, v). At this time Hogarth nourished a hope that things had gone as far as

Bearing in mind such critical positions, we can better understand the historical context for Chorley's reaction to Verdi.

The first notice Chorley took of Verdi is a substantial article published
on 31 August 1844. The article is remarkable mainly because in it Chorley
analyzes Verdi's early operas before he had had a chance to hear any of them.
He begins by noting that Verdi is newsworthy:

> Recent occurrences and appearances having called the attention of our English public to
> the modern style, or rather no-style, of Italian singing, it may be as well for the critic to
> see what is doing in the world of Italian vocal composition; and, since the name of
> Giuseppe Verdi has begun to circulate widely as the *maestro* most likely to become popu-
> lar, we avail ourselves of such opportunities as perusal of his compositions here published
> affords us, to offer a word or two concerning his operas.
>
> (*Athenaeum*, 31 August 1844, p. 797).

Chorley's essay proceeds from general to specific: first an analysis of what he
considered the basis of all Italian opera, then an analysis of how that basic
principle applies to Verdi's operas.

The general analysis is the widespread perception that the melody is
the basis for opera: the article then moves into a diatribe against all currently
active composers for their inability to understand that principle: Hector
Berlioz, Richard Wagner, and "[Vincenzo] Bellini's successors" ([Gaetano]
Donizetti and Verdi) are all guilty. Chorley sarcastically predicts that we may
someday see without regret "the Opera reduced to the shapeless recitative
from whence it arose" (*Athenaeum*, 31 August 1844, p. 797).

After some incorrect biographical information for transition ("It is
not many years since Sig. Verdi was in this country . . ."), the analysis moves
to specifics. Having examined several selections of Verdi's music recently published in England, Chorley laments that there is no melody, and that the
works' "varieties of form" show even less "original fancy" than those of
Giovanni Pacini, Saverio Mercadante, or "Donnizetti." Chorley's claim that
Verdi's first operas have no original melodies, here first stated, remains basic
to his criticism of Verdi for many years to come. Nor does this fact indicate
that Chorley was an extraordinarily poor listener. As Julian Budden suggests,
"the idiom of the time was as narrowly defined as at any period in the eighteenth century, so that to a casual ear all composers seem to be quoting from
each other."[21] Despite Chorley's feelings about Verdi's poor melodic gift, the

---

they could go: "The human *tympanum* can hear nothing beyond the beating of drums, and braying of
trumpets and trombones, introduced by the followers of the Rossini school; and the temporary vogue of a
fashion of composing which is a mere cloak for ignorance and incapacity, appears to be passing away"
(Hogarth, *Musical History*, II, 186).

[21] Budden also notes that "the London critic Henry Chorley accused Verdi of lacking originality and proceeded to ascribe to Donizetti what he thought to be Donizetti's, and likewise to Federico Ricci, Bellini,

"concerted" pieces struck him as "a shade worthier and more individual." Reluctant to seem too approving, he quickly points out that the striking effects had all been anticipated in various parts of Rossini.[22]

Despite his many reservations, Chorley is clearly trying to be open-minded. He even grants Verdi a share of grudging admiration: "There is a certain aspiration in his works which deserves recognition, and may lead him to produce compositions which will command respect" (*Athenaeum*, 31 August 1844, p. 797). At this point, Chorley's antagonism is tentative: he leaves open the possibility that he may actually come to like Verdi's operas when he has a chance to see them.

II

Six months after Chorley's *Athenaeum* article, Her Majesty's Theatre gratified public curiosity about the new composer by presenting *Ernani* in March 1845, a few weeks before the "brilliant" part of the season (which always ran from Easter into August).[23] The opera's first performance in London thus took place almost exactly one year after its premiere at La Fenice in Venice (9 March 1844). Chorley began his review of *Ernani* by remarking enthusiastically that "we do not remember so interesting a commencement of an opera season as that of this day week, when a new work by a new composer was executed by new singers;—and music, *maestro*, and vocalists alike stood the difficult test." He adds: "By its length, which extends to four acts, its subject, and the treatment, it would seem as if the Italians are looking to the Grand Opera of Paris for their model in serious musical drama" (*Athenaeum*, 15 March 1845, p. 275). Chorley was considering the opera carefully in the light of his own criteria as established in the article of the previous August, before he had seen any of Verdi's operas; the same three issues were central:

and Mercadante" ("Verdi and the Contemporary Italian Operatic Scene" in *The Verdi Companion*, eds. William Weaver and Martin Chusid [New York: Norton, 1979], p. 86). For a discussion of this issue in its Italian context, see Julian Budden, *The Operas of Verdi*, 3 vols. (New York: Oxford University Press, 1973), I, 3–41. For a twentieth-century perspective on some of the issues Chorley raises, see Winton Dean, "Some Echoes of Donizetti in Verdi's Operas," *Atti del III° Congresso Internazionale di Studi Verdiani* (Milan, Piccola Scala, 12–17 June, 1972) (Parma: Instituto di Studi Verdiani, 1974), 122–147, and Friedrich Lippman, "Verdi and Donizetti," *Opernstudien: Anna Amalie Abert zum 65. Geburtstag* (Tutzing: Hans Schneider, 1975).

[22] *Athenaeum*, 31 August 1844, p. 797. Chorley's next comment reveals his sensibility: "We must note, too, that the progression of keys, in one movement, with a view to entireness in construction (a point till lately thought worthy of attention), is most curiously managed; unless some of the remarkable sequences are ascribable to transpositions on the part of the English publisher. Sig. Verdi shall have the full benefit of the doubt."

[23] *The Times*, 17 February 1845, p. 5: "Moriani and Fornasari are to appear before Easter, and as Easter falls early this year, the brilliant portion of the season will be of longer duration than usual."

Verdi's lack of originality, his interesting "concerted music," and his disturbing treatment of voices.

"That he has made free use" of other composers' music is clear (that is, the musical ideas of Bellini and Donizetti, as well as a dozen other "commonplaces" of current Italian opera). "But there is something beside" which impresses Chorley favorably: "a disposition to study new effects in the concerted music. . . . Signor Verdi's choruses are spirited: they move." Nevertheless, in his writing for voices, Verdi's "uncouthness of interval" is "ruinous." "The soprano part is perpetually above the stave. . . . To make matters worse, the orchestra is for the most part at full strength—very frequently fortissimo, leaving the poor *prima donna* no choice, save scream or pantomime." Composers no longer have the "slightest right to complain of the short-lived date of the voices of the present generation" because it is "their own ruthless ignorance" of how to write for the voice which causes the problem. Under the circumstances, the level of singing attained by Angiolina Bosio (Elvira), Moriani (Ernani), Fornasari (Don Ruy Gomez) and Botelli (Don Carlos) ranged from adequate to good (*Athenaeum*, 15 March 1845, pp. 275 and 276).

When Chorley looked back on the 1845 *Ernani* from the vantage point of 1862 in his *Thirty Years' Musical Recollections*, he stated that *Ernani* had been "received with curiosity rather than sympathy." Recollecting his bitter antagonism toward Verdi in subsequent seasons, he added that the opera "gave hopes which have not been justified by its writer's subsequent operas, more popular though they have been" (Chorley, *Thirty Years'*, 1862, I, 256–257). Chorley's memory of the opera's reception agrees substantially with Lumley's own assessment in his *Reminiscences:* "That it excited the enthusiasm awarded to it so lavishly in Italy, cannot be asserted; that it was a failure, may be emphatically denied. . . . The general result of this first introduction of Verdi to the English public was a feeling of hesitation and doubt" (p. 103). Despite its only "moderate" popular success, Lumley had the opera repeated "for several nights during the ante-Easter season" (p. 105).

After the season ended in August, Lumley went to the Continent, as he often did, to make arrangements for the coming season. His decision to initiate negotiations with Verdi about the possibility of writing an opera for London was a creditable instance of managerial far-sightedness. Verdi's Italian success was great and growing; nevertheless, London's reaction to *Ernani* had shown that his success might not be exportable. Yet Lumley was apparently confident that the next opera by Verdi would be a greater curiosity for English audiences than the previous one (he must have known, too, that the great success *Nabucco* was then enjoying in Paris augured well for its London chances).[24]

---

[24] Garibaldi prints Italian translations of several favorable French press reports, pp. 227–231.

We know some details of Verdi's business dealings with Lumley because they are preserved in Verdi's *Copialettere*. Verdi's irritation with his publisher Giovanni Ricordi had reached a crisis: Verdi signed a contract on 16
October 1845, binding himself to write two operas for Ricordi's rival, Francesco Lucca.[25] Our picture of Verdi's life at this period is especially vivid if we
supplement the information in the *Copialettere* by that in another source: the
collection of letters written by Emanuele Muzio to Antonio Barezzi (see above,
note 6). Several years younger than Verdi, Muzio had come to Milan from
Verdi's hometown, Busseto, in April 1844, and had become Verdi's pupil. In
addition to being the only pupil Verdi ever had, he soon became a companion and functioned as Verdi's secretary as well. (He remained a close friend
for life.) Muzio idolized Verdi and his operas; his regular letters to Barezzi—
the generous merchant at Busseto, friend to both Muzio and Verdi—show us
Verdi from the perspective of an impressionable young man who was somewhat naive, but also sensitive, good-humored, and honest.

Writing to Barezzi on 27 October 1845, Muzio was amused by the foreigner who had arrived in Milan while Verdi was in the countryside:

> As soon as Lumley heard about the outcome of *Nabucco* he came from London along with
> Escudier [the French publisher], to sign up the Signor Maestro for next spring. Not find
> ing him in Milan, they went to Clusone, where he was [visiting Countess Maffei]; but as
> they were on their way there, he was coming back, so they keep running after him till
> they find him. They thought he was in Busseto, and wanted to go there directly. It is very
> likely they will sign him up for London, with a third more than the fee he would receive
> in Italy, plus lodging, because there two little rooms cost twenty francs a day.[26]

When Lumley and Verdi finally got together, the negotiations must
have gone smoothly. Although no document exists containing the exact
agreement (as far as I know), we have Muzio's excited report to Barezzi two

---

[25] "I undertake to compose for you an opera to be performed in a leading Italian theatre by a first-rate company during the Carnival season 1848, provided that I do not have to write an opera for a theatre outside
Italy for the same Carnival season: in that case I should compose your opera for a different season, to be
agreed upon with you, within the year 1849. For this you will pay me 1,200 (one thousand two hundred)
golden napoleons of 20 francs in four equal instalments: the first on 1 November 1848, the second on
1 December 1847, the third on 1 January 1848, the fourth on 1 February 1848. If these conditions are
acceptable to you, I will hold myself engaged for five months, provided that *Attila* has been produced by
that time" (Translation from David R. B. Kimbell, *Verdi in the Age of Italian Romanticism* [Cambridge:
Cambridge University Press, 1981], p. 191).

    Lucca published Verdi's next opera, *Attila* (first performance: La Fenice, Venice, 17 March 1846) and *Il
Corsaro* (first performance: Teatro Grande, Trieste, 25 October 1848). Lucca also published *I Masnadieri*,
although as far as I know there are no documents extant that explain why (the original contract calls for
only two operas). Verdi's relationship with Lucca was worse than it had been with Ricordi, as the following
letter to the librettist Piave shows: "Paris, 14 January 1848 . . . You are interested in Signor Lucca? Do you
know how I have been treated by that man after I dealt with him so generously, working hard to finish
*Attila* in a deplorable physical condition and after I honored the London contract even though I was not
bound to? . . . With me he has been insensitive, boorish, and demanding. . . . but enough of Signor
Lucca, and I hope that you will never again speak to me of him" *Carteggi Verdiani*, ed. Alessandro Luzio,
4 vols. (Rome: Reale Accademia d'Italia, 1935), II, 350 (my translation).

[26] Translation from William Weaver, *Verdi: A Documentary Study* (London: Thames and Hudson, [1977?]),
pp. 164–165. Original in Garibaldi, p. 227.

days later (29 October 1845) that the engagement was agreed on ("Il signor Maestro è proprio scritturato per Londra, ieri mattina"). Verdi was to write an opera a year for ten years ("volevano che si obbligasse per 10 anni!!! e dare un'opera per anno!").[27]

Meanwhile, something that should have been completely irrelevant to Verdi's London contract was becoming an issue back in England. The *Illustrated London News*, a mass circulation weekly, reported on 11 October 1845 that Jenny Lind's voice was magnificent and that she would be making her English debut, sooner or later, at Drury Lane under the management of Alfred Bunn, even though "most liberal offers have also been tendered to her by Mr. Lumley's agents for her Majesty's Theatre" (p. 233). Despite the contract with Bunn to appear in English-language performances of Giacomo Meyerbeer's *Feldlager von Schlesien*, Jenny Lind had changed her mind: on 18 October, Lind wrote Bunn asking to be released from her contract. Bunn's reply was to threaten legal action against Lind.[28] But this had nothing to do with Verdi and Lumley.

Not yet.

### III

The year 1846 began with two developments that affected the reception of Verdi's early operas in London: Chorley's attitude toward Verdi changed from tentative acceptance to complete hostility, and Lumley's management of Her Majesty's was threatened by a series of problems so acute as to be almost overwhelming.

Like many English periodicals, the *Athenaeum* at this time printed gossip about Jenny Lind in almost every issue (is she coming? what will she sing? where will she sing?). But on 17 January, Chorley turned his attention from this phenomenon to a consideration of Verdi's newly published *Sei Romanzi*. Headed "The Verdi Mania," the review elaborated Chorley's new line that Verdi was all bad. "We are led to pay more attention to this newest of Italian *maestri* than his merits demand, from the circumstance that, bad or

---

[27] Garibaldi, p. 232. For useful accounts of Verdi's dealings with Lumley and the journey to London, see Frank Walker, *The Man Verdi* (Chicago: University of Chicago Press, 1982), pp. 158–163; Budden, *The Operas of Verdi*, I, 318–322; and Kimbell, *Verdi in the Age of Italian Romanticism*, pp. 190–207. These accounts are based primarily on the material in Garibaldi and the *Copialettere* (Kimbell's account is the most detailed).

[28] Henry Scott Holland and W. S. Rockstro, *Memoir of Madame Jenny Lind-Goldschmidt*, 2 vols. (London: John Murray, 1891), I, chaps. 6 (pp. 228–236) and 12 (pp. 290–298). Subsequently cited as Lind-Goldschmidt. Holland and Rockstro say that Lind was at this time not contemplating singing at Her Majesty's even though Bunn and many others thought she was. Documents relating to Lumley and Verdi show no references to Lind at this time, a fact which tends to support the assertion in Lind-Goldschmidt.

good, his Operas contain certain elements of popularity. . . . How long Signor Verdi's reputation will last, seems to us very questionable." Some say that his rythmic tricks in *Nabucco* have been "found out" and that "little or nothing remains: little science—no melody" (17 January 1846, p. 73).

On 23 January, Lumley announced publicly that Michael Costa, the widely admired conductor at Her Majesty's, was being replaced by Michael Balfe. Whether Costa resigned or whether Lumley fired him is not entirely clear from the strongly worded letters both men released to the press (see the *Athenaeum*, 31 January 1846). Costa took a great deal of good feeling along with him, apparently including Chorley's. The same issue of the *Athenaeum* that printed the Lumley-Costa correspondence also printed a significant little rumor: "Our contemporaries now tell us that Covent Garden is forthwith to be arranged as a second Italian Opera House. . . . [W]e cannot but consider such a project as hopeful, and an inevitable result from the course pursued at Her Majesty's Theatre" (p. 129). Elsewhere in this same issue, Chorley enumerates a long series of grievances against Lumley's administration. He sums them up as follows: "We will thankfully concede that the Opera orchestra and chorus are better now than ever before [Chorley's concession flatters Costa, not Lumley]. In all other respects, however, the Opera has deteriorated year by year since it came under Mr. Lumley's control" (p. 128).

Throughout the season of 1846, Chorley returns to the poor artistic standards of the house. Fifteen years later, when he published his *Thirty Years' Musical Recollections,* he was somewhat calmer: "It would serve no good turn . . . to recall the green room tales and their contradictions, which agitated those who are concerned in such maters.—It is enough to have lived for a while in the cauldron of Scandal, without stirring its waters afresh" (*Thirty Years'*, 1862, II, 4). Chorley then complained that the press at the time generally whitewashed the problems by ignoring them: "There was no record of failure. . . . The so-called power of journalism had never a greater rebuke than in the downfall of Her Majesty's Theatre—day by day described as unparagoned in the splendour of its performances, and as enjoying a well-deserved prosperity!" (*Thirty Years'*, 1862, I, 273). Chorley felt that events vindicated his judgment about the rottenness of the house. How far this may be an overstatement prompted by Chorley's sense of self-importance is impossible to say precisely, but it is true that in other journals one reads constantly about the brilliance of the house, "crowded to excess with rank and fashion"—as they liked to say—with very little sense that rank and fashion may not be the only judges of the health of an opera house. Chorley's notices, week after week in 1846, appear sometimes simply cantankerous; there is, however, no doubt that their tone was caused by the frustration of a critic who took opera more seriously as art than critics were expected to.

Lumley, in his *Reminiscences,* traced his ultimate downfall not to Chorley's criticism but to problems with singers that began under his predecessor, Laporte, and finally came to a head in 1846. Certain singers, whom Lumley termed the *vielle garde,* or the cabal, or the "clique," were allegedly power mad (pp. 9, 14, 134 and following). The clique had temporarily triumphed in 1841 when Laporte fired Tamburini and replaced him with Filippo Coletti: members of the audience under the cabal's sway responded with "Tamburini riots" and Tamburini was re-engaged. Lumley felt it was his duty to reassert strongly the authority of the management. Of the heart of the *vielle garde* (Persiani, Grisi, Rubini, Tamburini, and Lablache), only Grisi and Lablache were under contract in 1846, and of the two only Grisi (together with the new tenor Mario) could be considered rebellious. Lumley, picturing himself as sinned against by the power-mad singers, did not explain very convincingly what terrible things these singers were actually doing. Explanations from other commentators of the period suggest that Lumley in some sense caused his own problems. C. L. Gruneisen, for example, gave the following explanation in a pamphlet, *The Opera and the Press,* published five years after Lumley published his *Reminiscences:*

> Mr. Lumley, to this day according to his book, dwells on a monomania that he was ruined by a cabal. His error was in supposing that ballet was in the ascendant over opera, and to uphold the former, he sacrificed the latter. The Tamburini and Persiani secessions were only the prelude to the projected dismissals of Grisi and Mario; the schism with Costa was another fatal miscalculation. . . . Mr. Lumley's downfall was chiefly owing to his infatuated belief in the power of the press. He conceived journalism to be omnipotent. Hence his neglect of the stage and his attention to the newspaper people before the curtain. . . . Mr. Lumley relied on the press, and was ruined by the press. Had he acted solely on his own unquestionable abilities, and had he not listened to those advisers, now dead and gone, whose basis of action was in turn corruption and intimidation of journalists, he might at the moment have been still the ruler of the Haymarket Opera House.[29]

Willert Beale noted that Lumley quarreled with Giuseppe Persiani, husband of the famous soprano and a composer, because he did not want to produce Persiani's opera: "To that quarrel, and to a reserved, autocratic bearing towards his artists, may be traced all the rivalry against which Mr. Lumley had subsequently to contend."[30]

In this climate of stress, Lumley had several plans to make his season noteworthy: the possible return of Rubini, a possible ballet on *Faust* to be written by Heinrich Heine, and Verdi's new opera, *King Lear* (Lumley, *Reminiscences,* pp. 142, 143). The *Athenaeum* announced on 7 February 1846

---

[29] C. L. Gruneisen, *The Opera and the Press* (London: Robert Hardwicke, 1869), p. 5.

[30] Willert Beale, *The Light of Other Days: Seen Through the Wrong End of an Opera Glass,* 2 vols. (London: Richard Bentley, 1890), I, 43.

(along with another public letter from Lumley complaining about Costa) that
"the opera to be written by Signor Verdi for her Majesty's Theatre is said to be
on the story of 'King Lear.'" Chorley is already skeptical about it: "As it is an
opera *to be* written, let us point out to all concerned, the risk of selecting a
story in which the female interest is subservient" (p. 157). Lumley was to be
disappointed in all his hopes: Heine's ballet, Rubini's return, Verdi's opera—
each was cancelled or postponed.

The reception of Lumley's season in the popular press this year seems
to bear out accusations by Chorley and Gruneisen that Lumley could do no
wrong according to other journalists. Thus when Lumley brought out two
more operas by Verdi, *Nabucco* and *I Lombardi*, the press received them favorably, for the most part. *The Times* praised the March 3rd opening night of
*Nabucco* (presented as *Nino* "in conformity with the feelings of the English as
to the unsuitability of Biblical subjects for theatrical representation"), noting
that "the work was received with a stronger feeling of approbation than has
been displayed on the production of any new Italian opera for a long time"
(4 March 1846, p. 5). The *Illustrated London News* found it "characterized by
merits of the highest order" (7 March 1846, p. 162). *Nino* was praised even
more fervently in the next issue: a "splendid chorus" here, a "glorious burst of
harmony" there, "charming melody" everywhere, and a "splendid crescendo"
which was "grandly effective." The unison in "Va Pensiero" gave the piece a
"wild simplicity of character" that was especially appealing (14 March 1846,
p. 175). The critic liked *I Lombardi* better each time he saw it, in particular
the "concerted pieces" (23 May 1846, p. 341), and *The Times* critic affirmed
that "the success is unquestionable" (13 May 1846, p. 5).[31]

But Chorley, unmoved by this kind of response—which he saw as the
product of Lumley's "army of trumpeters in the Press who play in any key the
manager pleases"[32]—attacked with severe and somewhat savage thorough-
ness. Of *Nino* he wrote: "But with every sympathy in favour of a new style,
and a new master, our first hearing of the 'Nino' has done nothing to change
our judgment of the limited nature of Signor Verdi's resources" (*Athenaeum*,
7 March 1846, p. 250). Verdi's occasional effective passages are ruined because there is not enough contrast: everything is noisy. Later in the season, *I
Lombardi* was even worse: "more tawdry in instrumentation than either
'Ernani' or 'Nabucco' and less substantial in idea." Grisi is uncomfortable in
the role of Giselda because "happily for the world, she was not trained in the

---

[31] Another report notes that the success of *I Lombardi* was increased by the fact that "the principal parts in it
are sustained by Grisi and Mario, while those of *Nino* and *Ernani* were filled by the mere before-Easter
*tolerables*" (*Examiner*, 16 May 1846, p. 308, italics in original).

[32] *Athenaeum*, 27 June 1846, p. 665.

unmitigated screaming in which Young Italy delighteth" (16 May 1846, p. 507).

Chorley's dislike of Verdi was matched by his contempt for Lumley's proceedings "which, up to this point, entitle the season of 1846 to be called the most meagre in interest of any during the last twelve years" (*Athenaeum*, 25 April 1846, p. 434). A little later (after a performance of *Barbiere*) he notes: "The orchestra is now more frequently before or after the singers, than with them" (2 May 1846, p. 459). And after major last-minute cast substitutions: "Those who have watched the courageous downward progress of the management of our Italian Opera, assuredly *should*, by this time, be almost beyond the reach of further surprise" (27 May 1846, p. 530).

On 2 May 1846, Chorley announced that he had wind of bad news for Lumley: "It is generally rumoured that the opera 'written expressly for London' is not to be expected this year" (*Athenaeum*, p. 459). Lumley could not deny it: "As evil fortune would have it," he remembered, "about this time Verdi's health gave way; he was unequal to the arduous task, and the opera was not forthcoming" (Lumley, *Reminiscences*, pp. 142–143).

In January 1846, while Verdi was in Venice preparing for the first performances of *Attila*, he became very ill (*Copialettere*, p. 16). Although it was not unusual for Verdi to have various symptoms of illness while he was preparing a new opera—his illness the previous year had delayed the production of *Alzira* at San Carlo in Naples[33]—this time the recuperation period dragged on longer than ever before. One might wonder whether the long convalescence was partly a psychological necessity: he was not really ready to write the opera for London and needed a pretext. Frank Walker disputes this possibility as "impertinent."[34] Whatever caused the illness and the prolonged recovery, an opera for London was out of the question. Verdi wrote to Lumley on 9 April 1846, with the bad news:

Milan, 9 April 1846

Signor Lumley,
    I know that the news I am about to give you will not be unexpected, namely that because of the illness suffered in Venice, I am not able to come to London, and still less to write the opera there. The same day Signor Lucca will send you two medical certificates given him, which will authenticate things. You cannot imagine how distressed I am to have to renounce the honour of writing for London. My health is improving so slowly that it makes me incapable of even the slightest occupation, and I am forced to remain here idle, scrupulously following a medical cure until it is time to go to Recoaro to drink the waters, etc. . . . .

[33] See the exchange of letters with the impresario Vincenzio Flauto, *Copialettere*, pp. 9–12.

[34] "In the face of all this evidence, suggestions that Verdi was not honestly justified in his action seem impertinent" (Walker, *The Man Verdi*, p. 147). Walker's point of view seems to be that if the illness were real, its origin could not have been psychosomatic.

I hope that this inconvenience will not cause any harm to our relationship, and praying you to respond with two lines about the matter, I style myself with all respect yours faithfully.[35]

Lucca forwarded this letter on to Lumley in London, enclosing a medical certificate from Dr. Giacinto Namìas of Venice (22 March 1846) and another from Dr. Gaspare Belcredi of Milan (6 April 1846) (*Copialettere*, p. 19). From Lumley came two letters—sympathizing but also urging Verdi to reconsider. In the first (14 April), Lumley hoped that Verdi would still come for the change of scene and the brilliance of the London season.[36] A month later, he wrote again with news of the great popularity of *I Lombardi*, proposing a non-medical cure—the enthusiastic English applause awaiting him.[37] David Kimbell feels that Lumley's first letter displays "effusive and insensitive breeziness,"[38] but it could just as easily be said to display the dignified but understandable desperation of a manager about to lose one of the main novelties of a season in bad trouble. For Lumley, Verdi's illiness could not have come at a worse time. Verdi himself, though, insisted that the trip was off, writing on 22 May that "the natural curiosity to see an extraordinary city like London, my self-esteem, and my self-interest would be sufficient motives not to delay the execution of my contract with Signor Lucca. But my health prevents me, and I have a need for absolute repose."[39]

Muzio, too, was disappointed that the London trip was off. Lucca had offered to pay his expenses as a travelling companion and 2,000 francs. But if Verdi could not go, Muzio wrote, so be it: rather than have Verdi suffer—to the devil "with all the money in the world, because to me he is dearer than the whole universe!"[40]

Muzio's effusive letters to Barezzi at this time—full of news about Verdi's stream of successes everywhere—make a striking foil to Chorley's grim

---

[35] Translation of first paragraph from Weaver, *Verdi*, pp. 165–166. Original in *Copialettere*, p. 19.

[36] "C'est avec un vif regret que j'ai appris votre maladie au moment ou je comptais avoir le plaisir de vous revoir ici presque immediatement. Je suis bien aise d'apprendre que vous y portez le soins que requiert une organisation aussi sensible que celle d'un genie créatif comme le vôtre. Veuillez agreer l'expression de toute ma sympathie . . .
Je suis sûr que le changement de scène et une visite à Londres pendant une saison aussi belle et aussi prospère (je n'en ai jamais connu de plus brillante à notre Theatre) vous fera plus de bien que tous les remedes imaginables" (*Copialettere*, pp. 20–21).

[37] "J'espère que cette nouvelle [success of *I Lombardi*] vous fera plaisir et qu'elle agira si efficacement comme antidote à votre indisposition, que vous viendrez ici en prendre une bien plus forte dose en forme d'applaudissement; ce qui ne peut vous manquer" (13 May 1846, *Compialettere*, p. 22).

[38] Kimbell, *Verdi in the Age of Italian Romanticism*, p. 193.

[39] Original in *Copialettere*, p. 22. That Verdi was doing nothing at this time is corroborated by Muzio's letter to Barezzi (16 April 1846) in which he reports that Verdi "does not do anything—he does not write, he does not apply himself, but just amuses himself by going for walks and drives" (Garibaldi, p. 238, my translation).

[40] Muzio to Barezzi, 14 May 1846, original in Garibaldi, p. 245.

summing up of the 1846 season at Her Majesty's: Verdi's operas are not likely to hold the stage much longer in London. "Let us here, again, repeat, in present substantiation of our prophecies with regard to Signor Verdi's career, that his four last operas,—'I due Foscari,' 'Giovanno [sic] d'Arco,' 'Alzira,' and 'Attila,' have more or less failed in Italy;—the last most signally" (*Athenaeum*, 22 August 1846, p. 869).

During Lumley's post-season visit to the Continent, he pursued Jenny Lind in earnest, knowing that she was determined not to honor her contract with Bunn at Drury Lane. Writing on 6 October 1846, to her friend Madame Birch-Pfeiffer, Lind announced that she was going to Vienna to sing in Meyerbeer's *Feldlager von Schlesien*—"and all the more, because it has fallen through in London [with Bunn]" (Lind-Goldschmidt, II, 3–4). She ended her letter with an indication of the direction in which her thoughts were moving: "Lumley (the Director of the Italian Opera in London), what has he not offered! And what an amiable man he is! He came here; but I have sent him to Italy, to look for a singer there. But, he still hopes to get me; and, if you should hear that I have really gone mad, I may then go to London" (II, 4). Three weeks later, it was definite, as she wrote her close friend, Madame Wichmann:

> Munich, October 27, 1846
>
> . . . Now let me tell you that I am going to London; and that Mendelssohn alone was able to induce me to do so. For you know what confidence I place in his advice; and, besides that, things have really so shaped themselves, that I can clearly see that God Himself has so ordained it—and, against one's destiny, one can do nothing.
>
> (Lind-Goldschmidt, II, 6).

Mendelssohn (although in his long letter to Lind dated 31 October 1846 he mentioned that he had a number of reservations about certain points in her contract) strongly supported this step in her career and predicted that "you will be greeted, in England, musically and personally, with such love, and jubilation, and rapture, as has seldom fallen even to you" (Lind-Goldschmidt, II, 7).

In the same letter Mendelssohn mentioned the frustration he was feeling about the libretto Madame Birch-Pfeiffer was supposed to be writing for him:

> I should indeed be glad if I could soon, in accordance with my most hearty wish, write something dramatic—and especially, for you. Of what I can do in that way I will neglect nothing; of that I assure you; for I should at all times have gladly written dramatic music, but now more gladly than ever. And then I have a secret foreboding, which tells me that, if I do not attain to the composition of a fairly good Opera, *now*, and *for you*, I shall never accomplish it at all.
>
> (Lind-Goldschmidt, II, 9–10).

News of Lumley's contract with Lind was clearly important for Verdi. He wrote Lumley on 11 November 1846 that he was willing to compose an opera and he must have the right to choose the best artists in the company, among them Lind and Gaetano Fraschini (*Copialettere*, p. 30). He mentioned it again in a letter to Lucca on December 2nd and again on December 3rd, telling Lucca moreover that he had finished about one-third of *Masnadieri* (*Copialettere*, p. 32). The next day he wrote to Lumley again that, since his illness had annulled the previous contract, he was no longer bound to compose *Il Corsaro* (which had replaced *Lear* as the subject for London). He was, however, willing to complete *Masnadieri*, of which he had already composed "about one half" (*Copialettere*, pp. 33–34). If Lumley would agree to the opera and would give Verdi the pick of the company, specifically Lind and Fraschini, then the contract was to be on again for the coming season.

Since either Shakespeare's *Lear* or Byron's *Corsair* would have been more obviously suited to the interests of an English audience, Lumley's acceptance of Verdi's new proposal was not enthusiastic. "Verdi now offered his 'Masnadieri,'" Lumley recalled later, "and with this proposal I was obliged to close" (*Reminiscences*, p. 192).

## IV

The developments of 1846 laid the foundations for the failure of *I Masnadieri* in 1847. This year Chorley intensified the battle against Lumley's house begun so forcefully the year before. Chorley announced in the January 23rd issue of the *Athenaeum* that Lumley was promising for the coming season a new opera by Verdi, an appearance by Meyerbeer, a new opera by Mendelssohn (this news genuinely pleased him), and the English debut of Jenny Lind.[41] But he turned this announcement against Lumley, implying (and later openly stating) that Lumley was using deceptive advertising in order to win subscribers to the season; on 13 February Chorley asked rhetori-

---

[41] On 12 April 1847, the critic for the *Morning Chronicle* (probably Gruneisen)—by this time Chorley's ally in the theater war—reprinted Lumley's prospectus for the 1847 season as evidence that Lumley had not kept his promises (Jenny Lind arrived in London on April 16th): "That great composer, the Chevalier MEYERBEER, has arranged to visit this country to bring out the *Camp de Silesie*, and another of his admired *chef d'oeuvres*. The principal parts in the Camp de Silesie by Mademoiselle JENNY LIND and Signor FRASCHINI. The celebrated Dr. FELIX MENDELSSOHN BARTHOLDY will likewise visit England, and produce an opera expressly composed for her Majesty's Theatre, the libretto founded on the *Tempest* of SHAKESPEARE, written by M. SCRIBE: *Miranda*, Mademoiselle JENNY LIND; *Ferdinand*, Signor GARDONI; *Caliban*, Herr STAUDIGL; and *Prospero*, Signor LABLACHE. It is likewise announced with great satisfaction that Signor VERDI, having recovered from his severe illness, has expressly composed for this theatre a new opera, of which the plot is founded on "The Robbers," of SCHILLER. ROSSINI's opera of *Robert Bruce* [a pasticcio], lately produced at the Academie Royale, has also been secured. Mademoiselle JENNY LIND, whose engagement commences in March and extends until the end

cally "what became of the promise of Meyerbeer, with his 'Camp de Silésie'—what of Verdi with his 'Robbers'—what, even, of the one substantial hope of the theatre, Mdlle Jenny Lind?" (*Athenaeum*, 13 February 1847, p. 179). It seems that Chorley was eager to criticize Lumley for not keeping his promises for the season, before the season had even begun. When Chorley did print something positive about Her Majesty's, it was often done in such a way as to praise Covent Garden at the same time, as in his concession that "on the whole, the amount of variety produced before Easter, and the general quality of the performances, have been creditable to the energy of the management—and, we think, without precedent. Great is the virtue of opposition!—let the monopolists be ever so shocked thereat" (27 March 1847, p. 344).

By 1847 a widespread perception of Verdi had evolved among most journalists. It can be summarized as follows: Verdi was crude and unable to write original melodies, but he was able to write highly dramatic and effective concerted pieces. Representative statements of what is in a way a consensus of opinion may be found in the *Examiner*:

> The invention of striking melodies is not Verdi's strong point, and herein he has a disadvantage when compared with the generality of modern Italian composers. But the richness of his instrumentation, the power evinced in the construction of his concerted pieces, and the dramatic colouring he gives them, will command admiration among all unprejudiced hearers. There is *writing* in his work, which shows that he is daring to soar above the petty trivialities that have so long held possession of the stage of his country.
>
> (*Examiner*, 7 March 1846, p. 149).

And again, a few weeks later:

> Of original melody, there is scarcely a bar to be found in his entire works. Nay, he perpetually repeats himself . . . His erudition, such as it is does not take him far, and he goes

---

of the season, will appear immediately after Easter. In addition to the above, several operas, new to this country, will be produced, and the repertoire will be selected from the *chef d'oeuvres* of MOZART, CIMAROSA, ROSSINI, DONIZETTI, MERCADANTE, BELLINI, &c." (*Morning Chronicle*, 12 April 1847, p. 6).

As early as 13 February 1847, Chorley called Lumley's announcement about *The Tempest* into question, wondering "whether even, any *libretto* has been accepted" by Mendelssohn (*Athenaeum*, p. 179). About a month later he announced: "It is now, too, known beyond mistake—Dr. Mendelssohn's letters, which we have seen, being our warrant—that there will be no 'Tempest' this year: there having been (as we mentioned some weeks since) no engagement on the composer's part to produce such a work" (*Athenaeum*, 20 March 1847, p. 315). Lumley seems to have had a clear conscience, recalling bitterly that "both these reports [that is, of Lind's engagement and Mendelssohn's opera] were denied with singular acrimony by the Covent-Gardenite sharpshooters of the pen—and yet both were substantially true" (Lumley, *Reminiscences*, p. 159). Lumley said that Mendelssohn did not write him until 21 February to say that the opera would not be ready (Lumley, *Reminiscences*, p. 167). But Chorley, too, had a clear conscience about his accusations, writing several years later: "I passed the last three days of August, 1847, beside Mendelssohn at Interlachen in Switzerland and heard first-hand of Mendelssohn's irritation at the 'unauthorized use of his name' in announcing *The Tempest*"("The Last Days of Mendelssohn," in *Modern German Music*, 2 vols. [1854; rpt. ed., New York: Da Capo, 1973], II, 388).

back to his darling unison. His merit—and every first opera confirms this opinon—is his feeling for the drama which his music is to illustrate . . . His attention is directed not merely to his principal vocalists, but to the choruses, which form, as it were, the substances to his drama; and he elaborates these, not so much by "writing," as by balancing masses of sound of different quality, one against the other.

(*Examiner*, 16 May 1846, p. 308).

Chorley's position is closely related to this one, except that he takes everything in an entirely hostile way, emphasizing the severity of the melodic failings and de-emphasizing the excellences of the dramatic interest—adding a special note of fury over Verdi's writing for (or against) the singers' voices.[42] He began the year with a fresh attack, occasioned by a letter he printed from an anonymous reader stating that *I Due Foscari* was successful in Paris: "I think it much to be regretted that you should, for some incomprehensible reason or other, *systematically* decry a composer who, with many defects, has great merits . . . On the whole he is far superior to all the living composers" (*Athenaeum*, 2 January 1847, p. 24). Chorley printed the letter in order to have the pleasure of replying. Verdi "represents the extremes of that extravagant school of writing which, under pretext of dramatic effect, has all but ruined the singers of Italy." Verdi "*tears* his voices" and uses "trombones in unison with the voices,—no matter what the subject." His melody is "simple and clear plagiarism of the most wornout commonplaces of modern composers" (*Athenaeum*, 2 January 1847, p. 24). Chorley's opinions that season were reinforced by what amounted to an early Verdi festival at Her Majesty's: *Nino, Ernani, I Due Foscari, I Lombardi* ("*matter-less* . . . flimsy . . . full of pretense"),[43] and, of course, *I Masnadieri*.

On 6 April 1847, the new company at Covent Garden opened its first season with Rossini's *Semiramide* and interest switched to the new house. The performance was a great success, with Grisi at her best and Marietta Alboni making a tremendously successful debut as Arsace. Chorley's praise for the orchestra is significant (he relished mocking Michael Balfe at Her Majesty's for beating his foot loudly to keep the musicians playing together[44]): "The Orchestra is unquestionably the best ever assembled in England . . . and the general *ensemble* . . . something never heretofore attained by any Italian per-

---

[42] This charge persisted. More than fifty years later, George Bernard Shaw wrote in the *Anglo-Saxon Review* (March 1901) that "until Boito became his artistic conscience he wrote inhumanly for the voice and ferociously for the orchestra. . . . He practically treated that upper fifth as the whole voice, and pitched his melodies in the middle of it instead of the middle of the whole compass, the result being a frightful strain on the singer" (Reprinted in George Bernard Shaw, *London Music in 1888–89 As Heard by Corno de Bassetto* [New York: Dodd, Mead, 1937], pp. 414–415).

[43] *Athenaeum*, 10 July 1847 (italics in original).

[44] "Mr. Balfe in the last impassioned scene [of *Norma*] *outstamping* the drums, by way of keeping matters together" (*Athenaeum*, 19 June 1847, p. 653, italics in original).

formances in this country" (*Athenaeum*, 10 April 1847, p. 394). This "ensemble" aspect of the new house elicited extensive comment. That from the *Illustrated London News* is particularly valuable for what it adds to our understanding of mid-century performance practice because of its details about the composition of the orchestra:

> To eulogize the band too strongly would be impossible. Costa has achieved a most important improvement in the balance of instruments; by adding to the strength of the stringed ones, the braying of brass has been balanced. We never heard such first violins for brilliancy, and the luscious tones of the tenors and violoncelli, and the power and crispness of the double-basses, were quite as delightful . . . and we rank the Covent Garden band as now the first in the world. There are fifteen first violins, with Sainton at the head; fourteen second, with Ella; ten violas, with Hill; ten violoncelli, with Lindley; nine double-basses, with Anfossi; with the usual complement of wind instruments [for a total of eighty players].[45]

Covent Garden presented two operas by Verdi during its first season: *Ernani*, in which Alboni sang Charles the Fifth,[46] and *I Due Foscari*, in which, according to the *Morning Chronicle*, the singers—Grisi, Mario, and Giorgio Ronconi—"created an immense sensation" (23 June 1847, p. 5). But Chorley, while granting that Ronconi's acting was "sublime" and his singing was not bad, felt that the performance generally "strengthens our judgment of the utter worthlessness of the music" (*Athenaeum*, 26 June 1847, p. 683).

Verdi and Muzio arrived in London in early June (Muzio first, in order to reassure Verdi that Jenny Lind was indeed going to be singing in the new opera). Muzio's view of the activities at Covent Garden is interesting. Although he was pleased by the excellent performance of *I Due Foscari*,[47] he

---

[45] *Illustrated London News*, 10 April 1847, p. 234. The string-brass balance was different from that of many pit orchestras in Italy, where there were frequently more basses than cellos. Kimbell, *Verdi in the Age of Italian Romanticism*, p. 48; see also Gregory W. Harwood, "The Nineteenth Century Italian Opera Orchestra" [abstract], *Verdi Newsletter*, 11 (March 1983), 26–27. A few days later, the *Morning Chronicle* announced: "This undertaking has commenced triumphantly. It has the support of royalty, rank and fashion—it has the entire sympathies of the musical circles, whether composed of artists or amateurs. . . . From *The Morning Chronicle* it will continue to receive every encouragement and support, so long as we conscientiously believe that the interests of the public, the promotion of art, and the protection of artists are the leading principles of action. We are neither the organ, the tool, nor the parasites of the new temple of art. We were firm believers in the imperious necessity for its formation, to put an end to a grasping monopoly, and to a most corrupt and degraded system of puffery, the success of which would not only have swamped lyrical art, to establish in its place the sensual ballet, but would also have destroyed every vestige of independent criticism. We have stood alone in our course of action, and now we find ourselves with many allies" (*Morning Chronicle*, 12 April 1847, p. 6). The shrill tone of these remarks is a good reflection of the touchiness that many journalists were feeling at this period.

[46] Muzio recorded matter-of-factly that in London there is no difference between contralto and bass ("A Londra contralto e basso è lo stesso"), Garibaldi, p. 337. Chorley, however, cautioned that "such experiments ought not to be made by a management professing itself careful of musical integrity" (*Athenaeum*, 10 July 1847, pp. 737–738). The reprimand is mild; substitution of a contralto for a bass at her Majesty's might have been seen as one more example of artistic bankruptcy.

[47] Muzio to Barezzi, 29 June 1847, Garibaldi, p. 336.

insisted that the old guard at Covent Garden "are all enemies of Verdi's music" and that they refused to perform *Foscari* more than twice because of their jealousy. Costa, moreover, was a Neapolitan and "since they are jealous, proud, and neither able to do good things nor sing well, they do not want others to do well either."[48]

The day after the first performance of *Masnadieri*, Muzio wrote to Barezzi that "the opera created a furor"—the orchestra, singers, and press reception: everything was "bietifol" (Garibaldi, pp. 344, 345, 349). Verdi himself clearly had expected success and was preparing to negotiate a very high price for his future services at Her Majesty's. To Clarina Maffei he wrote on July 17th (five days before the premiere): "It is true that they have offered me 40 thousand francs for an opera and that I have not accepted. But do not be amazed, because it is not an excessive sum and if I were to return I should want much more" (*Copialettere,* p. 459, my translation).

*I Masnadieri* was received with great applause on the first night; it was, however, not really a success and was never revived in Victorian England. Ivan Turgenev, then on his first of several visits to London, saw the opera and wrote to Pauline Viardot-Garcia that it "had a very nice little fiasco."[49] Queen Victoria confided to her journal that the music was "very inferior and commonplace."[50] Chorley told his readers that "we take it to be the worst opera which has been given in our time at Her Majesty's Theatre" (*Athenaeum,* 24 July 1847, p. 795), and later, in *Thirty Years' Musical Recollections* he insisted that it was "perhaps his [Verdi's] most paltry work" ("*Thirty Years'*, 1862, I, 296). Even Lumley, who had gone to so much trouble for so long, did not choose to defend it. He noted that, although it was given "with every appearance of a triumphant success," it was a failure, not just in England but also in Italy.[51] Lumley's comments on Verdi's use of the great but very fat bass

[48] Writing to Barezzi on 18 June 1847, Muzio claimed that Costa had accompanied Lind at a private performance in the presence of the Queen, and "avendo appositamente accompagnata male la Lynd, è caduto in disgrazia della Regina. . . . Da un *Napoletano* la Lynd non si poteva sicuramente aspettare delle belle cose, giacchè essi sono invidiosi, superbi, e non potendo nè fare belle cose, ne cantar bene, non vogliono neanche che gli altri facciano bene" (Garibaldi, p. 343). Queen Victoria took an interest in the theater war, as is demonstrated in one paragraph of a letter to her uncle (the King of Belgium): "To-night we are going to the Opera in state, and will hear and see Jenny Lind (who is perfection) in *Norma,* which is considered one of her best parts. Poor Grisi is quite going off, and after the pure angelic voice and extremely quiet, perfect acting of J. Lind, she seems quite *passée.* Poor thing! she is *quite* furious about it, and was excessively impertinent to J. Lind" (12 June 1847, *The Letters of Queen Victoria* [first series], eds. Arthur Christopher Benson and Viscount Esher [London: John Murray, 1907], II, 144, italics in original, my translation).

[49] Quoted in Patrick Waddington, *Turgenev and England* (New York: New York University Press, 1981), p. 10.

[50] Quoted in Vincent Godefroy, *The Dramatic Genius of Verdi: Studies of Selected Operas,* 2 vols. (London: Victor Gollancz, 1975–77), I, 164.

[51] Lumley, *Reminiscences,* p. 193. That the opera was, in fact, reasonably successful in Italy is suggested by the list of printed librettos published in "The Verdi Archive at New York University: Part II" by Martin

Lablache is often quoted: "Lablache, as the imprisoned father, had to do about the only thing he could not do to perfection—having to represent a man nearly starved to death" (*Reminiscences*, p. 193). But according to the *Morning Chronicle*, Lablache's portrayal of Maximilian Moor was a redeeming feature of the evening: his character "was the only one commanding the sympathies of the audience" (23 July 1847, p. 5). *The Times* greeted the opera with a long, respectful notice, citing points of similarity with Schiller's play,[52] and pointing out that the world of "rank and fashion" was in attendance. The critic's only negative remarks were somewhat tentative: "Whatever opinion may be entertained of the merits of this opera, this fact is certain,—that the manager in its production has acted in a manner worthy of the director of such an establishment" (23 July 1847, p. 5). The *Illustrated London News* reported that "the opera was highly successful" (24 July 1847, p. 58). But the *Examiner's* critic did not think that the opera had much chance of "living beyond the occasion" (24 July 1847, p. 469).

The reaction of the press was, therefore, not uniformly negative, though it was certainly not as enthusiastic as Muzio wanted Barezzi to believe. And yet certainly the fact that Chorley damned the opera so severely could not in itself have made it unpopular with London audiences, since his previous hostility towards Verdi, manifested over several years, cannot be shown to have had a decisive effect on Verdi's appeal to English audiences. It seems most likely that the reason for *I Masnadieri's* being dropped the next few seasons were basically twofold: the lack of concerted numbers in the opera and the relative unimportance of the prima donna's role.

As we have seen, Verdi had made his reputation in London largely though not exclusively on the strength of the excitement created by the con-

---

Chusid, Luke Jensen, and David Day, *Verdi Newsletter*, 9/10 (November 1981–82), 31. Escudier wrote Verdi about a successful revival of *Masnadieri* (as *Les brigands*) as late as 1870. Stephen Casale, "A Newly-Discovered Letter from Verdi to Léon Escudier," *Verdi Newsletter*, 11 (March 1983), 10, note 7.

[52] Since the 1780s, Schiller's *Die Raüber* had exercised a real fascination on many English writers and critics. It was, for example, one of the major influences on Wordsworth's long poem, *The Borderers* (1795–96). An English translation of *Die Raüber* was even still occasionally performed (in 1851 at Drury Lane, for example). (See Frederic Ewen, *The Prestige of Schiller in England 1789–1859* [New York: Columbia University Press, 1932], xii, 78, 142, and following.) The reviews of *Masnadieri* generally gave some attention to Maffei's adaptation: *The Times* notes that "the opening portion of the second act of the opera is taken from Schiller's third, with considerable alteration . . . Several incidents in the third act of the original play are here packed closely together" (*The Times*, 23 July 1847, p. 5). Nevertheless, many in the audience of "rank and fashion" at Her Majesty's would have seen the plot as quaint and the source as of no concern. Indeed, one reviewer claimed that the opera's final trio was "more provocative of hilarity than of tragic emotion" (*Morning Chronicle*, 23 July 1847, p. 5). Muzio, by contrast, called it the high point of the opera ("In tutte le sue opere il Maestro ha qualche terzetto che è un capo d'opera, ma questo è il capo d'opera di tutti gli altri capi d'opera" [Muzio to Barezzi, 23 July 1847, Garibaldi, pp. 348–349]).

certed pieces in his operas. In *I Masnadieri*, the energetic bandit choruses made a relatively weak impression compared with that produced by Verdi's earlier full-scale ensemble finales in operas such as *Ernani* and *Nino*. The audience's expectations were not met; the critics did not have time to hear what was there, being too busy noticing what was missing.

Furthermore, casting Jenny Lind as Amalia looked like a good idea on paper, but was in fact a big mistake. Although Lind apparently told Muzio that she was pleased with the way the role of Amalia suited her voice,[53] the critic for the *Illustrated London News* felt that the music seemed "written, we suspect, rather with a view to its performance by *prime donne* of a less extended compass of voice, and therefore not embracing Jenny Lind's higher notes" (31 July 1847, p. 78). There is, in fact, only one passage in *I Masnadieri* requiring extraordinary virtuosity: Amalia's cabaletta "Carlo vive!" near the beginning of Act II ("evidently based," the *Morning Chronicle* smugly remarked, on Bellini's "Ah, non giunge!").[54] Certainly, Amalia's role is by no means disproportionately small for an ensemble opera (and *The Times* felt it had to remind readers that "it must always be remembered that Verdi writes more for an *ensemble* than for bringing forward any single personage, and hence there are not those opportunities for individual display which are to be found in the works of earlier composers").[55] Nevertheless, Jenny Lind's unprecedented power over an audience made people eager to see her in roles like Marie in Donizetti's *Figlia di Regimento* or Amina in *La Sonnambula*, roles in which she was the center of attention. As *Masnadieri* progresses, the emphasis is placed increasingly on the tenor, not the soprano. The appetite whetted for Lind in the first two acts was largely disappointed by the last two. During any other season with any other singer, even Grisi, this issue might not have been crucial to the opera's successful reception. This season it was. By the time it might have been logical to think about reviving *Masnadieri*—after Lind's retirement—there was no reason to. For Lumley, the opera represented a major disappointment; for Covent Garden, an affront. And for audiences, it soon became irrelevant, as Verdi's thrilling operas of the 1850s—*Rigoletto, Traviata,* and *Il Trovatore*—came along, erasing most recollections of Verdi in the forties.

Verdi conducted two performances of *Masnadieri*, then left for Paris to begin preparing *Jérusalem*. From Paris on 2 August, he wrote Lumley, expressing his willingness to write an opera a year for the next three years (2 August

---

[53] Muzio to Barezzi, 19 [July] 1847, Garibaldi, p. 343.

[54] *Morning Chronicle*, 23 July 1847, p. 5.

[55] *The Times*, 23 July 1847, p. 5.

1847, *Copialettere*, p. 43). Lumley's reply was polite but evasive. No contract was offered.

Probably, Verdi did not understand what a disappointment this opera had been to Lumley. Nor, probably, did he care.[56] Only a few seasons later, he composed *Rigoletto*. And from that time on, the world realized that Verdi really was as important as he thought he was. Problems caused by an idolized singer, a desperate manager, and a hostile critic were easy to forget.[57]

---

[56] Verdi to Escudier, 11 December 1869: "As for the Masnadieri I hope it succeeds. I can tell you nothing about it as I do not have it before me and don't remember it. I know that the last two acts are better than the first two, and perhaps it will be necessary to make some cuts in these earlier acts, if only in the repetition of the so-called Cabalette—Keep me posted." Verdi clearly was not thinking of Amalia as the opera's central role. Translation from Stephen Casale, "A Newly-Discovered Letter from Verdi to Léon Escudier," *Verdi Newsletter*, 11 (March 1983), 9.

[57] The author wishes to thank the National Endowment for the Humanities and Diana Natalicio, Dean of the College of Liberal Arts, University of Texas at El Paso, for their financial support and the American Institute for Verdi Studies at New York University for providing research facilities, as well as Martin Chusid, Luke Jensen, and Julian Budden for their kindness in answering questions and suggesting improvements during the preparation of this article.

Nicholas Temperley

# MUSICAL NATIONALISM IN ENGLISH ROMANTIC OPERA

MUSIC HISTORIANS ARE AWARE OF A GROUP OF COMPOSERS OF THE LATER NINE-teenth century who are usually called the Nationalists. These men asserted their national identity in the face of German or Italian dominance by empha-sizing colorful aspects of their country's folk music, as well as by choosing na-tionally significant subject matter. The primary examples of the nationalist school are the five Russian composers sometimes called the "Mighty Handful," of whom the most famous are Modest Musorgsky (1839–81), Alexander P. Borodin (1834–87), and Nikolay A. Rimsky-Korsakov (1844–1908). Lesser nationalist schools of the same period include the Czech, led by Bedřich Smetana (1824–84) and Antonin Dvořák (1841–1904); the Hungarian, led by Franz Liszt (1811–86); the Norwegian, led by Edvard Grieg (1843–1907); and the Spanish, led by Felipe Pedrell (1841–1922).

In the most recent text of nineteenth-century musical history, Leon Plantinga's *Romantic Music,* there is an admirable chapter on Nationalism which includes a section on English music of the later nineteenth century. Plantinga makes the following point:

> The usual factors in the growth of cultural nationalism—status as a developing nation, struggle against a foreign oppressor, feelings of cultural inferiority—were of course lack-ing in England. It was mainly in a quickening of interest in the "Celtic fringes" that certain nationalist traits appeared in music, and this occurred only late in the century.[1]

As examples he refers to Charles Villiers Stanford's *Irish Symphony* of 1887, Alexander Mackenzie's *Scottish Piano Concerto* of 1897, and some late nineteenth-century orchestral pieces of Hamish MacCunn. English national-ism, as opposed to Irish or Scottish, is relegated to the twentieth century. I propose to challenge this interpretation.

[1] Leon Plantinga, *Romantic Music* (New York: W. W. Norton & Company, 1984), p. 400.

The word "nationalism" implies the existence of a nation, and so it is not generally used to refer to the efforts of minorities within a nation to assert their rights. The nationalism of the Russians had nothing to say about the various oppressed minorities that formed part of the Tsar's Empire. It accepted the existence of the Russian state, and resisted the cultural subservience of that state to Western European influences—to the French language that was still used at court and by many Russian aristocrats, and to the Italian opera and German instrumental music that enjoyed overwhelming prestige in the musical life of the great cities. Russian nationalism was a movement of the middle classes and intelligentsia. It made no difference to Russian peasants whether the operas performed at Moscow and Leningrad were in Italian or Russian, nor whether they were based on coloratura arias or Russian folk songs. But the newly powerful businessmen, professionals, and civil servants were riled to find that their own language and culture were excluded from the high position which they should rightly have occupied in the cultural life of the nation.

One can discern three stages in the process of throwing off a foreign musical domination. In the first stage, the primary goal is to establish that a native product can be as good as a foreign import. This cannot be done by writing nationalistic music, because such would be rejected by most of the public as primitive or irrelevant. For instance, in Russia in the eighteenth and early nineteenth centuries, the only kind of opera that enjoyed prestige was Italian. Russian musicians were forced to prove their worth by actually writing Italian operas, or at least by imitating Italian style. This was the path taken by Dmitry Bortnyansky (1752–1825) and his Russian contemporaries.

When the status of native composers has been established, the second stage sees the beginning of musical nationalism, in which elements of folk-song and dance are introduced, and subjects of national interest are chosen. This may be seen in the music of Mikhail Glinka (1803–57) and the more tentative works of the Mighty Handful; the folksong elements are imposed on a style that is still fundamentally of the "mainstream."

The third stage is marked by a radical change of style, in which the classical forms, harmonies, and compositional techniques are replaced by newly created ones inspired by the national folk material, or by actual innovation. In my view, *Boris Godunov* (1874) is the first work of any country in which this third stage is fully developed. In Hungarian music, for example, it was not Liszt in the nineteenth century, but Bartók in the twentieth, who forged a radically nationalistic idiom.

Let us see how some of these ideas apply to the Anglo-Saxon countries in, say, the 1860s. The situation in Great Britain and the United States was not unlike that in Russia, despite great political differences. Britain, like Russia, was a large and powerful empire and was in no doubt of its political strength and importance; the United States was not yet a world power but was sure of its ability to become one, and it was not politically threatened or dominated by foreign powers. In all three countries, progressive changes were taking place: the emancipation of serfs in Russia and of slaves in America; in Britain (after 1866), rapid extension of the franchise and social reform. Musically speaking, both Britain and the U.S. were subservient to the same forces that dominated Russian music—Italian opera, German instrumental music, and French ballet (and later operetta).

Of course, in both Anglo-Saxon countries, as also in Russia and Eastern Europe, there was a subculture of indigenous musical theatre. It was always possible to hear English-language plays with music, musical entertainments and spectacles, pantomimes, burlesques, and sketches, in the smaller theatres and in taverns, pleasure gardens, warehouses, and barns. But the high ground of musical theatre—the opera and kindred forms—is the arena of musical nationalism. It was in opera that the middle classes, confident of their new strength, wanted to mount a challenge to the foreign-dominated cultural hegemony of the aristocracy.

Italian opera, of course, was *the* aristocratic musical entertainment. It had been introduced in London in the first decade of the eighteenth century and consolidated by the success of Handel's operas from 1720 onwards. For a hundred years the King's Theatre in the Haymarket enjoyed a legal monopoly for the performance of through-composed opera and exercised that monopoly by performing exclusively Italian-language operas, which were composed by Italians (with an occasional German or Bohemian) and sung primarily by Italian singers. The King's Theatre was the only London theatre patronized to any extent by the nobility; even Covent Garden and Drury Lane were socially inferior, and they concentrated on legitimate drama without music, although a species of English opera did develop there. It was left for the low-class "minor" theatres to develop genres such as the burletta and melodrama.

The first successful challenge to the dominance of Italian opera in London was begun in 1834 with the opening of the English Opera House at the Lyceum Theatre, and the successful staging there of *Nourjahad* by Edward Loder (1813–65), *The Mountain Sylph* by John Barnett (1802–90), and *Hermann* by John Thomson (1805–41). Next year came the first opera of Michael William Balfe (1808–70), who with William Vincent Wallace (1812–65), George Alexander Macfarren (1813–87), Loder, and Julius Benedict (1804–85) formed the nucleus of an English Romantic school of opera. They were not quite such a mighty handful as the Russian five, and their music has not lasted until our time. But it should be recalled that they did have considerable and lasting success; their best-known works were popular on the Continent and in the United States and were still in the standard repertory in the 1930s.

To what extent can we call these operas nationalistic? When you study the scores you are not struck by much in them that is particularly English in character. There are usually three or four strophic ballads of the "music-shop" variety, like "I dreamt that I dwelt in marble halls" from Balfe's *The Bohemian Girl* (1843), and probably a glee; these are different in kind from anything you would find in a Continental opera of the time. There is spoken dialogue. But apart from these, the style is a mixture of Italian, French, and German, with Rossini, Donizetti, Weber, Auber, and Meyerbeer as the chief models, while the librettos are almost invariably adapted from Continental dramas that were already familiar on the London stage, through imported operas or ballets, or translated plays. They generally deal with times, places, and events far removed from the experience and cultural history of the audience.

For instance, the plots of Balfe's first two English operas, *The Siege of Rochelle* (1835) and *The Maid of Artois* (1836), were based on earlier French works, and their style was strongly Italian, with the exception of a few English-style ballads. *The Musical World* commented: "Let [Balfe] forget Donizetti and Auber, follow the example of Barnett, and much may be expected from his future efforts."[2] But Barnett's *Mountain Sylph* (1834), here held up for emulation, was admired not because it was more English, but because its models were German rather than Italian or French: namely, Weber's *Freischütz* (1821) and *Oberon* (1826). Its plot had been borrowed from the highly successful French ballet *La Sylphide*, made familiar to the London public two years before. In their musical forms these English operas took from Italy the overture, the *cavatina* and *caballetta* and *gran' duetto*, the *preghiera* and barcarolle, an occasional recitative, and the concerted finale; French influence was often found in comic patter songs, choruses, and dances. When gothic or supernatural effects were needed, Weber was often the model.

Evidently, then, these Romantic English operas are not truly nationalistic, but mark the first stage of national assertion. In the words of a correspondent to *The Times* (probably Barnett), "The cant that Englishmen did not possess sufficient genius to develop a consecutive drama, with appropriate melodies and corresponding harmonies, one short season sufficed to crush."[3] However, the triumph was fragile, and the next sixty years saw a series of

---

[2] *The Musical World* 1 (1836), 191.

[3] *The Times*, 12 May 1835.

attempts to set up a National Opera Theatre, all of which either led to speedy bankruptcy of the management, or had to compromise by introducing foreign operas in translation. Thus, the need to assert that English composers could write good operas in a foreign style was going to be a pressing one for several generations to come.

The accepted historiography of British music tells us that the second and third stages of English nationalism were not reached until after 1900. Then, we are told, the folksong revival accelerated to the point where composers such as Ralph Vaughan Williams and Gustav Holst could base a new style on its modes and scales, blended with a harmonic idiom inspired by that of the sixteenth century.[4] The discovery of folksong was seen above all as a means of salvation from the late Romantic or Wagnerian style. But I will maintain that a much earlier composer, sixty years older than Vaughan Williams, had already followed a path that in all respects qualifies as the second stage of musical nationalism. He belonged, indeed, to the generation of Balfe, Wallace, and Loder.

George Alexander Macfarren, born in 1813, was presumably of Scottish descent, but his immediate forebears were English, and he identified himself strongly with England rather than Scotland. His father, George Macfarren (1788–1843), was a London dancing master, fiddler, and dramatic author, evidently a self-taught man, but a man of many parts. Macfarren was one of the early pupils at the Royal Academy of Music, which he entered in 1829. Already by that time he had had trouble with his eyesight, which steadily worsened, until he became totally blind by 1860. Nevertheless, he continued his career as a musician and composed prolifically in every major branch of music, eventually winning honors and awards, and a knighthood in 1883.

His father seems to have been a strong influence on his English musical nationalism, which developed steadily from the 1830s until the end of his career. The father, according to the son, "was a thorough patriot, and this character had impelled him to some of his early poems during the war with Bonaparte; had given enthusiasm to his writing of 'Edward the Black Prince' and 'Guy Fawkes' [both theatre pieces]; and prompted the subject of the never-acted opera of 'Caractacus.'"[5] During the 1830s William Chappell (1809–88), who was preparing the publication of his pioneering *Collection of National Airs*, asked the elder Macfarren to supply verses to folk tunes for which the original words were not known. Perhaps at the father's suggestion, the son was also brought into the enterprise and was asked to provide harmonizations of some of the tunes.

---

[4] See for instance Frank Howes, *The English Musical Renaissance* (New York: Stein & Day, 1966), chap. 12.

[5] Henry C. Banister, *George Alexander Macfarren: His Life, Works, and Influence* (London: George Bell and Sons, 1891), p. 136.

By the time Chappell's work reached its more famous form, *The Ballad Literature and Popular Music of the Olden Time* (1855–59), Macfarren had entirely reharmonized all the tunes, replacing the versions of William Crotch, which had been found "incongruously scholastic," and the "trivial" versions of Joseph Augustine Wade,[6] and also revising his own harmonizations. By this time Macfarren had studied deeply in musical history and theory, and he was able to bring to his task an almost unrivalled knowledge of the English musical styles of the past. He had edited Purcell's *Dido and Aeneas* (1689) for the Musical Antiquarian Society in 1840, and also works of the Elizabethan and Jacobean composers Orlando Gibbons, John Dowland, and Thomas East. His knowledge allowed him to develop a stylistic awareness unusual in the nineteenth century, so that instead of forcing the old folk tunes into the Classical or Romantic idiom of the time (as Haydn and Beethoven had in their arrangements of Scottish tunes), he tried (with varying success) to develop styles of harmony suited to the probable periods of origin of the tunes he was dealing with.

Not surprisingly, this began to have its effect on his original compositions as well. In 1836 he had been asked to write the overture to a theatre piece called *Chevy Chase*, by J. R. Planché, and he "determined to introduce the old English tune, which, however, he did not know, at least in connection with its name." He got his brother to hunt it up, and it "proved to be an old acquaintance." The *Chevy Chase* overture became one of Macfarren's most popular works; when Wagner conducted it at the Philharmonic Society in 1855, he wrote appreciatively of its "peculiarly wild, passionate character," though he did not take to its composer, whom he called "Macfarrinc, a pompous, melancholy Scotsman."[7]

From 1831 to 1840 Macfarren composed music for at least ten theatrical works. In this early phase he does not seem to have attempted to give his works an English character except in the one instance of *Chevy Chase*. He wrote bitterly in 1840:

> We are all aware of the low esteem in which English music is held by English people. . . . In my opinion, . . . the only thing that could make English operas receivable by the world, or place their authors on a level with men of equal talent in any other country, would be to form a colony of British composers in some great continental town, whence their works, having met the encouragement they might deserve from the world at large, would find their way home with the credential of a foreign reputation—the best, if not the only, recommendation to English favour . . . I have a spirit red-hot for the cause, and am anxious for an opportunity to jump into the struggle.[8]

---

[6] Banister, p. 135.

[7] Richard Wagner, *My Life*, "authorised translation" (London: Constable & Co. Ltd., 1911), p. 630.

[8] *The Musical World* 13 (1840), 364.

In 1849 Macfarren boldly presented a grand opera on an English sub-ject, *King Charles II,* with a libretto by Desmond Ryan. It introduced an Elizabethan-style madrigal but was still predominantly in an Italian idiom, with strong Mozartian overtones. To Macfarren Mozart was "the greatest mu-sician who has delighted and enriched the world."[9]

In 1860 Macfarren returned to opera, composing six full-length works in the next five years. All were on English subjects. In *Robin Hood* (1860) we have an opera with a thoroughly patriotic theme that would have pleased Macfarren's father. It was written by Macfarren's close friend, John Oxenford. Robin is portrayed as an Anglo-Saxon leading the struggle against arrogant Norman intruders, and Oxenford had a field day with such verses as "English-men by birth are free" (example 1). Macfarren set this in a bluff, diatonic style that was conceived as typically English, and which was perhaps a good deal influenced by his long study of folk songs, dances, and ballads. Later, in a short male chorus of Robin's retainers, there is a blatant use of a modal chord at the words "Death to thy foe."

EXAMPLE 1

The music indeed suggests a *preghiera* of Italian opera, or of the rather similar scene in Weber's *Freischütz.* Macfarren is careful to make his melody largely

In the love-interest side of the opera, Macfarren's nationalism is much more restrained. In Maid Marian's song from the second act, she is anxiously awaiting Robin's return from a dangerous exploit:

> Power benign! the wish fulfil
> Of an anxious faithful heart;
> Not upon my lover's skill,
> Not upon his eagle eye
> Doth it rely, but on thine aid,
> ·· All-bounteous as thou art.

The music indeed suggests a *preghiera* of Italian opera, or of the rather similar scene in Weber's *Freischütz.* Macfarren is careful to make his melody largely

---

[9] From a series of articles on Mozart written by Macfarren in February 1849, and cited in Banister, p. 221.

pentatonic (example 2), but his harmony sounds thoroughly "Victorian."
The nationalism of this song, if present at all, is quite tentative, but in the
more extroverted parts of the opera the nationalistic flavor is strong. The
second-act finale depicts a country fair with an archery match, which of
course is won by Robin Hood in disguise. It is constructed on a refrain that is
first sung by a unison chorus (example 3). The melody is strictly diatonic, and
in places modal; the harmony makes full use of the diatonic chords on the
second, third, and sixth scale degrees, which had been downplayed in Romantic harmony in favor of secondary dominants and chromatic chords; and
the rhythms suggest the English country dance.

EXAMPLE 2

EXAMPLE 3

*Robin Hood* had a long run after its first performance at Her Majesty's Theatre in 1860, and it enjoyed critical acclaim and some popular success, though Macfarren was never able to match the phenomenal popularity of Balfe and Wallace. It is interesting that the English musicologist Edward Dent thought *Robin Hood* the best of the pre-Sullivan Victorian operas and suggested reviving it at Sadler's Wells in the 1940s. He said it was "very full of good fun and on the way to Sullivan." [10]

Perhaps the success of *Robin Hood* encouraged Macfarren in the direction of musical nationalism. His most thoroughgoing nationalist opera was *The Soldier's Legacy*, produced in 1864. This was "on the way to Sullivan" in a more concrete sense, for it was commissioned by the German Reeds for performance at the Gallery of Illustration in Regent Street, which only five years later was to be the setting of the premiere of *Cox and Box*. The previous year, Macfarren's *Jessy Lea* was also premiered there. Full orchestral scores of these works exist in manuscript, but Macfarren also arranged the accompaniments for piano and harmonium, and it is possible that they were performed in this way at the Gallery of Illustration. Both works carry the designation "opera di camera."

*The Soldier's Legacy* appears to be an original comedy by Oxenford, though it uses stock characters and situations: the heroine Lotty has a middle-aged guardian, Christopher, on the Bartolo model, who wants to marry her himself; there is a widow who is trying to get him for a husband, and there is a romantic hero, Jack, who finally gets the girl. The plot hinges on a vow which Jack had made to a dying comrade to take care of his child, and it is compounded with the usual misunderstandings, disguises, and revelations. Although the story is set in rural England, there is nothing particularly nationalistic about it. But Macfarren went further than before in putting an English stamp on his musical style, and he succeeded in giving some individuality to his characters in the process.

The music begins with a "motto" theme (example 4) that represents the soldier's legacy of the title—the vow made by the hero on the deathbed of his fellow soldier. This theme is a solemn series of chords, largely triads, and is a sequence of the kind recognized by the Victorians as "ancient" harmony by its avoidance of chromatic dissonance, its use of triads other than I, IV, and V, and its 4-3 suspension cadence without a dominant seventh. (A more conventional harmonization of the second measure would have called for an A-major secondary dominant followed by a D-minor triad.) [11] This motto re-

---

[10]  Hugh Carey, *Duet for Two Voices* (Cambridge: Cambridge University Press, 1979), p. 167.

[11]  Since this cannot easily be played on the piano as written here (in a direct quotation from the published piano/vocal score), it presumably represents the combined piano and harmonium parts.

turns during the melodrame in which Jack tells the story of his vow, and it also recurs at key points of the opera when his conscience recalls him to the path of duty.

EXAMPLE 4

ANDANTE

In addition to this principal motto Macfarren adopts a new device of introducing eight motives or tags, always accompanying Christopher, the guardian, who is a professional fiddler. Most of these motives were well-known English popular songs that were meant to be recognized, and they are identified by name in footnotes in the published vocal score. They are given with their labels in example 5. Despite the labels, I have failed to identify Nos. 3 and 4 from ordinary reference sources such as Chappell and the *National Tune Index.*[12]

1. "Off she goes." Macfarren mentioned this song when writing about his father, who he said had composed it, along with "many country dance tunes that had great popularity"; he said it "may sometimes now be heard on street organs" and has been "claimed as an Irish national melody".[13] Chappell also attributed it to the elder George Macfarren, but this is unlikely, as Samuel Wesley published variations on the tune in 1802 when the elder Macfarren was only fourteen. I learned the tune as "Humpty Dumpty," and a similar tune appears in a collection of country dances published in 1751 as "Johnny's Frolic."[14] In this case Macfarren has used it to suggest fiddling; it appears when Christopher is announcing his profession.

2. "When the heart of a man is oppressed with cares" appears in *The Beggar's Opera* (1728); Macfarren has slightly misquoted the first line, "If the heart of a man is depressed with cares." It goes on "The mist is dispelled when a woman appears; Like the notes of a fiddle, she sweetly, sweetly Raises the spirits, and charms our ears," although the original song from which Gay took

---

[12] William Chappell, *The Ballad Literature and Popular Music of the Olden Time*, 2 vols. (London: Chappell & Co., 1855, 1859); Kate van Winkle Keller and Carolyn Rabson, eds., *The National Tune Index* (New York: University Music Editions, 1980).

[13] Banister, p. 3.

[14] *A Choice Collection of 200 Favourite Country Dances*, Vol. 6 (London: Jno. Johnson, 1751). (Traced through the *National Tune Index*.)

EXAMPLE 5

[Tag 1] Off she goes (Old dance tune)

[Tag 2] When the Heart of a Man is oppress'd with cares

[Tag 3] The Tank

[Tag 4] Drops of Brandy

[Tag 5] Cease your Funning

[Tag 6] Cold and Raw

[Tag 7] Here's to the Maiden

[Tag 8] Here we go round the Mulberry Bush

the tune was "Would you have a young virgin of fifteen years old." The reference in the opera is ambiguous. Christopher, the fiddler, is instructing his young ward on how to fend off suitors.

3. "The tank." I have been unable to find this tune anywhere, by name or by incipit. It sounds like a fiddle reel. Christopher is telling his ward Lotty to lock her house door securely.

4. "Drops of brandy." Again I have had no success in finding this tune, and the phrases used by Macfarren seem to be fragments only. Christopher is coming home late and is commenting in spoken monologue: "Really, people should think twice before they make a musician and a man of business lose his precious time on a fool's errand. The sergeant's wedding is put off until tomorrow." Perhaps the tune suggests he is drunk.

5. "Cease your funning." Here Christopher is begging his ward to let him into his house, but she is taking his instructions literally and saying

"No!", thus giving her lover time to escape. The situation in *The Beggar's Opera*, from which this tune is taken, has no obvious bearing, and perhaps Macfarren was just referring to the words of the first line taken out of context.

6. "Cold and raw" [the wind did blow]. This tune also comes from *The Beggar's Opera*, but here Macfarren gives it its older name. Again the reference seems to be immediate and superficial, as Jack, the hero, is telling his story about how he was wandering late at night in rainy and cold weather.

7. "Here's to the maiden." This is a well-known drinking song which is a toast to the female sex—"Here's to the maiden of bashful fifteen, here's to the widow of fifty." The words are by Sheridan. Macfarren has used the refrain, "Let the toast pass, drink to the lass; I warrant she'll prove an excuse for the glass." This is used as a refrain to Christopher's principal song giving his cynical view of the female sex: "The man who is doomed of a lass to take care A burden of trouble is likely to bear." Macfarren first brings in the lower line of example 6, with its own harmonization; then this refrain is sung a second time, now forming the bass of the harmony, while Tag No. 7 is heard above it, as in example 6.

8. I have always known this tune as "Here we go round the mulberry bush," which is a standard nursery rhyme, though oddly enough it does not

EXAMPLE 6

appear in the *Oxford Dictionary of Nursery Rhymes.*[15] The tune is not in the *National Tune Index,* although a similar tune called "Jenny Sutton" is listed there from a 1788 collection of country dances.[16] The tune appears, changed into the minor mode, just at the point where Christopher is humiliated and exposed, and a mistaken identity is resolved.

These tags are used entirely in the comic situations which prevail in this opera. For the more serious or sentimental vein, Macfarren provided strophic ballads, outwardly of the type that had been traditional in English opera for a hundred years; but their style shows, much more strongly than Maid Marion's song from *Robin Hood,* the general influence of Macfarren's work with English folksongs. This is true of the opening number of the opera, sung by the Widow (example 7).

*EXAMPLE 7*

After 1864, Macfarren wrote no more operas, turning instead to cantatas and oratorios. But he continued to develop his ideas about English music. He contributed a weighty article to the *Cornhill Magazine* in September 1868 to refute "the almost proverbial saying, 'The English are not a musical people.'" In 1870 he delivered a series of four lectures at the London Institution on "the National Music of Ireland, Scotland, Wales, and England," which was substantially published in *The Musical Times* later that year. In each of the first three lectures he attempted to demonstrate that many of the tunes generally regarded as Irish, Scottish, or Welsh were really English in origin. He offered the following definition:

> A melody is national when it has been commonly sung by a people through several generations, and sung because it naturally expressed the people's feelings, not because of its artistic merit. Every melody must have had a composer, and that composer must have been a technically trained musician. . . . Thus, Dibdin, or Carey, . . . or Purcell, . . . may have made a tune; it is the people who . . . have made it national.[17]

---

[15] Iona and Peter Opie, eds., *The Oxford Dictionary of Nursery Rhymes* (Oxford: Clarendon Press, 1951).

[16] *Thompson's Complete Collection of 200 Favourite Country Dances,* Vol. 5 (London: S. A. & P. Thompson, 1788).

[17] *The Musical Times* 14 (1870), pp. 520; cited Banister, pp. 149–50.

This is a surprisingly modern notion of the nature of folksong. Later in the lecture he placed the blame squarely upon Italian opera, from Handel's time onwards, for the failure to establish an English national school of opera.

We can see then that Macfarren's motivation was not materially different from that of the nationalist composers of Eastern Europe, despite the great difference in the political standing of Great Britain from that of, say, Bohemia. His national pride was offended by the low prestige which the ruling classes of his country gave to indigenous opera, and he set himself single-mindedly to do something about it, first by demonstrating that he could write an attractive and successful opera in the accepted (i.e., Italian) manner, then by gradually introducing English elements into his style.

He did not reach the third stage of radically remolding his style. His nationalism is comparable to Glinka's or Smetana's. It is mild by the side of Mussorgsky's: of course he lacked Mussorgsky's genius and power, but there were other factors involved. Public support for English musical nationalism was weak, since Englishmen were successfully asserting their national character in other fields that were given much higher importance than music. Most were quite content to leave music to foreigners. Again, much English folksong was not far enough away in its idiom from the European mainstream to provide a radically distinctive style. The Englishness is grafted on to Macfarren's normal style, which is classical, or more specifically Mozartian. Fifty years later Vaughan Williams would blend English folksong with Renaissance-inspired harmony, making a composite that is more strikingly distinct from the ordinary romantic idiom.

But for all that, I believe Macfarren was the pioneer of English musical nationalism, unless one prefers to give that title to John Gay. One can see his influence as early as 1862 in Julius Benedict's opera *The Lily of Killarney,* a far more popular work than any of Macfarren's and one which held the stage until the 1930s. It had been called the first Irish opera. The story is based on Boucicault's *The Colleen Bawn,* and the libretto is by Oxenford. It is of course set in Ireland, but there is no trace in it of Irish national aspirations, which presumably would not have passed the Lord Chamberlain's scrutiny. Benedict was a German-born pupil of Weber whose early operatic experience was in Italy; he had no particular feeling for Irish style, but he succeeded in developing an Irish operatic convention by using Macfarren's methods, while borrowing a few specific formulas from Thomas Moore's *Irish Melodies.*

A more important successor to Macfarren was Arthur Sullivan. Although the Savoy Operas owe much of their musical resources to German, Italian, and French models, whenever Sullivan tried to be recognizably English in manner I think we may suspect Macfarren's influence, especially in the earlier works. In *Pinafore* there is "We sail the ocean blue," the glee "A British tar," and the modal strophic duet "Kind captain, I've important information"; in *Pirates* "Pour, O king, the pirate sherry" is strikingly pentatonic, and "When Fredric was a little lad" suggests one of Macfarren's folksong harmonizations. Of course, Gilbert's nationalism was satirical, and by the time we get to *The Yeomen of the Guard,* an English subject if ever there was one, there is little trace left of the Macfarren brand of musical nationalism, even in a song like "When our gallant Norman foe." Sullivan's style had moved in other directions. It was left for Stanford and Hamish MacCunn to take up the cudgels of musical nationalism and pass them on to Holst and Vaughan Williams.

# CONTENTS OF THE CASSETTE RECORDING

*Side One*

1. Five Victorian Songs
2. Piano Pieces
3. Six Songs by John Ruskin
4. Church Music by Samuel Sebastian Wesley

*Side Two*

4. Church Music by Samuel Sebastian Wesley (continued)
5. Arthur Somervell's Cycle of Songs from Tennyson's *Maud*

The cassette recording supplied here is a two-sided, 90-minute tape, encoded with Dolby B noise reduction. The copies were duplicated by PRC Tape Co. from a master prepared by Rex Anderson in the recording studio of the University of Illinois School of Music at Urbana.

The words of the songs, and the program notes found in the score of "The Battle of Prague," are given below, following the order in which the music appears on the cassette, which in turn follows the order of the chapters concerned. Except in the case of the *Maude* cycle, no attempt has been made to collate the song texts with those of the original poems.

**Side One**

### 1. FIVE VICTORIAN SONGS

*Phyllis Hurt, soprano; Nicholas Temperley, piano*
*Recorded at the University of Illinois, Urbana, May 1986*
*Recording engineer: Rex Anderson*

**Invocation to the Deep** (Felicia Hemans)        *Edward James Loder, c. 1845*

> What hid'st thou in thy treasure caves and cells,
> Thou ever sounding and mysterious main!
> Pale glist'ning pearls and rainbow coloured shells,
> Bright things which gleam unrecked of, and in vain.
> Keep, keep thy riches, melancholy sea;
>         We ask not such from thee.
>
> But more, the billows and the depths have more,
> High hearts and brave are gathered to thy breast;
> They hear not now the booming waters roar;
> The battle thunders will not break their rest.
> Keep thy red gold and gems, thou stormy grave;
>         Give back the true and brave.
>
> Dark roll thy tides o'er manhood's noble head,
> O'er youth's bright locks and beauty's flow'ry crown.
> Yet must thou hear a voice: restore the dead!
> Earth shall reclaim her precious things from thee!
>         Restore the dead, thou sea!

**Foreign Children**                        *Charles Villiers Stanford, 1892*
(Robert Louis Stevenson)

> Little Indian, Sioux or Crow,
> Little frosty Eskimo,
> Little Turk or Japanee,
> O! don't you wish that you were me?
>
> You have seen the scarlet trees
> And the lions overseas;
> You have eaten ostrich eggs,
> And turn'd the turtles off their legs.
>
> Such a life is very fine,
> But it's not so nice as mine:
> You must often, as you trod,
> Have wearied not to be abroad.

You have curious things to eat,
I am fed on proper meat;
You must dwell beyond the foam,
But I am safe and live at home.

Little Indian, Sioux or Crow,
Little frosty Eskimo,
Little Turk or Japanee,
O! don't you wish that you were me?

**A Widow-Bird** (Percy Bysshe Shelley)          *Liza Lehmann, 1895*

A widow-bird sate mourning for her love
    Upon a wintry bough;
The frozen wind crept on above,
    The freezing stream below.
There was no leaf upon the forest bare,
    No flow'r upon the ground,
And little motion in the air,
    Except the mill-wheel's sound.

**The Dream** (Alfred Bunn),          *Michael William Balfe, 1843*
from *The Bohemian Girl*

I dreamt that I dwelt in marble halls,
    With vassals and serfs at my side,
And of all who assembled within those walls
    That I was the hope and the pride.
I had riches too great to count — could boast
    Of a high ancestral name;
But I always dreamt, which pleas'd me most,
    That you lov'd me still the same.

I dreamt that suitors sought my hand,
    That knights upon bended knee,
And with vows no maiden heart could withstand,
    They pledg'd their faith to me.
And I dreamt that one of that noble host
    Came forth my hand to claim;
But I also dreamt, which charm'd me most,
    That you lov'd me still the same.

**Buy Me Some Almond Rock** (Joseph Tabrar)          *Joseph Tabrar, 1893*

   I feel so glad, I never had
    Such joy within my heart;
   I've been asked out, and without doubt
    I'm dying to make a start.
   I've never seen a ball, nor been
    Allowed out after dark;
   I'll mash the men, nine out of ten,
    Oh won't it be a lark!

(*Chorus*) Only fancy if Gladstone's there,
     And falls in love with me!
    If I run across Labouchere,
     I'll ask him home to tea.
    I shall say to a young man gay,
     If he treads upon my frock,
    Randy pandy, sugardy candy,
     Buy me some almond rock!

   I heard in truth that General Booth
    Is going to be M.C.,
   And if he is, 'twill be good "biz,"
    No end of fun there'll be.
   Ma said last week, I'm not to speak
    To even one young man,
   But just you wait, in spite of fate,
    I'll speak to all I can.

(*Chorus*) Only fancy, . . . .

   If Sir Charles Dilke sees me in silk,
    To dance with me he'll try,
   I'll sing "Tral la," Ha! "There you are,"
    Then "Wink the other eye."
   If by a "fluke" I meet a Duke,
    A Marquis or an Earl,
   I'll win all three, in fact I'll be
    A regular "Giddy girl."

(*Chorus*) Only fancy, . . . .

## 2. PIANO PIECES

*Philip Carli, piano*

*Recorded at Palomar College, San Marcos, California 1986*
*on a Mason & Hamlin Piano (c. 1890)*
*Recording Engineer: James A. Weld*

**The Battle of Prague**        *Franz Koczwara, c. 1788*

Slow March

Word of Command — First Signal Cannon — The Bugle Horn Call for
the Cavalry — Answer to the first Signal Cannon — The Trumpet
Call — Cannon

The Attack — Prussians: Imperialists — Cannon — Flying Balls —
Trumpets, Kettle Drums — Attack with Swords, Horses Galloping —
Trumpet, Cannons, Light Dragoons advancing — Heavy Cannonade —
Cannons & Drums in general — Running Fire — Trumpet of Recall —
Cannon

Cries of the Wounded — Trumpet of Victory

God Save the King

Turkish Music: Quick Step

Finale — Go to Bed Home — Tempo Primo

**Fantasia on a Favorite Irish Melody**        *Felix Mendelssohn, 1830*

"'Tis the Last Rose of Summer"

## 3. SONGS BY JOHN RUSKIN

*Paul Proveaux, baritone; William J. Gatens, piano*
*Recorded at Swarthmore College, April 1986*
*Recording engineer: Glenn Short (Crystalline Acoustics)*

**At Marmion's Grave** (Sir Walter Scott), 1881

But yet from out the little hill
Oozes the slender springlet still,

And shepherd boys repair
To seek the water-flag and rush,
And plait their garlands fair;
When thou shalt find the little hill
With thy heart commune, and be still.

### On Old Ægina's Rock (Lord Byron), 1881

On old Aegina's rock, and Hydra's isle,
The god of gladness sheds his parting smile.
Descending fast, the mountain shadows kiss
Thy glorious gulph, unconquer'd Salamis.
Not yet; — not yet. Sol pauses on the hill;
The precious hour of parting lingers still.

### Come Unto These Yellow Sands (William Shakespeare), c. 1880

Come unto these yellow sands,
And then take hands.
Curtsied when you have, and kissed,
The wild waves whist.
Foot it featly here and there,
And let the rest the burden bear.
Hark, hark,
The watchdogs bark.

### Faune, Nympharum (Horace), c. 1880

Faune, nympharum fugient' amator,
Per meos fines et aprica rura,
Lenis incedas, abeasque parvis,
Aequus alumnis.

Si tener pleno cadit haedus anno,
Larga nec desunt Veneris sodali,
Vina craterae, vetus ara multo,
Fumat odore.

Ludit herboso pecus omne campo,
Cum tibi Nonae redeunt Decembres,
Festus in pratis vacat otioso
Cum bove pagus.

Inter audaces lupus errat agnos
Spargit agres tes tibi silva frondes,
Gaudet invisam pepulisse fossor
Ter pede terram.

## A Note of Welcome: Joanna's Care (John Ruskin), 1880

What shall we say to her,
Now she is here,
Don't go away again,
Joanie my dear.

## Trust Thou Thy Love (John Ruskin), 1881

Trust thou thy love, if she be proud, is she not sweet?
Lay thou thy soul, full in her hands, low at her feet.
Trust thou thy love, if she be mute, is she not pure?
Fail, sun and breath, yet for thy peace, she shall endure.

## 4. CHURCH MUSIC BY SAMUEL SEBASTIAN WESLEY

*Medici Chamber Choir*
*Raymond Lewis, director; Justin Waters, organist*
*Recorded in Bromley Parish Church, November 1988*

*Jubilate* from the Service in E, 1841–1844

O be joyful in the Lord, all ye lands: serve the Lord with gladness,
and come before his presence with a song.
Be ye sure that the Lord he is God: it is he that hath made us, and not
we ourselves; we are his people, and the sheep of his pasture.
O go your way into his gates with thanksgiving, and into his courts with
praise: be thankful unto him, and speak good of his name.

For the Lord is gracious, his mercy is everlasting: and his truth endureth
   from generation to generation.
Glory be to the Father, and to the Son: and to the Holy Ghost;
As it was in the beginning, is now, and ever shall be: world without end.
   Amen.

**Anthem,** "Cast me not away," 1847

Cast me not away from thy presence, and take not thy Holy Spirit from me.
Restore unto me the joy of thy salvation, and uphold me with thy spirit.
The sacrifices of God are a broken spirit; a broken and a contrite heart thou
   wilt not despise, O God.
Make me to hear joy and gladness, that the bones which thou hast broken
   may rejoice.

*Side Two*

*Nunc Dimittis* from the Chant Service in F, 1848–1850

Lord, now lettest thou thy servant depart in peace: according to thy word.
For mine eyes have seen: thy salvation;
Which thou hast prepared: before the face of all people;
To be a light to lighten the Gentiles: and to be the glory of thy people
   Israel.
Glory be to the Father, and to the Son: and to the Holy Ghost;
As it was in the beginning, is now, and ever shall be: world without end.
   Amen.

## 5. CYCLE OF SONGS FROM ALFRED TENNYSON'S *MAUD*
### *by Arthur Somervell, 1898*

*Bart Lind Smith, baritone; Nicholas Temperley, piano*
*Recorded at the Unversity of Illinois, Urbana, May 1986*
*Recording engineer: Rex Anderson*

Note: the text of the song-cycle has been collated with that of the poem, as printed in Christopher Hicks, ed., *The Poems of Tennyson* (New York: Norton, 1972).

1. "I hate the dreadful hollow" (Tennyson: I, 1-4)

> I hate the dreadful hollow behind the little wood,
> Its lips in the field above are dabbled with blood-red heath,
> And the red ribbed ledges drip with the silent horror of blood,
> And Echo there, whatever is ask'd her, answers "Death."

2. "A voice by the cedar tree" (Tennyson: I, 162-189)

> A voice by the cedar tree
> In the meadow under the Hall!
> She is singing an air that is known to me,
> A passionate ballad gallant and gay,
> A martial song like a trumpet's call!
> Singing alone in the morning of life,
> In the happy morning of life and of May,
> Singing of men that in battle array,
> Ready in heart, and ready in hand,
> March with banner and bugle and fife
> To the death, for their native land.
>
> Maud with her exquisite face,
> And wild voice pealing up to the sunny sky,
> And feet like sunny gems on an English green,
> Maud in the light of her youth and her grace,
> Singing of Death, and of Honour that cannot die,
> Till I well could weep for a time so sordid and mean,
> And myself so languid and base.
>
> Silence, beautiful voice!
> Be still, for you only trouble the mind.
> With a joy in which I cannot rejoice,
> A glory I shall not find.
> Still! I will hear you no more,
> For your sweetness hardly leaves me a choice
> But to move to the meadow and fall before

Her feet on the meadow grass, and adore,
Not her, who is neither courtly nor kind,
Not her, not her, but a voice.

3. "She came to the village church" (Tennyson: I, 301-307)

She came to the village church,
And sat by a pillar alone;
An angel watching an urn
Wept over her, carved in stone;
And once, but once, she lifted her eyes,
And suddenly, sweetly, strangely blushed,
To find they were met by my own.

4. "O let the solid ground" (Tennyson: I, 398-411)

O let the solid ground
Not fail beneath my feet
Before my life has found
What some have found so sweet;
Then let come what come may,
What matter if I go mad,
I shall have had my day.

Let the sweet heavens endure,
Not close and darken above me
Before I am quite, quite sure
That there is one to love me;
Then let come what come may
To a life that has been so sad,
I shall have had my day.

5. "Birds in the high Hall-garden" (Tennyson: I, 412-427, 432-435)

Birds in the high Hall-garden
When twilight was falling,
Maud, Maud, Maud, Maud,
They were crying and calling.

Where was Maud? in our wood;
And I, who else, was with her,
Gath'ring woodland lilies,
Myriads blow together.

Birds in our wood sang,
Ringing thro' the valleys,
Maud is here, here, here
In among the lilies.

I kissed her slender hand,
She took the kiss sedately;
Maud is not seventeen,
But she is tall and stately. . . .

I know the way she went
Home with her maiden posy,
For her feet have touched the meadows
And left the daisies rosy.

6. "Maud has a garden" (Tennyson: I, 489-494, 516-526)

Maud has a garden of roses
And lilies fair on a lawn;
There she walks in her state
And tends upon bed and bower;
And thither I climbed at dawn
And stood by her garden gate. . . .

I heard no sound where I stood
But the rivulet on from the lawn
Running down to my own dark wood;
Or the voice of the long sea wave as it swelled
Now and then in the dim gray dawn;
But I looked, and round, all round the house I beheld
The death-white curtain drawn;
Felt a horror over me creep,
Prickle my skin and catch my breath,
Knew that the death-white curtain meant but sleep,
Yet I shudder'd and thought like a fool of the sleep of death.

7. "Go not, happy day" (Tennyson: I, 571-598)

Go not, happy day,
From the shining fields,
Go not, happy day,
Till the maiden yields.
Rosy is the West,
Rosy is the South,
Roses are her cheeks,
And a rose her mouth.
When the happy "Yes"
Falters from her lips,
Pass and blush the news
Over glowing ships;
Over blowing seas,
Over seas at rest,
Pass the happy news,
Blush it thro' the West;

Till the red man dance
By his red cedar tree,
And the red man's babe
Leap, beyond the sea.
Blush from West to East,
Blush from East to West,
Till the West is East,
Blush it thro' the West.
Rosy is the West,
Rosy is the South,
Roses are her cheeks,
And a rose her mouth.

8. "I have led her home" (Tennyson: I, 599-610)

I have led her home, my love, my only friend.
There is none like her, none.
And never yet so warmly ran my blood
And sweetly on and on.
Calming itself to the long wished-for end,
Full to the banks, close to the promised good.

None like her, none.
Just now the dry-tongued laurel's pattering talk
Seemed her light foot along the garden walk,
And shook my heart to think she comes once more;
But even then I heard her close the door,
The gates of Heav'n are closed, and she is gone.

9. "Come into the Garden, Maud" (Tennyson: I, 850-867, 902-923)

Come into the garden, Maud,
For the black bat, night, has flown,
Come into the garden, Maud,

I am here at the gate alone;
And the woodbine spices are wafted abroad,
And the musk of the rose is blown.

For a breeze of morning moves,
And the planet of Love is on high,
Beginning to faint in the light she loves
On a bed of daffodil sky,
To faint in the light of the sun that she loves,
To faint in his light, and to die.

All night have the roses heard
The flute, violin, bassoon;
All night has the casement jessamine stirred
To the dancers dancing in tune;
Till a silence fell with the waking bird
And a hush with the setting moon. . . .

Queen rose of the rosebud garden of girls,
Come hither the dances are done,
In gloss of satin and glimmer of pearls,
Queen lily and rose in one;
Shine out, little head, sunning over with curls,
To the flowers, and be their sun.

There has fallen a splendid tear
From the passion flower at the gate.
She is coming, my own, my dear,
She is coming, my life, my fate;
The red rose cries, "She is near, she is near;"
The white rose weeps, "She is late;"
The larkspur listens, "I hear, I hear;"
And the lily whispers, "I wait."

She is coming, my own, my sweet;
Were it ever so airy a tread,
My heart would hear her and beat,
Were it earth in an earthy bed;
My dust would hear her and beat,
Had it lain for a century dead;
Would start and tremble under her feet,
And blossom in purple and red.

10. "The fault was mine" (Tennyson: II, 1-5, 34-35)

> "The fault was mine, the fault was mine;" —
> Why am I sitting here so stunned and still,
> Plucking the harmless wild flower on the hill?
> It is this guilty hand!
> And there rises ever a passionate cry, . . .
> a cry for a brother's blood,
> It will ring in my heart and my ears, till I die, till I die.

11. "Dead, long dead" (Tennyson: II, 239-258, 334-342)

> Dead, long dead, long dead!
> And my heart is a handful of dust,
> And the wheels go over my head,
> And my bones are shaken with pain,
> For into a shallow grave they are thrust,
> Only a yard beneath the street,
> And the hoofs of the horses beat, beat,
> The hoofs of the horses beat,
> Beat into my scalp and my brain,
> With never an end to the stream of passing feet,
> Driving, hurrying, marrying, burying,
> Clamour and rumble, and ringing and clatter,
> And here in the grave it is just as bad.
> For I thought that the dead had peace, but it is not so;
> To have no peace in the grave, is that not sad?
> But up and down and to and fro,
> Ever about me the dead men go;
> And then to hear a dead man chatter
> Is enough to drive one mad. . . .
>
> Ah me, why have they not buried me deep enough?
> Is it kind to give me a grave so rough,
> Me, that was never a quiet sleeper?
> Maybe still I am but half dead;
> Then I cannot be wholly dumb;
> I will cry to the steps above my head
> And somebody, surely, some kind heart will come
> To bury me, bury me
> Deeper, ever so little deeper.

12. "O that 'twere possible" (Tennyson: II, 141-144)

> O that 'twere possible
> After long grief and pain
> To find the arms of my true love
> Round me once again!

Epilogue: "My life has crept so long" (Tennyson: III, 1-5, 9-11, 15-17, 34-37, 53-55, 58-59)

My life has crept so long on a broken wing
Thro' cells of madness, haunts of horror and fear,
That I come to be grateful at last for a little thing:
My mood is changed, for it fell at a time of year
When the face of night is fair on the dewy downs, . . .

That like a silent lightning under the stars
She seemed to divide in a dream from a band of the blest,
And spoke of a hope for the world in the coming wars — . . .

And it was but a dream, yet it yielded a dear delight
To have looked, tho' but in a dream, upon eyes so fair,
That had been in a weary world my one thing bright. . . .

And I stood on a giant deck and mixed my breath
With a loyal people shouting a battle cry,
Till I saw the dreary phantom arise and fly
Far into the North and battle, and seas of death. . . .

The blood red blossom of war with a heart of fire.
Let it flame or fade, and the war roll down like a wind,
We have proved we have hearts in a cause, we are noble still, . . .
I have felt with my native land, I am one with my kind,
I embrace the purpose of God, and the doom assigned.

# CONTRIBUTORS

ROBERT BLEDSOE is an Associate Professor of English and Director of Literature at the University of Texas, El Paso. His articles have appeared in a number of publications, including *PMLA, Studies in the Novel, Women in Literature, Mosaic, The Dickensian* and *Victorian Studies.*

MARY BURGAN, Professor of English and Chair of the English Department at Indiana University, is a member of the *VS* Editorial Board. She has authored articles on Jane Austen and father figures in Lawrence and Joyce. Her current research involves her in the areas of children's literature and the family in Victorian fiction.

WILLIAM J. GATENS is the author of *Victorian Cathedral Music in Theory and Practice* (1986). He has written articles and reviews for *Music & Letters, The American Organist,* and *The Diapason.* Professionally, he combines practical and scholarly interests, particularly in the fields of organ and choral music.

PETER HORTON is Assistant Reference Librarian at the Royal College of Music, London. His special interest is nineteenth-century English church music, and he is currently editing the complete anthems of S. S. Wesley and working on a full-length study of the composer.

LINDA K. HUGHES, Associate Professor of English at Texas Christian University, is author of *The Manyfacèd Glass: Tennyson's Dramatic Monologues* (1987). She and Michael Lund are completing a book on Victorian serial literature. While teaching at the University of Missouri-Rolla, she was a member of the Collegium Musicum and played recorders and krummhorn.

BERNARR RAINBOW is President of the Curwen Institute in London and the author of numerous books, including *Land without Music: Musical Education in England, 1800–1860, and its Continental Antecedents* (1967), *English Psalmody Prefaces* (1982), and *Music in Educational Thought and Practice* (in preparation). He currently edits the continuing series *Classic Texts in Music Education,* which has issued 24 facsimile volumes to date.

NICHOLAS TEMPERLEY is Professor of Music at the University of Illinois at Urbana-Champaign. He is the author of *The Music of the English Parish Church* (1979) and has edited *The Blackwell History of Music in Britain,*

*Volume 5, The Romantic Age* (1981) and a 20-volume series of piano music, *The London Pianoforte School 1766–1860* (1984–87). In 1966 he revived a Victorian opera, *Raymond and Agnes* by Edward Loder, on stage at the Arts Theatre, Cambridge. He is currently writing a book about the piano in European life.

# Index